Simon P. Lock, owner and CEO of The Lock Group, is known for his key role in the implementation of international fashion week showcases in the Asia Pacific region. Founder of the Mercedes Australia Fashion Week, Lock currently serves as creative director of Dubai Fashion Week and acts as a creative consultant to fashion and retail brands including Marc Jacobs and Stella McCartney. Credited as the 'Godfather' of Australian fashion, in 2011 Lock was the recipient of the prestigious Australian Fashion Laureate award in recognition of his enduring contributions, marking the first time the award was presented to an individual who was not a designer. He has recently established ORDRE, a global online wholesale platform for the ready-to-wear fashion industry.

IN THE FRONT ROW

HOW AUSTRALIAN FASHION MADE THE WORLD STAGE

Simon P. Lock

MELBOURNE
UNIVERSITY
PRESS

MELBOURNE UNIVERSITY PRESS
An imprint of Melbourne University Publishing Limited
11–15 Argyle Place South, Carlton, Victoria 3053, Australia
mup-info@unimelb.edu.au
www.mup.com.au

First published 2015
Text © Simon P. Lock, 2015
Design and typography © Melbourne University Publishing Limited, 2015

Cover design by Emilia Toia
Typeset by Cannon Typesetting
Printed in Australia by McPherson's Printing Group

National Library of Australia Cataloguing-in-Publication entry

Lock, Simon, author.

In the front row: how Australian fashion made the world stage/Simon P. Lock.

9780522867916 (paperback)
9780522867923 (ebook)

Mercedes Benz Australia Fashion Week—History.
Fashion—Australia—History
Fashion shows—Australia—History.
Fashion design—Australia—History.
Fashion designers—Australia.

746.920994

Contents

In the Front Row *is dedicated to my father, David Price Lock Senior,*
who passed away while I finished the final chapters.

He was and will remain the inspiration and the driving force
for my ambition, enthusiasm and passion for life.

He taught me two things that have been guiding forces in my life:
Don't be fearful of change or scared of failure.

He sat next to me many times in the front row and let me know how
proud he was. These are some of the most cherished memories of my life.

Preface

WELCOME TO *In the Front Row*. I'm Simon. Simon P. Lock to many, SPL to the chosen few, Si to my closest family, and Lockie to my darling wife, Kirsten. I'm the guy the Australian fashion industry still loves to hate all these years later for being the upstart outsider who dreamed of building an international fashion week in Australia and dared the world to come and see the talent of our best designers. I've been tempted to write this book many times in the past. When I first thought I would, the title was going to be 'I Quit', because I thought after the book was released I would never be able to work in the industry again! A few years on, the stars aligned. Mercedes-Benz Fashion Week Australia, as the event is now known, will soon celebrate its twentieth anniversary and I feel what I am currently doing in fashion is going to help put into perspective a forward-facing vision of the industry instead of purely a retrospective one.

This is the story of the trials and tribulations of building Fashion Week, replete with intriguing insights into the Australian industry, its characters, superstars and supermodels, the dramas, the divas, the tantrums, the challenges, the failures and the traumas. This is also the story of a new beginning and the start of an equally exciting adventure. Coinciding with the anniversary of Fashion Week is the launch of our new business ORDRE, a world-first online wholesale platform. Simply put, it takes the best designers from the best fashion weeks around the world and shows their collections online to fashion buyers in over ninety-three countries and 543 cities around the globe. It's an additional channel for the fashion industry to sell its wholesale collections and it will sit alongside traditional fashion weeks. It will change the way our industry works forever and in many ways will put Australian designers on an equal platform with the best in the world.

I am writing this book while I travel the world with Kirsten as we launch this new business and you'll soon see as you read that the similarities and relevance to what I did twenty-five years ago to launch Fashion Week are astounding. Only now I'm doing it in a global context and it is fascinating.

I hope you enjoy being *In the Front Row* with me.

1
The University of DPL

TODAY WAS A pretty big day for our little business. It doesn't seem like over twenty years ago that I had the same emotions when the very first Australian designer committed to what was then known as Mercedes Australian Fashion Week (MAFW). I am in New York trying to get the most famous designers in the world to buy into something just as new and exciting to grow their businesses. The similarities between now and all those years ago are incredible. The feeling I have now when three of New York's most applauded designers join our new global wholesale platform ORDRE is every bit as sweet as when the designing duo Peter Morrissey and Leona Edmiston became the first Australian designers to commit to what was then just as radical an idea. The world of fashion has changed since I came up with the crazy idea to launch a new stop in Sydney on the international fashion week circuit, but in many ways it's still the same. It's all about the designers—you can't live with them and you can't live without them!

*

My mother says that I was a born entrepreneur. Apparently when I was about five and growing up in the Melbourne suburbs in the early 1960s I filled used jam jars with soil from the garden and sold them to the neighbours as special potting mix. Only a few years later I was running a bottle collection depot out of our backyard and going head to head with the local scout bottle drive. My business sense was always strong.

In later life this trait was to brand me as a megalomaniac of sorts in the fashion industry, especially when I established a range of marketing agencies around Fashion Week to capitalise on the investment I had made in the event. The truth of the matter is that at the time it was necessary just to survive financially. Still, my ever-present competitive nature didn't hurt. This inherent characteristic has always been coupled inside me with a feeling that I'm not afraid to fail and that I can achieve anything—driving forces I carry to this day.

If I'm going to tell the story of Fashion Week I don't think I can do so honestly without explaining where my drive and passion come from. At the end of the day it has been this focused feeling, energy and attitude that has made the difference between success and failure. In my case it is all due to an incredible force of nature and human dynamo known as David Price Lock, my father and hero. Every designer who has ever launched a business through Fashion Week, or secured an international order, or a front cover of *Vogue* has my father to thank, because without his radical way of addressing life and business I doubt very much I would have had the foresight, skills and determination to pull off what many thought was impossible.

David Lock was born in Melbourne to a Welsh coalmining immigrant father and a mother who died when he was very young. Basically he was a kid born on the wrong side of the tracks who grew up in the working-class suburb of Port Melbourne while dreaming of a wide world that had to be conquered. His father was the original Lock entrepreneur—when he came to Australia he traded his coal pick for a squeegee and set up his own office window-cleaning business in Melbourne. Growing up in the docklands of Melbourne my father dreamed of the exotic locations the cargo vessels sailing in and out of the harbour visited and, determined to see beyond the horizon of Port Phillip Bay, embarked on an apprenticeship to become a fitter and turner. This would lead to the first of his three careers, as a marine engineer. It was a career that not only led him to discover the travelling life but to cross paths with a man who would change the course of his life: Alan Franklin Rudd.

Alan lived in a Victorian mansion on Guildford Road in the upmarket Melbourne suburb of Canterbury. He was one of four children, but the only son, of a well-to-do Melbourne builder, a man who must have been broken-hearted when Alan chose to become an apprentice in Melbourne's docklands rather than join the family business when he left Camberwell Grammar School. I think maybe Alan had also seen those boats leaving Port Phillip Bay. The boy from the wrong side of the tracks met the silvertail and immediately they became unlikely best friends. They completed their fitter-and-turner apprenticeships and soon signed up as engine hands on cargo ships heading north. Not long after, to the complete shock of their respective families, the two, who had now become inseparable in their shared dream, decided to move to Hong Kong. This was the early 1940s and not at all like today, when many travel to Hong Kong on bankers' contracts. For my father and Alan, it was exotic going to the Far East, a far-flung colony next to a growing communist waking giant, full of pigtailed men pulling rickshaws and beautiful Suzie Wongs in cheongsams.

Before the boys left, however, there was a fateful meeting. Alan had been taking Dad home to Guildford Road for dinner on a pretty regular basis. David eventually met Alan's sister Joy, who had left her pigtails of Canterbury Girls' behind and was now a secretary to a professor at Melbourne University. She was a stunning young woman. By all accounts she was responsible for a never-ending queue of young men to the professor's office to see if he was 'in by chance', especially on his rostered days off! I don't quite know whether for her it was love at first sight, intrigue about the good-looking, well-mannered 'kid from the wrong side of the tracks' or that by then my grandmother had clearly declared my father as her favourite among Alan's friends, but a deep bond formed between them around that dining room table and as the dishes were washed at Guildford Road. It only grew stronger the closer it came to my father setting sail.

David and Alan set off on their great adventure. From Shanghai to Borneo the pair lived the life. My father was always incredibly sketchy about the details. The occasional reference to a daring gold-smuggling racket that 'apparently' some of the boys were involved in on the Shanghai run. The parties with the daughter of the chairman of Jardine Matheson, the boys' employers. The descriptions of opium dens they had never been in! One can only imagine. These experiences opened up my father's mind, life and attitudes about how the world was an amazing place. He discovered new cultures, he made new friends easily, he learnt respect for traditions and to appreciate what he had and understand what he wanted. He developed a work ethic that saw him continually promoted, one that would stand him in good stead for the rest of his life and one he would instil in me. Above all he developed a belief in equality and justice. His convictions would remain with him all his life and they were always central themes in our dinnertime 'classrooms' at home in the years to come.

When the boys' time in Asia was up, an optimistic and growing economy in Australia was calling them home, as were their families. Alan arrived first to find his sister Joy had just turned down her sixth proposal of marriage. She confided in her brother that she couldn't hold out much longer and if David P. Lock didn't show up very soon the spark that had been ignited years before would finally go out. One telegram later, and like a scene from *An Officer and a Gentleman*, my father was on the doorstep of Guildford Road and the rest, as they say, is history. My mother and father married soon after, with Alan as best man. The three were inseparable.

Having lived a life few would dream of the thought of a nine-to-five job held no appeal. What to do? Like their fathers before them, there was only one course to take: open their own business. ARA Engineering was born. It was a welding works for a number of manufacturers, registered in haste using Alan's initials that got jumbled up on the form and never corrected. Despite the protests of my grandfather—it was obvious to him from day one that welding sparks and wooden floors were never going to be a great foundation for success—the boys somehow convinced him that the stable in the backyard of Guildford Road was the best place for their operations. It wasn't long before my grandfather arrived home one evening to smouldering ruins. Not deterred, the boys found a factory in a new industrial estate in Clayton, then on the outskirts of Melbourne, and the business took off. Mum and Dad had by now moved out of Guildford Road and into a brand new AV Jennings home in Albert Street, Mount Waverley, a bright shiny new suburb in Melbourne that looked exactly like something out of a 1960s American sitcom.

Business was booming. The boys were the best of partners, complementing each other in many ways. Alan had also got married and it was nearly time for me to enter the world. But when Mum was in early pregnancy the unimaginable happened. Alan had been on a weekend break with friends down at San Remo near Phillip Island in Victoria and a group of them were fishing from the rocks. Two small boys fishing on a rock ledge nearby were suddenly swept away into a nasty ocean by a freak wave. Without a care for his own safety Alan dived into the swirling mess and attempted to rescue the boys. With great effort he managed to shove one back up onto the rock shelf to safety, and returned in search of the other. The two bodies were never found. I was born soon after with a strong physical resemblance to my uncle.

A beloved and only son was dead, a husband was gone, a brother who was a kindred soulmate was never to return. My father had lost his best friend and his business partner. Where does a man go from there? If you're my father, you dig deep. A handshake between friends—'If anything ever happens to one of us let's make sure the other's family is looked after'—becomes your driving force. For the next half a decade my father worked day and night, sacrificing time with his own young family and sometimes his own health, until he knew he could honour the commitment he had made to his best friend. ARA was sold and half the proceeds went to Alan's widow. As far as I know she never had to work again.

By this time my father was in his mid thirties, having already had a successful career as a marine engineer and sold a thriving business. At this point, most people would invest some of the proceeds from the business's sale, start a new business or get a job. Instead, my father gathered up his young family, which now included my younger brother, Richard Alan Franklin Lock, leased out his home and went on a five-year road trip around the world, and spent the lot!

Welcome to my formative years. We left Australia and sailed to London, where my father leased a beautiful home in Surrey, close to where the Beatle George Harrison lived, purchased his dream car, a Mark II Jaguar, and brought his mother-in-law over. We then spent eight months living in hotels in France, then in Cardiff to understand his heritage, and then on the Costa Del Sol in Spain. He returned to university in London to complete his engineering degree and then bundled us all into a cool caravan and traversed the Continent for eighteen months before travelling the long way home to Melbourne via Miami and the Caribbean.

I returned to the final years of primary school with a proper English accent and a completely different attitude from everyone else. Nothing was impossible because my father had shown me that. The world was full of culture and people to be celebrated and embraced, not feared or discriminated against. Mount Waverley Primary School and the trials and tribulations of the schoolyard were another world for me at that time, and I guess from that moment on I knew I was never going to have a normal life.

This amazing journey at such a young age left me with an uneasy feeling that I couldn't quite put my finger on until much later in life, something that was to be a driving force in creating Australian Fashion Week. As a kid in foreign lands I was often ostracised because I came from the land down under. No one seemed to have the view of our country that I had formed from a young age, which was a combination of the newness and opportunities epitomised by the bright shiny new suburb I had left behind and the refined sophistication I knew through my grandparents. It seemed from my childish point of view that the only opinions the world had of Australia were that it was completely unworldly, was great at sports, had a wealth of natural resources and that was about it. It was a country devoid of any creative culture or place in the arts.

In the mid 1980s, the Australian Tourism Commission released their Paul Hogan 'throw a shrimp on the barbie' campaign. I first saw it on a business trip to the United States and was horrified. It hit me in the heart and head. It was the same feeling I'd experienced as a child when I was teased because to all these posh little English kids I appeared as an uncouth Antipodean who spoke funny and wore shorts in winter. I wanted to tell the world we were more than this stereotypical version of Australia. One of the major reasons I was so passionate about making Australian Fashion Week a success internationally was because it sends a very different message to the world about who we are as Australians. It tells the world we are creative, innovative, sophisticated and able to compete in the luxury world of ready-to-wear fashion alongside New York, London Paris and Milan. These are attributes that add value to the DNA of brand Australia, in addition to the casual openness of our culture, our sporting prowess, wonderful environment and our two greatest assets: Indigenous culture and natural resources. Like our emerging artists, filmmakers, winemakers and chefs, fashion has a role to play in promoting a more accurate perception of us as a nation. And I'm very proud to say that Australian Fashion Week has been a part of that.

*

The next phase of my life was going to give me the tools I needed to get Fashion Week off the ground and instigate my initial intrigue in the fashion industry. As always, my father was leading by example. Having arrived home from our extended worldwide travels we were broke. My father soon landed a job at the Royal Dental Hospital, before he found a career at the Royal Melbourne Hospital, where he would stay until he retired at the age of fifty-six as a board director—he subsequently went on the road again with my mother. Along with my grandmother, we moved to Doncaster into what I have always considered our family home.

These were the years, I guess, when my father prepared me for what lay ahead. The art of open debate on every subject was encouraged and often compromises were hard fought and won. The evening dinner table was seminal in my development as a young man, from the manners expected of me to my contribution to the conversation to the undeniable impact my father's business news of the day would have on us all. We would listen to how my father negotiated with the union or superannuation companies on behalf of the thousands of employees at the Royal Melbourne Hospital, his daily criticism of those poor souls who didn't pull their weight around him or his continuous commentary on politics and world news. Just imagine growing up when Gough Whitlam was in power and the controversy that came with every political discussion. Daily I learnt how to handle people in a work environment, how to create a like-minded team to achieve a common goal, what was fair and just in life and business and what wasn't. The University of DPL was open daily. It was to become the only university degree I was ever going to finish.

It was during this part of my life that my mother also became much more of an influence. My mother is the creative one in the family. She is the feeling one, the incredible portrait artist, the poet, the singer, the writer and the actor. If Dad was the commerce, then

Mum was the art. As it turned out, later in my fashion career I realised that ultimate success in the fashion world comes from a balance between art and commerce. There was also another talented and strong-willed woman living in that household: my grandmother, Lillie Emilie Mary Rudd.

My grandmother was the most endearing snob you could ever meet. She moved through life as if she was born to royalty. She loved the 'little people' and was known to help them out through her endless charity work. She was a man's woman and my father adored his mother-in-law, the mother he never really had. I was spellbound from an early age. She was larger than life: she had an opinion on everything, went on the most extravagant outings, had the best fun and was always the favourite of my mates. Much to my mother's annoyance, she often ruled the roost at Vine Court in Doncaster, and during my difficult teenage years she became my confidante on all things. There was nothing I couldn't discuss with Nan and nothing she wouldn't advise me on—often to my complete shock! One of the most special times in my life was when my parents were travelling on an extended trip and I was 'between' marriages. I moved back in with Nan on the premise of looking after her. If the truth be known, it was the other way around.

Emily, as she was known to all, was the reason for me being interested in fashion in the first place. Every season I witnessed a ritual that fascinated me. When the latest collections arrived at Venn Gowns, then one of the only multi-label designer boutiques in the eastern suburbs of Melbourne, my grandmother would take herself off to buy her new season's wardrobe. Twice a year Nan returned with up to six new outfits perfectly selected to mix and match for her social outings and charity work. The new outfits would be laid out on her bed while she removed all the current season's outfits from her wardrobe. These were then sorted into two groups: those that might make an appearance the following season and those that were off to St Vincent de Paul. European designer names that I am now so familiar with were packed into boxes and, season after season, dispatched to the 'little people'. If only back then I had had the foresight to open a vintage store!

A seed, however, was planted. What was this thing called 'fashion' that required constant renewal and reinvention? What could possibly make a seemingly sensible woman behave in what I thought then such an illogical manner? The clothes my grandmother was dispatching were perfectly good and in some instances almost brand new, but they had been deemed 'unfashionable', forever banished from her sight. Little did I know then that the intrigue and astonishment of this seasonal ritual was going to lead me to create a platform for Australian designers.

*

From the safety net of Camberwell Grammar I headed out into the real world. After years of pursuing a dream of becoming a doctor I missed getting a place into medical school by a country mile—what was I thinking?! I tried applied science instead but dropped out halfway through my first year. That's when it dawned on me: if I couldn't become a doctor why not the next best thing: a hospital administrator like my father? I applied for a job as a stock clerk in the supply department, and having my father as a well-respected member of the management team didn't hurt my chances. That was the last time Dad was to open a door for me, but once opened there was no turning back.

I threw myself into my new career; I was 'Simon everywhere'. I'd finish my job on the stock cards at 10.30 in the morning—my predecessor had made it last all day—and then it was on to whatever needed doing or not. I soon came to the notice of my first mentor, Bob Green, the department head. He just kept putting the challenges in front of me and I kept knocking them out of the ballpark. First it was assistant purchasing officer, then purchasing officer, and then, to the surprise of the entire hospital executive, I was appointed the youngest-ever assistant department head of the Royal Melbourne

Hospital Supply Department. I had a staff of about thirty-five people and was involved in helping to oversee an acquisitions budget of $80 million. I was studying for an economics degree and the junior manager most likely to succeed. The perfect company man.

At twenty-one I was wearing three-piece suits to work every day, and my hairline was rapidly receding, so with my late-1970s moustache I looked about thirty-five. In many respects I was acting that age as well, which would cause me problems later in life as I felt as though I had basically missed all of my twenties. I had been going out with my high-school sweetheart—well, actually, I was in high school and she was in teacher's college—since I was sixteen. Mary is one of the nicest people you are ever going to meet in the world, and she was one of my first girlfriends and my first wife. It all happened very fast. I had moved out of home, my career was exploding, I popped the question and the next thing I knew a white Rolls Royce was out the front of our house in Doncaster, picking up myself and my 16-year-old brother to whisk us off to the full-scale church wedding, followed by a lavish reception at the newly opened Victorian Arts Centre, all courtesy of the wonderful Pattison family in celebration of the marriage of their first daughter. Bloody hell, I *was* thirty-five! And I had the life to prove it.

That's when I had what might be called a quarter-life crisis. This is not me, I thought. Where is the adventure? Where is the risk-taking your father taught you? Where is your Far East? I knew then that I wanted to make a living out of what I loved doing the most: skiing. I had been obsessed with it from a young age, since my father introduced me to his own passion for skiing and his lifelong association with Mt Buller—he and his friends even built one of the first ski lodges there, called Caribou. My life as an entrepreneur was about to begin.

In September 1981, during one of the best ski seasons on record in Australia, I quit my job at the Royal Melbourne and with my good friend Steve Blenheim opened the coolest ski shop in Melbourne, Pro Ski. Our business plan attracted funding from two well-known

Melbourne businessmen and the shop in Glenferrie Road was to trade for the next seventeen years. It was the ultimate small business and it taught me everything: how to buy and manage stock, hire and manage staff, balance accounts, deal with the bank and financiers and, above all, sell and promote. It also introduced me to writing, which was my entry to public relations.

After a number of years working at Pro Ski I was writing about skiing for various ski magazines and newspapers and it came to the attention of a well-known Melbourne PR firm, Welbeck PR. Out of the blue I got an offer to join them by the then managing director, Peter Sterling. Then came one of the most defining moments of my career: I followed Peter Sterling to Saatchi & Saatchi PR, where he had been appointed as managing director. His role in the business was soon declared a disaster and he departed, while the head of Saatchi Australia in consultation with the infamous Saatchi brothers, Maurice and Charles, in London contemplated the fate of the two offices in Australia and the small staff of about half a dozen people, including myself. I saw an opportunity and pounced on it. Having been in PR for less than a year I got on the phone to London and told the Saatchi brothers that I was the man for the job in Australia and if they gave me a chance to be MD I would, with my team, turn the agency around in six months. To my and everyone else's surprise they gave me a shot and with the support of the intrepid staff we actually did it. It was here that I also met my most loyal lieutenant, Jodi Pritchard, who would travel the fashion journey with me over the next twenty years.

From the Saatchi opportunity I went to The Promotional Market to learn sales promotion and from there to Harrison Communications in Sydney as general manager. It was here I learnt from one of life's great spinmeisters, Peter Harrison. He had me fooled right up until the liquidators walked in and closed the business down. Foolishly I thought he was the real deal and a true mentor. When the doors closed I pledged my financial support to open an agency with him as a partner. He basically laughed in my face and said

I could never be his equal. The next day, in April 1989, I started The Lock Group and invited all my key staff to join me. It was to become the vehicle for everything I was to do in my business life from then on.

Over these years the person Mary had married had changed. I was no longer the sure-footed rising corporate executive. I had become the ultimate risk-taker, putting everything back on the table time and time again and rolling the dice, first with Pro Ski and then with my emerging career in marketing and fashion. While I have many regrets about the way we grew apart the one thing we will never regret is having our beautiful and talented son, David Price Lock Jnr. Mary and I separated shortly after I established The Lock Group. It was not an easy time for any of us. We were living in Sydney and had offices in both Sydney and Melbourne. Mary moved back to Melbourne with young David to be around her family and I started the weekly commute back and forth between the cities, which was to become a feature of my life for the next fifteen years.

Between 1989 and 1992 the Lock Group established its first PR company, The Lock Partnership, and it amassed a growing list of increasingly fashionable clients. This company was later rolled into the famed fashion and youth marketing agency I started with Simon Bookallil called Spin Communications. By 1992, under the umbrella of The Lock Group, the key players who would form the support and catalyst for me to create Australian Fashion Week were now in place. They were Marguerite Julian, Simon Bookallil, Jodi Pritchard and Lorraine Price.

2
Fashion Unity

KIRSTEN AND I are travelling from London to Paris on the Eurostar after a hugely successful week. We are talking about the moment we'd had this week that reminds me of a number of similar ones I'd had in the lead-up to the first Fashion Week in Australia. It was at a presentation with Jonathan Saunders, one of the UK designers we admire the most. After we'd finally received confirmation of the meeting we were extremely eager to involve him and his crew in ORDRE, and so we did our best job pitching the concept and showing them through our new clickable demo of the platform. Then we paused for the inevitable stream of questions and queries that we thought would follow, only to be met with: 'We are in … we love it.'

Times like these, when designers immediately see your vision and believe that you can deliver, are priceless. It was these sorts of moments that I'd had with designers with whom I had grown up and greatly admired that kept me going some twenty years earlier. The standout memory for me is Joe Saba. He introduced many of the great Japanese designers to Australia through his boutique, and then he took the 1970s by storm with his Staggers Jeans brand. After that he slowly went about building his own ready-to-wear collections. Joe knew the industry and understood the risks we were facing in trying to set up our venture back then. After I'd presented the idea to him, he had simply looked me in the eye, shook my hand and said, 'We're in.'

*

I'm not too sure who had the original idea for what was to become Australian Fashion Week. I don't know if I can actually claim it was mine, which will come as a surprise to those who have worked alongside me for long enough to know that I usually lay claim to all the good ideas! The early 1990s was an exciting time in the fashion industry in this country. Internationally some interest had been generated by Jenny Kee and Linda Jackson and a few other Australians who had made their way to the fashion capitals of the world and were experiencing firsthand the phenomenal rise of various international fashion weeks, especially in London. But the Australian industry was still reeling from the total embarrassment of an event produced to celebrate the Australian bicentennial in 1988 that was attended by Princess Diana. Leading Australian designers mounted a fashion 'parade' at the Sydney Opera House in front of an international audience of fashion media and designers. The latter included French fashion designer Claude Montana who, on seeing the show, immediately accused the majority of the designers of ripping off European designs. It was a moment of great shame. It also defined which designers would be asked and which would not be asked to participate in the inaugural Australian Fashion Week.

There were a number of other things shaping the direction of the Australian fashion industry at the time. One was a human dynamo called Christine Bookallil. Her son Simon was to join me as a partner in The Lock Group around then, but it was Christine who kicked down doors in the industry. A contemporary of Ita Buttrose at *The Daily Telegraph*, Christine reported on women's issues, including everything from rising hemlines to interviewing The Beatles. She was one of the first powers in fashion PR in Australia, long before the Roxys and Hollys came on the scene. Christine's defining role in my mind was when she was queen PR at what was then Myer Grace Bros. She conceived a showcase of Australian designers the likes of which had never been seen before. Taking the seasonal launches that everyone is now very familiar with, she moved this demure event from the Myer Mural Hall in Melbourne to the Royal Hall of Industries in Sydney and proceeded to produce what, in my mind, was the first world-class fashion 'show' in Australia.

Thanks to the undeniable talents of boy genius Simon Bookallil and the generosity of his mum, I got an opportunity to work on the event alongside Ali Newling, a fashion show producer who had just returned from London. The show was a spectacular success. It put Australian designers in a spotlight they had never experienced before, and it also embedded in me a confidence that I was to draw on in the coming years. In 1992 Simon B had returned from London where, at only twenty-three years old, he had been directing some incredible fashion campaigns and editorial for bands like Bloodstone and Soul II Soul. He now felt the Australian industry was ready for something bigger. He walked into my office with two of his buddies to pitch the idea of launching Australia's first 360-degree marketing communications agency, to be called Spin. For anyone who knows what Simon B is like today, can you just imagine him back then? I can't begin to describe what an incredible creative and intellectual force he was. I was blown away.

Straight after the meeting I registered the name Spin, set up a company and offered Simon a 5 per cent stake, telling him I didn't want his mates. This was to set the tone of our tempestuous and successful business relationship, which would span the next twenty years. He was beyond furious but he saw he needed me as much as I needed him. Obviously Simon became a major shareholder in both Spin and The Lock Group but the intensity and dynamics of our personal relationship were to be the foundation of not only one of Australia's most revered and loved agencies but also a catalyst for the creation of Australian Fashion Week.

We started The Lock Group on two trestle tables in the basement of the Remo Building (now American Apparel) on the corner of Oxford and Crown streets in Sydney. We gathered together there with a crazy bunch, including circus acts and music legend and artist Reg Mombassa, who was in the process of creating the dog trumpet icon for the new punk-surf brand Mambo. We also opened a Melbourne office in Bridport Street, Albert Park. The original staff of the group had joined me from Harrison Communications, which included my soon-to-be wife Lorraine, trustworthy Jodi Pritchard and original business partners Sam Elam and the eccentric, amazing, legendary, one-of-a-kind Ms Marguerite Julian. Lorraine's former boyfriend, Martyn Pointer, also came on board as a silent partner, although in years to come he became not so silent. We soon outgrew Remo's basement and moved to the corner of Liverpool and Palmer streets, which was to become the original home of Australian Fashion Week.

Simon B was a big fan of Lynne Franks, the PR guru who will forever be remembered as the inspiration for Eddie in *Absolutely Fabulous*. The Lock Group had now been going for about three years and, on one of our first jobs for Spin, Simon and I travelled to London to shoot a Lee campaign with model Emma Balfour. While there, I took myself off to meet the said Ms Franks to find out more about her agency. At the time she was heavily involved in London Fashion Week. I came back to Australia, having stolen much of the DNA of Lynne Franks PR to inject into Spin, including the establishment of Australia's first fashion showroom. Showrooms had become commonplace in Europe and the United States—they are great for generating editorial content in the media.

Around this time a number of other fashion girls had landed in Sydney, including Elise Garland and Jessica Finch. Along with Ali Newling, Simon and me, we all began to talk about an Australian fashion week. I decided one day to convene a meeting at our Palmer Street office to discuss what might be possible. At first we thought we couldn't fit one into the international format of a fashion week and needed to create a different event strategy that was perhaps more flexible in what season designers showed and how the event was staged. Somehow I came up with a name for the event: Australian Fashion Innovators. I saw this as an opportunity to be more than a fashion week but I didn't quite know what that was. Regardless, I registered the name and The Lock Group formed a new company called Australian Fashion Innovators Pty Ltd, which I was later to sell for millions of dollars.

At around this time Jarrad Clark had joined Spin in our show-room. At the time he was the boyfriend of Jayson Brunsdon, the creative director at Morrissey Edmiston, who had asked us if we would give his young boyfriend from Melbourne a job. That phone call was the start of a twenty-year relationship that was the catalyst for a great many things to do with Fashion Week. The first of these was when I asked Jayson to design the logo for Australian Fashion Innovators as a favour. He did a beautiful drawing, the style of which is still immediately associated with his own label, Jayson Brunsdon.

Over time, an idea and strategy formed in my head. The weird seasonal changeover in my grandmother's wardrobe, the business opportunity I saw from what Christine had created, the chance to push a cultural message internationally, the fascination of working with the design community I had already experienced through Saba, who had now become a client, the Spin showroom … it all started to add up. But I needed more, I needed to understand the business of fashion and everything there was to know about the international fashion week circuit—and there was no internet!

Taking a punt, I convinced my business partners to allow me to invest in researching fashion weeks around the world. This would be the first of many, many, many, many, many times that I would need Marguerite's support for my harebrained schemes. While not the biggest shareholder in the group, she was in many ways the balance between the voice of reason and the risk-taker. As long as I had MJ's support I had everyone's support. I honestly believe if it had not been for MJ's belief in what I was doing, and her continually agreeing to let me throw good money after bad, Australian Fashion Week would never have happened.

I then set off on a huge fact-finding mission but, as much as I would have liked to have been the one to travel around the world investigating all the international fashion weeks, the business was growing so quickly I just couldn't leave Australia. Through a series of interviews, phone calls, reading and researching I fast-tracked my training in every facet of the fashion industry and its supply chain, all from the safety of my office. In the meantime, we footed the bill for Ali Newling to take off on a round-the-world trip to report back on what was happening at all the major fashion weeks. From memory, it was an eight-week trip covering New York, London, Paris and Milan.

I discovered a lot through my research. One thing I uncovered in particular was going to be the ace up our sleeve in the years to come. Many, but not all, in the Australian fashion industry had for many years been simply reinterpreting US and European designs from last season's collections and reproducing them at a lower cost in Australia and calling them their own. They usually got the ideas from the print editions of *Collezioni* magazine, which arrived in Australia about three months after the collections were launched overseas. So the spring/summer collection shows in New York, London, Milan and Paris in September and October would arrive via airmailed magazines in Australia in November/December. Australian designers would copy the fashion and make samples to show to retailers in March/April, to be produced to arrive in-store for our summer retail season in August/September. But the European and US versions of the same had already arrived in-store the previous February/March, in time for the northern hemisphere summer season. In every sense, we were six months behind the rest of the world, and many in our industry were plagiarists. This was exactly the issue experienced at the bicentenary fashion parade. Through my research I discovered this timing was a huge advantage for the Australian fashion industry. But it was not something I was going to shout from the rooftops. I would let the world—and the Australian fashion industry—find out for itself with a gentle nudge in the right direction.

The fashion design process follows an exacting timetable in both the northern and southern hemispheres. It all revolves around the need of department stores and speciality fashion boutiques to have new season collections arrive in-store before the start of summer and the start of winter. In the northern hemisphere, spring/summer collections need to arrive in February/March. In the southern hemisphere, they arrive in August/September. In the northern hemisphere autumn/winter collections need to arrive in September/October and in the southern hemisphere in March/April. To be able to maintain this six-month cycle designers need to keep to a rigid schedule. This process includes the creative inspiration for a collection—often illustrated through sketches but nowadays through digital images—the selection of fabrics, the making of patterns and then samples, the presentation of these samples through fashion weeks and showrooms to retail buyers, the production of orders placed and the delivery in-store. The whole undertaking is then repeated twice a year to make the retail in-store deadlines.

Around 1993–94 the foundation strategy for Australian Fashion Week came to me. I had found out that the entire world's new season fabrics were presented globally to the leading designers at a huge fabric fair in Paris called Première Vision. The spring/summer fabrics were presented in February and the autumn/winter in September, a whole year before finished garments were due in-store. It dawned on me that if Australian designers were the first in the world to present new fabrics in their collections earlier than the northern hemisphere, we could turn around the perception that we were six months behind the United States and Europe. If I could encourage Australian designers to source their fabrics at Première Vision in February, airfreight sample fabric to Australia and then make up collections to show at what was then still to be called Australian Fashion Innovators, we could legitimately lay claim to being the first international fashion week in the world to show a spring/summer line. A brave claim; however, technically true.

The next step was to identify the commercial opportunity for Australian designers both domestically and internationally. There was, I discovered, a little-known seasonal delivery known as Cruise or Resort. These were collections that major department stores in the northern hemisphere wanted to have in-store before Christmas. They needed to be lighter than the autumn/winter collections that were already in-store because they were for their wealthy clientele who were off to warmer climates to get away from the northern winter over Christmas and the January holiday period. For years department stores had been complaining that US and European designers could not get their cruise/resort collections in-store early enough. They were often delivered after Christmas. It seemed to me that this was an opportunity to introduce the spring/summer collections of the Australian designers.

It was now time to turn to the international fashion week calendar to find a slot for Australia to fit into, knowing what I had discovered about Première Vision and the cruise/resort collections. Paris is the last to show autumn/winter at the end of March. There was no way I was going to get buyers and media to come to Australia straight after Paris. They would be already exhausted from their buying trips to New York, London and Milan and they would have no budget left. My idea was to allow them to go back to their offices and complete their autumn/winter orders and then wait for them to start to think about placing their cruise/resort orders, albeit smaller, which they normally did in June for delivery in-store in November/December. What if I was to propose to them that they come to Australia after the autumn/winter collection shows but before they finished their cruise/resort orders? *Perfect*, I thought.

Now I had to look at the southern hemisphere buying cycle. In Australia no one was really buying Australian designers; the department stores were focused mainly on the internationals. When they wanted to buy the collections it would be in March or April, when the northern hemisphere shows were on. So I decided to put a stake in the ground and tell everyone in Australia and the world that Australian Fashion Week was going to happen in the first week of May. This would not be too late for designers to deliver in-store in Australia for spring/summer in August/September and was perfect to deliver in the northern hemisphere for cruise/resort from October onwards.

At about the same time Ali returned from her trip and provided some startling news. She fronted up to my office with her report that basically said what I was attempting to do was impossible and also that I would never be taken seriously because I was not part of the fashion industry. She promptly quit her involvement with us and left. At the time I was furious. How dare she take all our hard-earned money, deliver a very superficial report and tell me I was dreaming? To this day I still don't understand why she did this but, as so often is the case with me, it only made me dig my heels in further to prove her and the rest of the world wrong. I took her hit on the chin because Ali was pretty influential, along with her then photographer boyfriend Steve, and I didn't need any enemies—enough of them would come later. I also had another idea up my sleeve in which I would need Ali's involvement.

I now had my blueprint in place for a strategy for Australian Fashion Innovators but by this time everyone who was in the know was telling me to call it what it was and not to go against the trend. The event from here on would be known as Australian Fashion Week and Australian Fashion Innovators became the company that owned and produced it. This was 1994.

Ali to a certain extent was right. In Australia I was a fashion outsider, a pony-tailed PR whiz kid who had landed some pretty big clients thanks in most part to MJ and her reputation and Simon's creative genius. At the time it was really Simon B who had the fashion credentials and a relationship with design team Morrissey

Edmiston, which would be crucial. Before Simon left for London he was one of the Sydney club kids and through infamous hangouts like Kinsella's Middle Bar and the Freezer he had met the Morrissey Edmiston posse. And when I say posse, I mean it. This crew went en masse everywhere: Peter Morrissey, Leona Edmiston, Jayson Brunsdon, Bradley Perkins and Cheryl Collins were the leaders of a cast of fabulousness that followed. Morrissey Edmiston were like nothing that had ever come before and I think ever will again. They weren't just the hottest fashion designers of their generation, they were rock stars. Peter was buff and skin-tight with the swagger of James Dean and the attitude and ego of Brando. Leona was an enigma: one-part femme fatale, one part Bette Davis, and wrapped up like Audrey Hepburn with the body of Gina Lollobrigida. They surrounded themselves with people like Michael Hutchence, Kylie Minogue, Elle Macpherson, Helena Christensen and every other cool cat in Sydney and beyond. Seriously, no one could touch them. Not even me, as it turned out.

My calls to them went unanswered. My only 'in' was Simon B. He is canny, though, and he wasn't about to introduce me to fashion royalty until he was actually convinced that my crazy scheme of starting a fashion week had a hope of working. Simon, even in his mid twenties, had an amazing intellect and was in tune with every part of popular culture. While he may not have been convinced that the industry was able to support a fashion week, he certainly knew innately that Australia was ready for such a cultural event. He'd seen it firsthand in London and knew that a momentum could be built behind it in Australia. Eventually, he offered to introduce me to the king and queen themselves: Peter and Leona.

I had already started to pitch the idea to those designers who would let me into their studios. They sat, not very passionately, and listened to my crazy idea to start an event that the best fashion buyers and media in the world would attend. Some squirmed in their seats at the idea because if this ever got off the ground they might be found out as the copycats they were. Others were inspired by the possibilities. But no one was making the leap of faith to say they would support it. Not one designer.

Simon and I went to the inner sanctum of the Morrissey Edmiston design studio in Sydney's version of a New York loft in Potts Point. The whole posse was there. We were all crowded around a table in their tiny studio. Sexy images of the latest Morrissey Edmiston campaign directed by Jayson hung on the walls. Peter was in a skin-tight black silk shirt and jeans, Leona in a draped and wrapped dress that in later years would define her own label. Simon B, the club kid they had all known for years, introduced his business partner and off I went, delivering the fully informed, passionate and enthusiastic pitch that I had been practising on lesser mortals for months.

Bradley Perkins was first with the questions, which were intelligent and probing. Jayson lent his support, having seen what fashion weeks can do for an industry. Leona, as she often does, let others make the running. Peter said nothing. I can still remember the emotional tension I felt. This was it. If Morrissey Edmiston said no I had a big hill to climb that maybe was impossible. Every designer I had pitched to wanted to know who was in. No one wanted to be the frontrunner. No one wanted to be that first domino that was going to create the momentum. There was only a handful of designers in Australia at the time who had the respect of the industry to be leaders, and I was surrounded by two of them and their inner cabinet.

The questions stopped and the attention turned to Peter, who until this point had been silent. Following a dramatic pause he looked straight at me and basically said, 'I don't really know who the hell you are and I don't know how you are going to pull this off but I love your vision and your passion. We are in. Tell whoever you need to.'

There were many other milestones to be reached and hurdles to overcome to make Australian Fashion Week possible but, in all honesty, this was the building block that laid our foundations. I knew others would follow. To this day I owe much gratitude to Peter and Leona. As partners they agreed to support me and in doing so they created a domino effect that soon saw Bettina Liano, Scanlan Theodore, Wayne Cooper, Alex Perry and many others follow, but not without a lot of arm twisting. And some of that twisting came from the highest office in the land: our first lady of fashion at the time, the prime minister's wife, Annita Keating.

Having started the designer push I now needed to fund this giant beast and there was no way our little private company, even with our mortgages on offer, could do that. My first port of call was the federal government. It would be the first of hundreds of trips to Canberra and the offices of various state governments to plead for support on behalf of the Australian fashion industry. No government department oversaw anything to do with the design capabilities of the fashion industry. We were lumped into various portfolios—basically, the industry had been to a certain extent relegated to the scrap heap. The only real economic value of the industry at the time was the manufacturing sector. That industry was represented by the Council of Textile & Fashion Industries of Australia (TFIA), and it was battling to slow the reduction of the tariffs that had kept the industry alive against an onslaught of cheap manufacturing from around the world, particularly China. Australian workers were protected because the Australian Government added huge tariffs to imported goods, which allowed Australian-made garments to compete. As the Keating Government moved towards opening up the Australian market, no doubt one of the casualties was going to be the Australian manufacturing industry. I had another idea.

If we could grow the design and creative part of our industry, the added-value part of the supply chain, we could still expand even if most of the manufacturing was done offshore, as it is today. I worked with the TFIA to slow the reductions in tariffs and presented a huge showcase in the Great Hall at Parliament House illustrating the value of the industry, which needed support until it could generate international markets through Australian Fashion Week.

On one of my early trips to Canberra I ended up in Senator John Button's office. He was Minister for Industry and Commerce—a visionary and all-round nice guy. At the time he was trying to establish through Austrade the Export Market Development Grant Scheme. This scheme was to eventually give back fifty cents in every dollar spent overseas promoting Australian designers. It was originally going to be set up to include the marketing funds of Australian Fashion Week but the legislation in the end only allowed international marketing funds expended by the official industry association, which we could never become because we were a private company. However, the most valuable thing John Button did for me was to introduce me to Annita Keating.

She is a very private person and I guess everyone was looking to her during the Keating rule to see how she was going to make the role of first lady her own—her predecessor, Hazel Hawke, was loved and adored and hers were big shoes to fill. I met Annita and we immediately hit it off. She was passionate about creativity and was developing as a photographer in her own right. After a few conversations, she agreed to be the first patron of Australian Fashion Week. Can you imagine how I felt? I now had Morrissey Edmiston and Annita Keating. There was no stopping me.

Annita very kindly agreed to host a series of afternoon teas at Kirribilli House in Sydney. The invitations were sent out on her government-created cards, requesting 'your pleasure to discuss Australian Fashion Week'. There was now nobody in the Australian fashion or media industries that I couldn't engage with. Who was going to turn down an invitation to the prime minister's residence? Yes, you got your chance to meet Annita and check out the view, but then I had you for the best part of ninety minutes to convince you to support what I was doing. A lot of influential people had afternoon tea with me and Annita. The support was building.

At the time, the promise of an Export Market Development Grant from the federal government was one thing, even though it was never to eventuate, but I needed a lot more cash than that.

By this stage I had set the dates for the first Fashion Week as early in May 1995 and I was hatching plans for a huge industry launch. I needed a total industry show of force that would amalgamate our industry and build confidence. People were starting to freak out that the world might be coming to check them out and everyone was worried about the report card, especially those who had an airfreight subscription of *Collezioni*.

It was around this time that two amazing women entered my life: Nancy Pilcher, who was the editor of *Vogue Australia*, and Jane de Teliga, who at the time was the curator at the Powerhouse Museum and prior to that the fashion editor at *The Sydney Morning Herald*. These women of substance and power took me under their wings. Nancy was making calls to designers who were sitting on the fence and basically telling them to get with the program, while Jane introduced me to some members of the state government, where she had been a ministerial advisor.

I needed government funding if Fashion Week was going to happen. The original financial model was to try to get a balanced budget that was made up of revenue from government support, corporate sponsorship and designer contributions. Nothing was going to happen if I didn't have a substantial government grant. Before Jane came along I had been knocking on every state minister's door in both Victoria and New South Wales. I had purposely named the event Australian Fashion Week so it was never going to be city-centric, a break in global precedents, where fashion weeks are named after the city in which they are held. Jeff Kennett was in power in Victoria and he had a vision for supporting the fashion industry but no one in New South Wales seemed to get it until Jane introduced me to Peter Collins, then treasurer and arts minister. With the Kennett Government definitely interested I used this as leverage to get New South Wales involved. I knew that Sydney was going to be hugely promoted in the lead-up to the Olympics in 2000 and if Fashion Week was up and running it would be a cultural event that could be supported alongside the global push for Sydney.

Secretly, I had also decided on a venue and I needed the NSW Government to pay for it.

Jane organised my meeting with Peter Collins and he totally got it in one. He understood the economic value, the cultural value and the promotional value to the state. Above all he understood me. From day one he was one of our biggest supporters. He didn't hesitate, just pulled out his chequebook and guaranteed a three-year grant. Another major building block was now in place. Peter Collins in every sense can lay claim to creating the reason why Fashion Week is in Sydney. It has added hundreds of millions to the economy, if not billions, it has promoted Sydney as a regional creative hub and it has helped Australia establish its sense of style.

Morrissey Edmiston – check.

Annita Keating – check.

State government funding – check.

Now the big one: to sell the first-ever naming-rights sponsorship for an international fashion week.

I knew instinctively that we all had to come together, complete with our insecurities. This included our creative stars, our behind-the-scenes purists, our growing public relations players, the media, the retailers, everybody. Separately we could only be fleeting sky-rockets; together we could be the Milky Way, and I was shooting for the stars. Corny, I know, but that was me at the time! So thanks to my long-suffering partners, who were still allowing me to spend our company's hard-won profits, as well as the generous support of Susie Stenmark—the future head of Chanel's public relations department but at the time doing PR for the Regent Hotel Sydney, now the Four Seasons—I declared in the ballroom of the Hotel InterContinental that we were launching Australian Fashion Week. Seven hundred and fifty people showed up for that late-morning launch, which starred *me*—oh, and yeah, the prime minister's wife.

This was the first time I got up on my soapbox, and it would be by no means the last, and told the Australian fashion industry I needed their support, passion, determination and creativity if we were going to put Australia on the global fashion map. Annita added the style and the cred. For me it was more like a political rally, telling everyone they had to be true believers if we were going to pull this off together. My words might have helped, but it was an unexpected piece of creative genius that was conceived by the youngest creative director in Australia at the time, Simon B, and produced by none other than Ali Newling, that won the hearts and minds of the Australian fashion industry that day.

With almost no money in the bank I took a punt on spending over $50,000, a fortune at the time, on a four-minute piece of film that portrayed the essence of the Australian fashion industry. Beautifully shot by Oscar-winning director of photography Dion Beebe, the film starred Annita, Peter, Leona and Nancy, and used iconic Australian images as a backdrop to these stars of Australian fashion as they appeared to be describing their favourite piece of Australian landscape.

'It runs through your fingers like bejewelled crystals,' Leona said, presumably to describe the sands on Bondi Beach.

'Its silhouette is timeless,' a quietly spoken Annita seemed to have said of the Sydney Opera House.

In the end, the reveal of the film showed everyone was actually describing Australian fashion and not, as assumed, our most famous landmarks and scenery. It struck a chord in the industry's hearts and minds. Almost at once it galvanised those in attendance into believing that we did have something unique and inspiring to show the world, and it was time to stand up and make this happen. There was no turning back. The industry was now behind Australian Fashion Week.

By this time I had travelled the world several times, sneaking into fashion week shows to spy on production, door-stopping buyers to get their reactions, and introducing myself to everyone from Suzy Menkes to Anna Wintour. I had met with the heads of all the major fashion weeks, including Fern Mallis (New York)—who was later to become my colleague at IMG Fashion—the head of the British

Fashion Council, and the head of the *Camera Moda* in Milan, at the time Beppe Modenese. The *Fédération Française de la Couture, du Prêt-à-Porter des Couturiers et des Créateurs de Mode* in Paris have never agreed to meet with me, to this day. Mr Modenese was an industry icon and he graciously listened to my plans for an international fashion week on the other side of the world. For the life of him he could not understand why anyone would want to travel outside of Europe, or even Milan for that matter, for fashion. He was both amused and bewildered at the same time. He laughed openly out loud when I told him my plans for naming-rights sponsors of our events. Never, ever, ever would that happen in Milan. But sponsorship was the next building block I needed, and while I originally launched the event in early 1995 with the intention that it would be held in May of that year, I had to pull the plug and postpone for another twelve months. Many lost faith in the idea over this time but my passion was unabated, perhaps even strengthened by the disappointment.

When I studied all the other fashion weeks around the world it was obvious to me that these events were the perfect vehicles for corporate sponsorship. There was huge media attention along with every trendsetter in the country attending—the perfect showcase for an array of fashionable products. I had my heart set on a luxury brand to help position the event globally. For me it had to be a car and my choice at the time was BMW.

When I finally got BMW to the table in 1996 it was only months away from the first event. At this time I had made commitments all over town and all over the world that I had no way of keeping without them. My back was so against the wall it was coming through the other side. It was D-Day. Here I was in the Melbourne headquarters of BMW about to sign a five-year contract with them to sponsor BMW Australian Fashion Week. The price had been negotiated, the contract drawn up, and I had my pen in hand when I walked into the BMW boardroom. But something didn't seem right. It was then proposed to me that while BMW saw the merit in the sponsorship they would only sign a five-year contract on the basis that they received the first event for free. If they then deemed the event a success they would pay the agreed sponsorship fee. What the …?!

It was February, the event was in May and there was no way MJ and the others were going to let me go ahead with the event with no sponsors apart from ourselves. In a moment of clarity I didn't react to them. I quietly told the gathered executives and their lawyers that I needed twenty-four hours to consider their proposal and excused myself. Outside I was furious. This was beyond a joke, given the months that had gone into these negotiations. They knew I was too close to the event not to accept their terms. They had actually proposed the first payment for the next year soon after the first event so they knew exactly what they were doing.

I rang directory assistance and asked for the number of the Mercedes-Benz headquarters. It took me a few days to arrange a meeting with Bernt Schlickum, the then head of Mercedes-Benz for Asia Pacific and a visionary executive who was in his twilight years at the company. He was a true gentleman and a gracious host. When we finally sat across from each other a few days later I calmly told him we had something great in common: we both hated BMW with a passion. I told him exactly what had happened only a few days previously. We bonded over our competitive nature but, more importantly, he had been hatching a new direction for Mercedes-Benz in Australia. He knew that the company needed to appeal to a younger market—it could no longer be seen as producing expensive cars for old people. He saw in Australian Fashion Week the perfect promotional vehicle. Within a number of days we had a signed contract and the event was now officially Mercedes Australian Fashion Week. One of the sweetest calls in my life was to BMW to thank them very much for their offer but we would be working with Mercedes-Benz.

3

The Italians
Are Coming

MY CURRENT JOURNEY continues to mirror the early years of getting Fashion Week off the ground all those years ago. I'm still living out of a suitcase, but this time travelling to the fashion capitals of the world, trying to convince the world's most famous designers to be a part of the ORDRE portfolio. This time most people know who I am or, at least my experience and reputation is easy to find on the internet. Thank heavens twenty years ago no one could Google me!

In a matter of weeks ORDRE will be launched globally. It will allow almost three thousand of the most prestigious retailers in the world to be able to view and place wholesale orders for the world's best designers. In one fell swoop I will have done what I set out to do twenty years ago: put our industry on a level playing field with the rest of the world. No longer will the limitation of travelling to a fashion week or showroom on the other side of the world put Australian designers at a disadvantage.

*

In early 1996, the foundations to launch the inaugural Mercedes Australian Fashion Week were laid. In years to come it would be known as Rosemount Australian Fashion Week and Mercedes-Benz Fashion Week Australia, but it will always be MAFW to me. The deal with Mercedes-Benz provided us with much-needed funds to start confirming production for the event, and the NSW Government money promised by Peter Collins soon started flowing. This meant I could now start to build the first event. But we only had months, not years, as it had taken so long to confirm this initial funding.

My years of developing events for Spin clients had taught me that when it comes to any event, venue is king. It is the starting point for everything. My first vision for the home of MAFW was the Victoria Barracks Parade Ground on Oxford Street in Sydney. London Fashion Week had used Chelsea Barracks in London and I thought hosting our event in a similar space would help our positioning on the world stage. At the same time my friend Fern Mallis had established what was then called Seventh on Sixth, now known as New York Fashion Week, in Bryant Park behind the New York Public Library, and so open spaces with the use of massive tents was also the style of the day for the leading fashion weeks. Thanks to my growing connections within the NSW Government I got an audience with the brigadier general in charge of the barracks. I was amused to hear that an event for the fashion industry was being thought of as a threat to army security at the site. In the end I received a firm 'no' from upon high as a result of the supposed sacred nature of parade grounds. It seems no tent stakes could be inserted into its precious green turf. Years later, while attending a United Nations event at the barracks, I smiled to see stakes holding a white tent in place.

I needed a big space. At the time there was lots of talk about the Sydney Royal Easter Show moving out to what was to become Olympic Park. Moves were also afoot by News Corp to take over the showgrounds site at Moore Park and turn it into a film studio. Kim Williams, one of Rupert Murdoch's key lieutenants, and his 2IC, the indomitable Sandra Chipchase (now the head of Destination NSW),

had been put in charge of overseeing the transformation of ancient
cowsheds into multipurpose film studios, an entertainment precinct
and an exhibition space. Instantly I thought Australian film and
fashion were going to be great bedfellows. Cate Blanchett, Russell
Crowe and Hugh Jackman were all on the rise, along with Bruce
Beresford, George Miller and Baz Luhrmann. They were sending
signals around the world about a new creative place called 'Stralya'.
It was a bandwagon I wanted to jump on. I was passionate about
Australian fashion making an international creative statement about
who we are as a country, and catching a ride on the film industry's
coat-tails would be a good start. In years to come some of Australia's
film stars became our industry's biggest supporters. The wonderful
Cate Blanchett would go on to spend one Fashion Week as a special
guest editor for *Harper's Bazaar*, which had a huge impact at the time.

I created a vision in my head that the inaugural MAFW would
be held at the newly minted Fox Studios Australia. What an international calling card that would be! The reality as it turned out was
a long way off the glamorous image in my head. The Centennial
Park and Moore Park Trust controlled the Hordern Pavilion and
the Royal Hall of Industries and these venues were in the middle
of complete and much-needed renovations. The Fox Studios film
spaces were fully booked in May. But thanks to the support of Kim
and Sandra we managed to secure one venue under their control,
the Byron Kennedy Hall. It was small by comparison and had
demolished cowsheds on one side, two huge construction sites on
the other, and a field of mud in between. That was until one fateful
day in early February when I had a call from Spin employee Jarrad
Clark: 'You better get down to the old showgrounds now.'

When I arrived I saw, growing out of the mud between the
Hordern and what is now the entertainment precinct, two of the
biggest sprung structures in the world. One was as long as a football
field and 40 metres high; the other, standing next to it, was a mini
version of the same. Both were beautiful and gleaming white, with
huge clear-span spaces on the inside. They were a gift from heaven!

As it turned out they were from the organising committee of the Sydney 2000 Olympic Games. To our amazement the powers that be had decided they would need these huge temporary venues for the Olympics and bought them to try out on the Royal Easter Show before Olympic Park was ready to host the event. We would eventually move into the Hordern and the Royal Hall, but for then, for our first year, we had finally found our home in two tents and a hall.

In the meantime, work had continued in earnest to lock down the designers who were going to present collections at the inaugural MAFW. After Peter and Leona had said yes, a number of major players followed suit. These included Melbourne's reigning fashion queen Bettina Liano; our beloved founding client at Spin, Joe Saba; bad-boy Wayne Cooper; the tulle king at the time, Alex Perry; the ever-in-fashion Scanlan Theodore; the sweetest tough guy on the planet, Mark Keighery; good friend Michael Bracewell; queen bee Collette Dinnigan, who had just showed in Paris for the first time; and the nicest sisters in fashion ever, Simone and Nicole Zimmermann. They joined a cast of Australian fashion luminaries including Jenny Bannister, Jodie Boffa, Jonathan Ward, Leonie Levy, MJM Lifestyle, Nelson Leong, Robert Burton and Third Millennium, all of whom were there to present individual collection shows on the four-day schedule.

Things appeared to be gathering momentum and then I was to experience my first encounter with Theo Onisforou. Years later Theo was to become a good friend, but at this time he was the feared corporate lawyer for the one and only Kerry Packer. Theo had called to aggressively put Mr Packer's point of view across that he in fact owned the name Australian Fashion Week and that it had been registered by Australian Consolidated Press to protect future publishing endeavours. Our mouse of a company, Australian Fashion Innovators, was about to get a cease and desist order from the Goliath himself. I was stunned. We had already registered the name, along with a number of other versions, and we were in the process of seeking trademark protection. It was one of the first times in my professional career, and unfortunately not the last, that I paid a top-five law firm to reply with certainty that ACP had no leg to stand on. As it turned out it was a calculated bluff by them to try to muscle in on the media environment they felt sure was about to engulf MAFW. It confirmed in my eyes we were onto something that everyone else wanted.

The schedule is always the bedrock of any fashion week. It determines when and who shows, on what day and in what venue. In the beginning it was simply a matter of who wants to show when and it developed in a pretty amicable way and directly with those who were soon to become my designer friends and family. By the time we had got to year ten the schedule was a battleground for fashion editors to promote their power, PR gurus to promote their own egos, sponsors to get bang for their bucks and designers to showcase their best diva impersonations. For much of the first decade, though, my say-so was final. I think I can honestly say I never played favourites, always focused on the designers first and tried to build the best level playing field for the industry I could. At times a lot of people just thought I wielded the power of the schedule as only a true megalomaniac would … well, maybe just a little on some days!

By the time MAFW came around in 1996 I had circumnavigated the globe a number of times pitching to buyers from New York to London and fashion editors from Paris to Singapore to come and attend what was going to be a truly memorable first outing. During these travels I had also researched many of the other fashion weeks and figured out what they were doing right and wrong. Sometimes I went to extraordinary lengths to go behind the scenes to find out how everything worked. I can remember one London Fashion Week when I had no designer invitations and couldn't get into any shows—and my days of pretending to be an eager fashion student and being allowed to slip through had passed. But then I spied at the front door the biggest security guard in the world, who was on a first-name basis with everyone from Anna Wintour to Hilary Alexander. In a break from his velvet-rope duties I went straight up to him, shook his hand and gave him two hundred pounds. I looked him square in the eye and said next time you see me in the back of the queue wave me through, then I turned on my heel and left. An hour later, as everyone queued for the Vivienne Westwood show, our eyes met as I waited patiently at the back. To my sheer delight he waved to me to approach him and dropped the velvet rope of the VIP entrance to let me in. I gave him another handshake at the end of the week after I had seen every show I had wanted to.

From my ambushes of various fashion weeks around the world I slowly put together what we could build as a competitive advantage for our fashion week. At the time, fashion week organisers didn't really see themselves as customer service providers with a focus on the buyers and media who attended. Instead, they felt their role was to play to the needs and wants of designers. This meant that a very old-fashioned system had evolved where there was no central management of invitations and, with most fashion weeks around the world, designers were able to choose their own venues, often meaning that buyers and media had to travel across town through peak-hour traffic and arrive at a fashion show exhausted and frustrated—not an ideal frame of mind to take in new creative ideas. For years I have seen buyers sitting in the front row exhausted, with arms crossed, hungry and upset about all the inconveniences they have had to suffer during that day of that particular fashion week. This didn't seem to me a good way to get them to open their order books or for the media to be in a good mood to write a positive story. Something had to change and I wanted to be the one to do it.

First, I devised a four-day official schedule for MAFW that absolutely forbade any designer from showing anywhere else except in one of our three venues, which were all conveniently located next to each other. Next, I established a central delegate registration system so that buyers and media could sign up with us as an organisation and we would handle all their invitations to each collection show and set up a seat-allocation process. These two simple strategies turned MAFW over the first few years into the most user-friendly fashion week in the world. What people didn't immediately recognise was that it also handed control of the front row to us. One of the most powerful tools at our disposal to grow Fashion Week had been secured. Never before had organisers been given this power and in years to come our seating directors were able to establish their own companies off the back of this strategy.

Today a lot of these tactics are globally accepted. Well, except the front row bit! To media and buyers coming to MAFW in 1996 it was revolutionary in some senses, but certainly not all. All I wanted to do was to ensure buyers weren't too tired to write orders or go to every show on the schedule. This is still one of my legacies to this day with the exception of a few off-site shows, which ultimately needed to be held elsewhere for various reasons.

As we locked in designers the bones of the schedule came together. There was now only one small problem we had to solve. Australia had never produced an international standard fashion show, with the exception perhaps of Christine Bookallil's, and we only had a few months to pull it together. A solution came in the form of an Italian magic man, a Mediterranean Elvis and fashion royalty: Marco Maccapani.

I knew from the outset that I couldn't look within the Australian fashion industry to lead the production of MAFW. I don't want to give the impression that no one in Australia had experience in any element of producing international standard fashion shows, but very few did at the time. We had decades to catch up on in terms of the quality of the execution of other fashion weeks and we had to come out on day one with all guns blazing, looking and feeling like an authentic and professionally produced international fashion week. It could not be a repeat of the bicentennial year. Nor could it be a series of shopping centre 'parades' and well-meaning Australian choreographers with girls swinging their hips and twirling like they were at some RSL dance night. Kate Moss had just made her debut in London and the style was sleek and deadpan. We had to be seen as fashion contemporaries and not as hicks and outsiders.

This was as much a personal statement as it was a professional one for me.

For months on my travels I had been briefing all the big production companies around the world, including KCD in New York, who Jarrad now works for. Most were amused by our vision and I think they saw an opportunity to take a greenhorn for a bit of a ride. In a chance conversation with Collette Dinnigan she suggested a guy she knew in Milan who, along with his then girlfriend, ex-model Jennifer Surness, had built a fashion production company that was getting rave reviews. This was my introduction to the maestro himself, Marco Maccapani. Marco had married into fashion royalty when he wed Angela Missoni in 1982, and is the father of Margherita Missoni, the international model and ambassador for the family house today. As far as I know he has always been involved in the fashion industry as both a show and fashion video director. With his set designer partner Angelo and Jennifer as his manager of casting they had become a formidable and effective team working on some of Milan Fashion Week's biggest shows, including Versace, Armani and Missoni, of course. Collette organised an introduction and we started our discussions on the phone. It wasn't long before I found myself in Milan with Marco and his posse for the first time, on the first of many long and sometimes drunken nights together.

From the start, Marco and I were totally transparent and upfront with each other, both with what I expected and what he wanted. It was a weird but perfect fashion partnership that continues to shape the fashion industry in Australia to this very day. As a result of our collaboration nearly every fashion show producer currently working in Australia can trace their career roots back to Marco. They either learnt directly from Marco, like Jarrad did, or worked directly for Jarrad or someone who has worked for Jarrad. The family tree all leads back to Marco Maccapani. There are very few exceptions.

After the first few days of getting to know each other in Milan we got down to brass tacks. I wanted Marco to build the best catwalks in the world in my beautiful big white tents in Sydney and produce world-standard fashion shows. I wanted to surround him with a team of Australians who over time would suck the last bit of knowledge out of him. I wanted him to show us how to design a fashion showroom. I wanted to know how to prepare a designer to present a collection on the runway from concept through to execution. I wanted to know how to cast properly, manage running orders, prepare hair and make-up briefs and teams to execute them, program music and work with DJs, design and program lighting and sound systems, organise backstages, shoot videos and teach models to walk properly. I wanted the lot, and I wanted it right now with only months to go!

Marco studied the venue plans, discussed them with his team and then presented me with a plan that basically over the next three years was going to drive me to within an inch of personal and professional bankruptcy. But I nearly knocked him over in my haste to sign the contract. What I didn't realise then and what I found out the hard way was that Marco thought big. The sheer scale of what he had in mind would not only put us on the fashion map but also nearly wipe me off it. I signed a three-year deal with him to produce MAFW for 1996, 1997 and 1998. The essence of that contract was that he would teach anyone I surrounded him with and then after three years graciously retire to the relative safety of Milan. I think by the time he was back there it was we who were safe! Jarrad had outgrown the confines of the Spin showroom and he was on my case for new opportunities. Well, he certainly got them. With Simon B's support Jarrad was to become Marco's right-hand man in Australia and a lifelong friend. From the moment Marco and his team arrived Jarrad shadowed his every move—except for a few late-night ones when Marco was particularly elusive!

While we were waiting for Marco and his team to arrive in Sydney for the first time I started to put the rest of the production team together so that they could learn from the maestro. I turned to my connections in the music industry, Michael Gudinski and

Michael Chugg, and they recommended I speak with Meri Took, the boss at Staging Rentals, who was a straightforward, no fuss, rock-and-roll production legend. He basically said on our first meeting he'd give me lots of rope but if I didn't pay my bills he would break my legs … and I believed him. Another key player also entered the scene at this time: the 'Man in the Hat' Iain Reed from 32 Hundred Lighting. He became our lighting director and also had experience both in the rock and TV industries. I had a gut feeling that people from the music scene would suit us best and I was right.

Appropriately, when I went to meet Marco at Sydney airport it was like watching a rock star walk out of customs. Having flown straight from a bitter winter in Milan, Marco arrived to a Sydney summer in a fur coat, tight jeans, boots, dark glasses and a permanent cloud of cigarette smoke around his very Italian five o'clock shadow. He could have been Bono arriving for a U2 concert. I knew instantly that, as soon as he walked into any room, designers were going to believe in his production vision, queen bees were going to fall at his feet in submission—much to Jennifer's constant frustration—and Australian fashion would know we had a major international player in our midst.

Marco's first job was to finish the designs of our collection showrooms. The larger of the sprung structures was to house two perfectly designed runways, the likes of which had never been seen before in Australia. They would be mirror images of each other, with a central production control unit. Marco had bought Angelo Jelmini with him, who was part architect, part mad scientist and part CAD genius. To this day he reminds me of the Italian film director Roberto Benigni. Marco had the production vision in his head and his heart and Angelo would transform it into CAD drawings and lighting plots that our team could follow.

Creating the perfect collection showroom requires great skill. The venue needs to be the right combination of intimate physical viewing room, where buyers and media can get close enough to the collections to see the details and fabrications, and a state-of-the-art photographic studio capable of producing high-quality video and still images to promote the collections through all channels of media coverage. It also requires a catwalk wide enough to allow models to pass each other without colliding and long enough so silhouettes and fabric drape and flow can be appreciated; seating suitably tiered to enable a large audience to view the collection, as no one can see from the third row on the same level; a backdrop to protect the audience from the chaos and distraction of backstage; a lighting rig that illuminates every special detail of the collections while creating the perfect balance for video and still photography; a production console that is invisible; a sound system that can balance both pumping beats and background ambience; and, most importantly, an overall environment that creates the theatre of the front row in all its sought-after glory. A collection showroom like this had never been built in Australia until May 1996, the first year of MAFW.

Some people at times have had an issue with my 'control freak' attitude in relation to the early years of Fashion Week but I just wasn't prepared to let any element of visual production out of our grasp. It seems incredible now but twenty years ago our industry just didn't have the experience it now does in producing world-standard fashion shows. We had to learn the international language of fashion as well—I banned the word 'parade' from passing our team's lips, insisting presentations were named a 'fashion show' or 'collection show'. Part of the control I exerted extended to the formula I put in place for designers to participate in the event. I asked them to contribute a once-off total venue and production fee that was hugely underwritten by the NSW Government, our sponsors and me, as it turned out! For this fee, designers received use of a collection show-room and its backstage facilities, all the production and equipment operators that go with it, a producer, music director, casting director, models, hair and make-up teams, backstage dressers, ushers and the maestro himself to direct and call the show. Back in the day design-ers got all this for a little over $10,000 each. Today a single budget on a show produced at any international fashion week averages out at about $100,000, and in the case of the Chanels of this world, about $5 million.

All this allowed us to totally control all the production elements of each show with the A team I had put in place. The long-term plan, though, was that each year we would hand one production element back to the designers as we learnt together from the best. The designers were also encouraged to surround themselves with people who wanted to acquire the skills of both the production and business of fashion. We had just three short years to learn what had taken other industries decades.

This system, while good in theory, put tremendous financial pressure on our organisation, as we were ultimately responsible for every single cost involved in the production and marketing of MAFW. This required us to negotiate cross-industry model rates, which at the time was very controversial. I couldn't and wasn't prepared to pay current standard rates so I set an MAFW rate and went about selling it to the four big agencies—Chadwick, Priscillas, Chic and Vivien's. Fortunately for me, Peter Chadwick, Priscilla Leighton Clark, Ursula Hufnagl and Vivien Smith were true believers from the beginning. They accepted the $375 per show rate under duress but knew if we could build the event they would have a steady annual revenue stream for years to come.

Jennifer Surness really came into her own with models, hair, make-up and backstage management. She introduced me to her cousin Selina Robinson, who was to become our backstage manager for years and then go on to become an internationally respected producer who, years later, I would work with again on Dubai Fashion Week. Jennifer was beautiful, tempestuous and knew exactly what she expected of a model on the catwalk. At one of the first castings she undertook she realised quickly she had her work cut out for her as model after model insisted on putting their hands on their hips. She must have walked a thousand miles herself in showing them the 'new style'. She was also responsible for bringing into the fold perhaps the most defining hair director of the era, Renya Xydis. I believe they had worked together on Collette's first show in Paris and Renya was one of a few in our local industry who had international experience. Jennifer also searched our industry for the leading make-up directors and helped them to work in this new show environment.

As the MAFW team came together other heads of department were secured, including inaugural music director Andy Glitre, who hit it off immediately with Marco through a number of shared common interests, and the Grucci brothers Mick and Tim, who came on board to manage video production. Within the first months of the year the bones of the production team had come together and Marco and Jennifer along with Jarrad and myself had started designer production meetings. In the early years these were quiet, simple affairs, as the designers didn't know the capabilities of our production team, so Marco and I helped develop the concepts and themes for many shows based on the inspiration behind the collections. In the first year we really filled the roll of creative director for many designers, with the exception of the usual suspects who were never going to be told what to do: Morrissey Edmiston, Collette Dinnigan and Wayne Cooper. They knew exactly what they wanted to do and we immediately fell in behind them as their production team to build their vision. Wayne was always going to give Marco a run for his money in the rock god stakes.

It was around this time that the editor of *Vogue Australia*, Nancy Pilcher, contacted me with an extraordinary offer. Nancy had been one of my biggest supporters, working with Annita Keating, myself and Jane de Teliga when we were trying to encourage everyone in the industry to get on board. She did things behind the scenes that made a huge difference. I was often in her office, seeking her advice and politically putting all the elements and players together. I fondly remember when searching for a venue dragging her and Jane to a disused pier at Walsh Bay, now beautifully restored, in an attempt to support my push to the premier to do a makeover of the pier and then give it to me as the permanent venue for MAFW … dream big, I say.

Nancy was hosting an event in Sydney for Jonathan Newhouse, chairman of Condé Nast, the international owners of *Vogue*, and wanted to use it to support MAFW. The event, held at Le Trianon restaurant in Potts Point—run by my good friends Peter and Bev Doyle—was just a few months before the first Fashion Week and the who's who of the industry would be rolling up to meet Jonathan. He is an amazing executive who always seems capable of balancing the fine juggling act between art and commerce in the publishing world while keeping the loyalty of some of the smartest people in the industry, including *Vogue* editors Anna Wintour in the United States and Alexandra Shulman in Britain, and Nancy and the woman who was to eventually replace her, Kirstie Clements. Kirstie would, in the years to come, also have a huge influence on MAFW.

On that evening at Le Trianon a hush fell over the fashion crowd, which is quite unusual in itself, as Nancy introduced Jonathan. Steely eyed, he looked around the room and to my amazement and sheer delight spent the better part of his speech telling the Australian industry that what they were about to embark on with MAFW was both brave and innovative and that he and Nancy intended to put their full support behind it. He went on to announce *Vogue*'s commitment to the first-ever runway report for Australian Fashion Week. He left the podium and walked directly to me and shook my hand, wishing me good luck.

It wasn't only me who was left wide-mouthed and speechless—everyone in the room was. It sent shockwaves through the industry. This thing called Australian Fashion Week *must* be real: *Vogue* had just publicly backed it. It also put the fear of god into every Australian designer who usually hid behind their past editions of *Collezioni* because the international spotlight was going to be shining brightly on the catwalks of Australian Fashion Week and there would be nowhere for them to hide.

Once Marco, Angelo, Jennifer and Jarrad were well established in designer production-meeting hell I turned my attention to whatever else needed doing. It was like turning around and being faced with

Everest from the airport car park in Kathmandu! My first job was to complete the schedule. While all the leading Australian designers at the time had been slotted into individual shows, the overall program needed more balance. Instinctively I created three new events—just because we didn't have our hands full enough with all the individual collection shows.

We needed a huge high-profile Opening Ceremony to sound the starting gun to the nation that MAFW had begun. I turned to Jane de Teliga, who was able to secure the Powerhouse Museum as the venue. The Powerhouse still holds much of the Australian Fashion Week archive and, a decade and half later, staged the 15th Anniversary Frock Stars Exhibition.

I had purposely not invited any of the old guard of the Australian fashion industry to present individual collections at MAFW. Most of these designers had vertical retail businesses and weren't interested in wholesale or exporting. I did, however, feel a need to pay tribute to all they had contributed to the industry and to this end I created the first of many group shows at MAFW, called the Australian Designer Collections. This included Adele Weiss, Anthea Crawford, Brian Rochford, Carla Zampatti, Covers, George Gross, Harry Who, Jane Lamerton and Jill Fitzsimon. My only one regret to this day was including Carla Zampatti in this group. She deserved in every sense to be offered her own Fashion Week show from the very beginning and it was my inexperience in the industry that meant I didn't see that. She joined the schedule years later to my great joy and relief.

The other event I added to the schedule in the first year is still a central foundation to Fashion Week: the showcase of emerging talent. I knew from day one we had a huge responsibility to the industry to ensure we used our spotlight generously on not just the established designers but also the future of our industry. Thus the group show New Generation Collections was born and, in conjunction with Simon B and others, we created a vetting process to invite the best new talent in Australia to become a part of MAFW.

Those selected in 1996 included Akira Isogawa, Billion Dollar Babes, Glamour Pussy, Jac Allen Couture, Jaclin Chouchana, Miss Gladys Sym Choon and Paablo Nevada.

There seemed at least another five thousand elements that had to be completed before the Opening Ceremony rolled around on 6 May 1996. The checklist included chasing all the international delegates who said they would come, designing and sending out the national delegate registration forms, accrediting all the media, selling the first MAFW Exhibition that was going into the smaller sprung structure, designing a seating allocation system, creating an international host program, establishing an international and national publicity program, continuing to sell sponsorship and managing the sponsors, creating a courtesy car program using the demos we had been given by Mercedes-Benz ... the list went on. This doesn't even account for the daily list of production requests coming from Marco's team: we need more Vari-Lites, we need 5-metre-wide seamless fabric for catwalk covers, we need more power, we need, we need, we need ... OMG! Who was going to pay for all this?!

Spin at this time was slowly developing into the dynamic entity it was to eventually become. At that stage we had about twenty staff along with MJ's and Simon B's support, and everyone got dragged onto the MAFW team in some capacity. Australian Fashion Innovators, the company I had set up to run MAFW, had also started to employ a number of key staff, many transferring from the Spin team. One of the first was Jodi Pritchard. Jodi had been with me since the Saatchi days, following me to Harrison Communications and then becoming one of the first employees to join The Lock Group's first company, The Lock Partnership, in Melbourne in 1989. She had since become the general manager of Spin, but as we developed in Sydney I asked her to take on the GM's role at MAFW. In my mind she was in many respects the lynchpin of the success of Fashion Week's early years. Her strengths in creating structures out of the chaos and reality out of the dreams are enormous. As the ultimate quiet achiever I still don't think, to this day, the debt the Australian fashion industry owes this amazing woman has been recognised.

The other heads of department had also come together around this time. I had roped in Christine Bookallil, of course, to be the inaugural communications director; John Flower, my old friend who had been working for us in Melbourne, to be in charge of all delegate registration and seating; Lucia Labbate as receptionist, who went on to become event director during our time at IMG in later years; and even my brother Richard, who was to run the courtesy car program. We all sprinted together towards the Opening Ceremony. There were late sessions at Palmer Street until two or three in the morning, with visits from Lucia's mum with homemade lasagne to keep us going, for seven days a week and for months and months on end. Even so we hadn't even got to base camp ... and still the requests came from Marco.

I remember one of the requests that most astonished me. In a very matter-of-fact way Marco asked me when he would be able to brief the backstage dressers and ushers. He estimated that about one hundred and fifty or so would make do! In my naivety and inexperience and whirlwind state of mind I had completely overlooked the need for this huge staffing requirement. We were four weeks out from the event and had already spent every cent I had raised ... and a lot I hadn't. When I said I was onto it Marco casually explained that at other fashion weeks the roles were usually filled by student volunteers. Great idea, I thought.

While I hadn't as yet met a crazy guy called Nicholas Huxley, who was then the head of East Sydney Design Studio, I knew his reputation through designers like Alex Perry and Nicole Zimmermann, who had studied under him. I arranged a meeting with him and told him of my dilemma. Even though MAFW fell during school semester, Nicholas closed down the fashion school, rounded up his Whitehouse and TAFE colleagues as well and promised he would deliver all the students I needed. It was to become a partnership with Nicholas and the other fashion schools in Sydney, and eventually around the region, that is now the backbone of Fashion Week. The industry today couldn't afford to run the event if it wasn't for the students. We get the manpower we need to run this huge beast and they get firsthand experience in the business of fashion.

On a personal level, things were growing in more ways than one on the home front. Lorraine and I had married shortly after we started working together, and had started a family. Hannah Emily Rose had been born in 1994 amid negotiations to get Fashion Week off the ground and two months out from the inaugural event our son Julian (Jules) Thomas was to arrive. I will never forget, and nor will Lorraine I suspect, being dragged away from her bedside when she was in early labour to approve the artwork for the first MAFW delegate brochure that Louisa Gent from Spin had designed. Fashion week was certainly going to be a big part of my children's upbringing! For the next twenty years the Lock children, including my first son, David, were never too far away from the front row or backstage. Lorraine was very supportive during these years. She managed the children while still juggling clients in her own company, Planet Communications (part of The Lock Group), and accepted me being away for weeks at a time chasing buyers and media around the world.

In the lead-up to the event I hadn't been able to spend much time down at Fox Studios, as I was running around town putting out fires, such as figuring out who was going to represent the government at the Opening Ceremony, managing about a hundred daily media requests, juggling cash flow with our embattled finance director and now partner Greg Gleeson and trying to sell the last spots. Then I got a call from Jarrad: 'I think it is time you got down here to see what is going on.' I jumped in my brand new Mercedes-Benz, which I had very kindly been provided by Mercedes on an ongoing basis as part of our contract, and headed to Fox Studios. The phone rang again and I presumed it was Jarrad.

'Hi mate ... what's happening?' The voice on the other end was a little surprised.

'Hello Simon, this is Lachlan Murdoch.' He had been watching with interest as the industry prepared itself for the first Fashion Week and had called to personally wish me good luck. I felt pretty chuffed with myself, having gained the attention of two of the country's media moguls. I didn't realise then, though, that you need to be careful what you wish for when it comes to the Australian media—an article in Lachlan's family newspaper *The Daily Telegraph* a few weeks later nearly precipitated the downfall of the event before it had barely got going.

I drove into Fox Studios and wandered straight into the back door of the largest sprung structure. Nothing could have prepared me for what I faced. It is an image that is still crystal clear in my memory to this day. Stretching for over 80 metres under the sky-high arched spans of this amazing structure was the scaffold framework of my dreams. The skeletons of what were to become known as the Blue Room and the Yellow Room had taken shape. They were bigger, bolder and on a scale that I had never imagined. Angelo's plan on a computer screen gave me no perspective as to what I had just walked into. The sheer size took my breath away. This was bigger than New York. It was bigger than London. Marco greeted me with the usual cigarette in the corner of his mouth and a grin that said it all … *You wanted to make a statement; well, you got it!*

If we could fill these rooms with buyers and media, if we could make the catwalks come alive with the talents of the Australian designers and fill these huge voids with applause that would lead to orders placed and media promotion, we had a chance to pull off the most unlikely international fashion coup of the decade. Marco and his team had delivered us the platform that for the first time gave our industry an equal footing with the best fashion weeks around the world. The rest was now up to us.

In the last few days leading up to the first event it became clear to me in some sense what I had achieved over the past four years: I wasn't so much the circus ringmaster—which I have often been accused of being—but the catalyst. Somehow, as a fashion outsider,

I had been able to get others to believe in my vision, to become passionate about what we could achieve as an industry and importantly to have the self-confidence to believe that together we could do it. Along the way I had led from the front, never too proud to staple a press release, to get on my knees and plead my case on behalf of the industry, always the last to leave and first to arrive, and always trying to keep a sense of humour and build a team spirit. Around me I had gathered an equally passionate, loyal and hard-working group of hundreds of people who were the ones delivering on my huge promises.

As I walked out the back door that day after seeing my dreams come alive for the first time Iain Reed quietly came up to me, looked me in the eyes, as always with his hat firmly in place on his head, and said, 'SPL, if this isn't the best I can possibly make for you, you'll find me in that dumpster over there with my wrists slashed. On the day I promise you it will be everything you want.' Iain, that day, I believe echoed the feeling of the whole team. Somehow I had managed to engender this sort of loyalty in those around me. It made me immensely proud, but above all drove me to make sure I didn't let anyone down in return.

I left Fox Studios with the full weight of an industry on my shoulders.

4

'We Did It'

THIS WEEK KIRSTEN and I arrived back in New York. ORDRE is now live and in this first week we are excited to be actually letting the world see our new platform. We have created headlines in WWD.com, the international authority on the fashion industry, and more designers are showing interest in what we are doing, including majors like Derek Lam, Thom Browne, Phillip Lim and Marc Jacobs.

Twenty years ago, the same thing happened. So many designers sat on the fence and waited to see if we could pull it off before they jumped on board. It is a true leap of faith to sign up to someone else's vision. The Zimmermann sisters had that faith twenty years ago and were there at the start of Mercedes Australian Fashion Week and here they are now with us at the start of ORDRE.

*

There was no doubt in my mind or anyone else's that we had done the best possible job we could in attracting attention to the inaugural MAFW in 1996. Christine Bookallil, managing publicity, was already

attracting a huge amount of interest from the media. Over the previous four years my media presentation skills had also improved and
I now found myself quite comfortable in front of a television camera
or a reporter's microphone. I was being called on to speak not just
on behalf of the industry but also for Australia more broadly. I was
once even asked via the prime minister's office to assist with the
Australian Republican Movement and for a while I worked alongside
Malcolm Turnbull and Mark Ryan to generate community interest
in this important issue for the country. It was one I felt was aligned
to the international promotion of Australia's coming of age in the
fashion industry. I also spoke to world leaders at the Commonwealth
Heads of Government Meeting about the meaning of Australian style
and the fashion industry's impact on Australia's image.

In that first year, I was certainly becoming recognised for my
enthusiasm for the local fashion industry and building high expectations of what our Fashion Week could achieve. Many promises had
been made. I appeared bullish about which international guests were
going to be attending the first event. So by the time we were ready
to fire the starting gun we had the Australian media in a feeding
frenzy. Newspapers, magazines, television stations, current affairs
programs and radio stations were all chasing us for stories. Sydney
was entering the international fashion week circuit alongside New
York, London, Paris and Milan and the world was coming to see us.
And there I was standing on my soapbox telling anyone who would
listen that we had an amazingly talented industry and together we
were going to take on the world. I was so boldfaced that even before
the event started I had estimated we were going to do millions in
wholesale orders and actually sent out a press release to that effect
to throw petrol on the fire.

The media in the lead-up were overwhelmingly positive; little did
I realise then it was the calm before the storm. Over the next twenty
years, the media had a field day with me and me with them. I spoke
up for the game of the Australian designers like I was the coach of
the Wallabies. I promoted sales figures and media coverage statistics,

and paraded a never-ending series of celebrity designers and fashion superstars. I orchestrated parties on luxury yachts, media launches in famous spaces, took over Government House on more than one occasion, crowned new supermodels, launched the careers of up-and-coming designers, paid tribute to founding fashion fathers and all the time left myself wide open for criticism. And boy did I get it.

It was inevitable that I would be portrayed as the all-singing, all-dancing circus ringmaster. I would be applauded and vilified as both the saviour of the Australian fashion industry and its self-appointed international ambassador, as both a clever business person and a controlling egomaniac driven at all costs to achieve success without letting anything or anybody stand in my way. My enthusiasm was going to be portrayed as arrogance, my passion as greed and my caring as insincerity. I was going to be called manipulative, a spin doctor, obviously, and a megalomaniac. News Limited referred to my bald head as resembling another part of the anatomy.

The end result in my opinion was absolutely worth it. After all these years of working with the media and having suffered my fair share of tall-poppy slurs I can honestly say I do not regret one moment or resent one word said or written about me. The media environment that was created around Fashion Week was actually the industry's most powerful asset. In April 1996 there were only a few Australian designers recognised by the general public. Australian Fashion Week made Australian designers famous and household names. It put them up there alongside famous international designers and positioned them as equals. It is the reason why our department stores fight over them today.

But when I walked out of the sprung structure at Fox Studios Australia on that Sunday night, 5 May 1996, I was feeling nervous, scared and, quite frankly, a little sick. After four years of planning it was about to happen. It seemed like there was still so much to be done, but as I was to say for many years to come, 'The train is about to leave the station and you just have to hang on for the ride.'

International guests started to arrive on the weekend of 4–5 May via Qantas thanks to the sponsorship deal we had struck with the airline, which had in fact been the very first sponsor to commit to Fashion Week due to then communications director Ken Groves. I wanted to personally meet all the international buyers and media as they arrived and so over that weekend I made what seemed like a never-ending series of trips to the airport to meet around twenty-five guests, including those from Liberty (London), Lane Crawford (Hong Kong), *Elle* (United States), Harvey Nichols (Britain), CK Tangs (Singapore), *Collezioni* (Italy) and *South China Morning Post* (Hong Kong). There were also two international delegates who out-shone everyone else that first year: Mrs B, or Mrs Joan Burstein, the influential owner of Browns in London who discovered Galliano and introduced Donna Karan and Armani among others to the United Kingdom; and the equally influential Marion Hume, the fashion editor of *The Financial Times* and a contributor to *Vogue*. In the years to come, both would have a major impact on the event and the industry, Marion in a most unexpected way.

Apart from welcoming them personally, all the international guests were given a mini tour of the city and invited to a series of welcome dinners. For many years we would follow this same course of action on the weekend before the event. In between fashion shows, after-parties, sponsor events and press conferences, Jodi Pritchard and I would also spend as much time with the internationals as we could, consistently in their faces about this designer or that and doing everything we could to encourage them to get out their cheque books or to provide media support.

The first official event of the schedule was a press conference held at Fox Studios on Monday, 6 May: a group photo call of all the designers involved that year. It was a momentous occasion and the first time the media had seen inside the sprung structures and what Marco, Jarrad and the team had built. From the very beginning people were impressed. The designers themselves were blown away by the sheer scale of the collection showrooms, many feeling daunted by the prospect of filling both the catwalk and the seats.

The next twenty-four hours were a complete blur. The production team literally ran in every direction. It had rained and this left a number of muddy pathways between our venues that had to be dealt with. The exhibition area was being bumped into the middle-sized of the three sprung structures, finishing touches were made to the signage, display cars were delivered and positioned and designer walk-throughs and technical rehearsals were conducted. This was not a well-oiled team—far from it. Everything from backstage layout to focusing lights on the catwalk was being done by us for the first time and on such a grand scale.

The core team of myself, Alannah Bermeister, Lucia Labbate, John Flower, Mary-Anne Seymore, Anthea Loucas, Clemence Harvey and our still long-suffering finance director Greg Gleeson was in a state of panic combined with apprehension, excitement and expectation. Each of us hadn't had a decent sleep for days, often working through the night. What I thought would be essential and great attributes for Fashion Week, like a central seating program and an international host program, often took thousands of hours to deliver. There is no doubt in my mind some of our early success was a direct result of the thousands of hours of often unpaid work by a whole range of unsung heroes who believed in my vision and lent their own passion to help.

Tuesday, 7 May, loomed large and three preliminary events before the many shows were planned. The very first Fashion Week Seminar and the all-important Opening Ceremony were both staged at the Powerhouse Museum thanks to Jane de Teliga, then fashion editor at *The Sydney Morning Herald*, Powerhouse curator Glynis Jones and our major benefactor Peter Collins, who was now opposition leader as a result of a change of government in New South Wales. The third was a designer dinner to be hosted at the Regent Hotel.

The seminar was amazing. *Vogue Australia* editor Nancy Pilcher agreed to chair the event, and Jane de Teliga and a number of international guests spoke to the enthusiastic MAFW delegates. Collette Dinnigan also spoke about the challenges of launching a fashion brand from Australia. The Opening Ceremony that evening was a huge challenge logistically. Our production team was already up to its eyeballs in final preparations at Fox Studios and they basically had to relocate to the Powerhouse to produce what also needed to be a world-class event—believe me, the eyes of the world were upon us.

I was determined to personally shake the hand or kiss every single person who showed up. I had no idea what a huge task that was going to be. The original five hundred invitations for the Opening Ceremony had gone out weeks before and the phones hadn't stopped ringing since: 'Can I bring a plus one?', 'We need to invite such and such', 'The sponsors want more guests', 'My mum wants to come' … the requests went on and on. By the time my wife Lorraine joined me at the end of the red carpet there was a queue around the block. The fashion industry had turned up in force. The Turbine Hall at the Powerhouse was overflowing—the hors d'oeuvres were hoovered up in a matter of minutes—but thanks to my always over-generous drink catering we just about got through the night with enough bubbles. By the time I was literally dragged from the welcoming position to start the official proceedings I had greeted over one thousand five hundred people—three times more than we had expected.

When I rose to the podium to make the official welcome, a silence fell over the crowd—that almost never happens at a fashion event. A lump formed in my throat as I looked out over the heads of every designer in Australia, every fashion media person and major retailer, leaders of fashion schools, hairdressers and make-up artists, models, agents and stylists, PR people and sponsors, our own production team—everyone in the industry, every one. I knew right then and there it was going to be a success. This success wasn't going to rely on how good we were as event organisers or how good an individual designer's collection was. It was going to be based on the fact that we had come together as an industry with a singular determination. In that room on that night there was a collective feeling that was amazing. This wasn't about petty issues like whether Sydney or Melbourne was the centre of the fashion industry in Australia or which designer was the hottest at that minute. Instead, we felt each other's strengths and creativity, and joined together in an ambition to be more than the sum of individual parts, in the knowledge that together we could do more. In my mind the Australian fashion industry, as we know it today, was born on that night, Tuesday, 6 May 1996, at about 9 p.m.

My heart was pounding so much and I was so excited and enthusiastic about the opportunity I'm sure I sounded like an evangelical preacher as I introduced Bob Carr, the then premier of New South Wales; Bernt Schlickum, the head of Mercedes; Matt Handbury, who, along with his marketing director at Murdoch Magazines, Mark Kelly, had become one of the most influential early supporters and sponsors of the Opening Ceremony; and Stephen Bennett, the much-loved founder of Country Road, whom I had recently appointed as my chairman. The night was a blur of well wishing and great expectations for the four days of shows that lay ahead.

Straight after the Opening Ceremony another early supporter hosted her first Fashion Week event. Karin Upton Baker, the stylish editor of *Mode*, which was to become *Harper's Bazaar*, hosted a swanky dinner at Kable's Restaurant for all the VIPs and internationals. It was one of a number of traditions that started that night. And the main event was now only twelve hours away.

*

Early on the question was asked, 'Who is going to put up their hand to be the first designer ever to show at MAFW?' It would be a brave person. I can still hear Wayne Cooper with his East End London accent saying to me, 'Sure, Lockie, I'll open your Fashion Week', and open it he did, with a collection called, you guessed it, Brave.

I turned up on-site about 6 a.m. on that first day dressed head to toe in my signature look at the time: dark suit set off by a mono-coloured shirt and a tie that matched the colour of the shirt exactly. It was to become my fashion uniform for some years. I walked back-stage at Wayne Cooper to find the Italians had taken over. Music blared, make-up mirrors lit up the place like Luna Park, steamers hissed and models giggled. Marco and Andy grinned and smoked. Jennifer was on a rampage about missing running orders, Selina was rounding up dressers, Iain was climbing around the rigging adjusting lights, Jarrad was chasing down every direction from Marco, and the Jands and Staging Rentals boys were just rolling their eyes, having seen it all before backstage at Rolling Stones' concerts. It could only be described as organised chaos. For me the excitement was intoxicating. Everything was happening everywhere and right in the middle of it were our three Australian supermodels as casual as you like, going, 'Yeah, we're used to this, it's just like Paris.' Well, I wasn't used to it and I was loving every minute. I might have been a fashion fan before but now I was a groupie!

I really owe a huge thanks to Sarah O'Hare (now Murdoch), Emma Balfour and Anneliese Seubert. These three Australian models had been hugely successful overseas but were little known in Australia. They had each left good paying work behind in the United States and Europe to head home at their own cost and to work for the modest rates we had set. They were to become, along with the designers in that first year, the stars of the entire event. The other Australian models, only a handful of whom had actually worked overseas at this stage, really looked up to these women and were eager to hear stories of the international circuit.

All of a sudden it was time for the doors to open and for our first day of delegate registration. The process had been a controversial one in the lead-up. In order to try to balance the budget I felt that industry representatives, including media and buyers, should pay a registration fee to attend. In exchange, we would provide a centralised ticket and seat-allocation services to ensure that once a delegate was registered they were invited to each collection show and allocated a seat where appropriate. A few snobs in the industry who had attended fashion weeks in the United States or Europe, where all the invitations are individually extended by designers and there is no central registration service or fee, complained to anyone who would listen. David Jones actually refused to pay their registration and tried to go around the system to the designers directly. As a result, it was a great shame that DJs hardly had a presence in the first year; however, this was to change once visionary executives like Colette Garnsey and David Bush became more involved.

I left backstage at Wayne's to see how things were going at registration. Beyond chaos! Queues out the door, under-staffed desks, seat allocation not complete and everyone who was too precious to pre-register now doing so on the day. Frustration was rising, tempers were building and a phrase we were going to hear a million times over the coming years emerged: 'Don't you know who I am?' The whole crew just looked at me in desperation. The crowd was five hundred people deep and the start time of the first show was rapidly approaching. I walked out into the crowd and was basically pulled every which way—'Where is my front row ticket?', 'I need to get my photographer in' and 'Can I get a backstage pass?' This was heaven to me. Without a model setting foot on a catwalk we were approaching fever pitch and we hadn't even got past registration. Action, however, had to be taken.

I had an innate sense that if I lost it and started running around screaming and shouting, we were not going to get anywhere. So, with the team holding the frontline at the registration desks, I calmly took myself off, borrowed a megaphone from security, got a chair, positioned it near the front door, rose above the crowd and with a blast from my megaphone brought the crowd to attention. To everyone's surprise, not least my crew's, there was a huge grin on my face. I welcomed everyone and tried to put them at ease by saying that no show would start until everyone was inside. I then asked them all to take a few steps back from the registration desks while

John and I figured out what to do. I also told them that I had been backstage and what they were about to experience was amazing.

The crowd took a collective deep breath and stepped back. I went behind the desk, pulled John and the team together, at which time we decided to abandon registration before the first show and make everyone general admission except for the front row, whom John and I would personally seat. It was not an ideal start, I admit, but it was going to allow us to get the first show off on time. So I climbed back on my perch, not for the last time that day, and calmly told everyone the way it was going to be. Within twenty minutes all the delegates were seated in the Blue Room awaiting the first-ever collection show at Mercedes Australian Fashion Week.

Sorting the front row was an interesting challenge for that first event. Luckily John pretty much knew the seating plan back to front and we arranged the VIP buyers, media, internationals and the few random celebrities who attended. It was so funny to see many in the Australian media who had only experienced 'parades' as social entertainment now at a professional industry show and expected to work. I can clearly remember Edwina McCann, who at the time was a junior with *Vogue* but is now its editor, looking across at Marion Hume from *The Financial Times*, who was readying herself with pen and pad in hand to take notes on the show. Edwina quickly realised she was there to do a job and hunted for a pad and pen. Everyone was learning.

I quickly slipped backstage to wish Wayne and the crew good luck and find out why we hadn't yet started. I was not prepared for the scene that greeted me. The Italians and Wayne had taken it upon themselves to help liven up the models before the show and had already broken out the good champagne intended for the backstage after-party. The girls were high-fiving and posing for the backstage photographers, Marco and Wayne were acting like rock stars who would only perform when they were damn well ready, and only half the models were in their first outfits with the rest still getting final touches to hair and make-up. I was beginning to feel nervous, but as it turns out that is just how Marco wanted it. When I went to him and asked if we were ready to go, he just smiled and said, 'Not just yet. We need to build, to create the theatre, to lift the energy.'

He knew exactly what he was doing. He had taken all the nerves away from everyone. The bubbles had added a new false bravado and every girl and boy felt like a supermodel because Marco had told them they were, and Wayne was playing the role of designer diva along with his trusty lieutenant Jean. Outside the energy was building as everyone in the audience just waited. The scene was set. I took my seat at the end of the runway, which I was going to do for the next twenty years! Then the most famous guitar riff in the world—the Rolling Stones' 'Satisfaction'—exploded into the Blue Room.

A 30-metre-wide, 5-metre-high light backdrop burst into action with 2-metre-high letters spelling out B R A V E. Everyone in the room knew just who was in the house. The bass from the incredible sound system literally rocked people in their seats. Then the hundred PAR can lights shone bright and white, turning Australian Fashion Week's first catwalk into a searing intense runway long enough for a 747.

On Marco's cue and to the beat of the Stones, Sarah O'Hare strode out and stood wide-legged, hands on hips, at the beginning of the catwalk with the illuminated backdrop behind her. Wayne's designs had never looked better as Sarah in a pantsuit strutted with a composure that was an incredible mix of sheer elegance and sexual intensity, the likes of which had never been seen before in Australia. It was electric. Everyone in the room felt it—the production team felt it, the girls backstage felt it, the rest of the world felt it. Australia had arrived on the international fashion week circuit. It was not going to take any prisoners!

The tone that Sarah set from the outset just gathered momentum as Emma and Anneliese, Jonathan Skeats and all the great Australian male models did Wayne proud. The rock 'n' roll soundtrack created by Andy Glitre set the perfect backdrop to Wayne's attitude and the party favourites that Wayne is still known for today were centre stage. He may have been a little heavy-handed on the lime green but at the time it didn't matter. Wayne had delivered a world-class performance, and showed in a world-class venue in front of an international audience. It was astonishing in so many ways.

In twenty years I have only given three standing ovations at a fashion show. The first was at the end of Wayne Cooper's first show. I have only ever cried once, and that was at the end of Wayne Cooper's first show. I was overcome with relief and I was exhausted and proud and everything in between.

*

If I thought it was a nightclub backstage before the show I can't describe what it was like after. It was sheer madness. Champagne, photographers, television cameras, half-dressed models, air-kissing fashion editors, proud family and exhausted producers and direc-tors. I just stood for a moment to the side taking it all in. It was magic. Even though I was already exhausted, it was only about 1 p.m. on the first day and in a few hours' time we had to do it all again. And then over and over and over again for the next four days. How on earth was that going to happen?

Christine Bookallil then ran up to me and asked what we were going to do with all the media and people until the next show, which was two hours away. We didn't want anyone leaving the venue. Good point. We really hadn't taken into consideration what delegates would do in between shows, which were in the first year sometimes three or four hours apart—by the second year we started staging shows on the hour but we just didn't have the logistics or staff or know-how to do this on our first outing. We had mounted a small exhibition of fashion accessories for buyers and media to review but with only fifteen exhibitors it didn't take long to check out. We had a Fashion Café and VIP bar but there is only so much fashion chat you can stand in one day. So as quick as you like, on the spot, Christine created post-show media conferences with each designer. In later years these were to become my own sort of talk show in front of delegates and media, with often hilarious results. They became known as 'On the couch with SPL'—I fancied myself as the fashion version of Oprah and Michael Parkinson rolled into one.

As fast as she could following Wayne's show, Christine managed to arrange a temporary stage with mics and a riser and an Oprah-style couch. Wayne and the crew were dragged from backstage to be interviewed live by me. The media loved it and lots of the grabs were used in the television news coverage that night. We soon got into a routine of show, backstage pics and then media interviews on the couch with me. Media complained from the beginning that they couldn't get a question in because I just wouldn't shut up—I was so excited. Christine was adept at anticipating what content the media would want, making sure we delivered in some way or another.

The day then rolled on to another milestone: Joe Saba's first show in his thirty-year career. Joe was an early mentor and hero of mine. I was a fan from an early age when he ruled the denim world with Staggers Jeans in the 1970s and was the first retailer to bring the famous Japanese designers to Australia. Simon B was also creative director on this show and we had both been working with Joe for a few years already at Spin. It was now an absolute honour to help him present his first collection at MAFW. His unique styles and silhouettes shone through in that first show, cementing his position in the Australian fashion industry as one of its enduring great talents. Having suffered a mild stroke in years past Joe walked with a limp, but the purpose with which he strode to the end of the catwalk was recognised by all. This was a man who had waited a lifetime for this and nothing was going to stop him from walking the full length of that catwalk!

A rising star was also present that evening at Fashion Week: Alex Perry. It was also the first time he showed in a group evening wear section. Alex that year brought new meaning to the word *froufrou* but somewhere hidden deep inside all that tulle were the beautiful designs we know today, waiting to emerge. It was to be the first of a continuous eighteen-year run of fashion week shows for him.

The second day started with Mela Purdie and MCM Lifestyle and was followed by the debut of the Zimmermann sisters, Nicky and Simone. Mark Keighery took to the catwalk with his eponymous label MARCS, which was in years to come to steal the show. Then it was time for the long-awaited arrival of Morrissey Edmiston. They turned up the heat in every sense. Their first show at 8 p.m. on Thursday, 9 May 1996, set the benchmark for what was to become a coveted evening time slot—not too late to miss the late evening news and perfect to get the next morning's news coverage in the papers and news broadcasts. The show was sheer sex and rock 'n' roll from beginning to end. It was also the first time we introduced a number of new production elements, including a revolving opening reveal at the start of the show. This huge white platform turned and there she was, Sarah O'Hare in a Morrissey Edmiston white leather suit. It is still an iconic image of her. She struck a pose and then headed off into the white light of the catwalk. The show was a huge success and generated a massive amount of media coverage.

That evening, a decade-long rivalry was about to start. To our company's dismay Peter and Leona had engaged the services of Peter Metzner from The ARC Factory to produce their after-party. We provided the smaller sprung structure as the venue and Peter and his ARC crew basically turned it into Studio 54. Spinning disco lights and mirrored surfaces were everywhere. An invitation to that after-party was the hottest ticket of the week and ARC knew it. The party was attended by every hot model and music and media celebrity in town. ARC at the time was a big competitor to Spin and Peter was doing all he could to maintain complete control over the invitation list. He was the door bitch from hell and was refusing entry to the guests I wanted to bring to the party. At that stage I thought I was the king of Fashion Week and I had the keys to the city. Peter was furious when he learnt I brought my crew in through the back door. We were very much like elks butting heads. It wasn't going to be the last time.

The third day rolled out with Bettina Liano and her trademark denim catching the attention of international buyers. She was followed by Michael Bracewell, who used the catwalk for the first-ever political statement at Fashion Week, sending models, including singer Kate Ceberano, down the catwalk with 'No Guns' T-shirts in the wake of the Port Arthur massacre. Claire Dickson-Smith followed with her beautiful Third Millennium collection, which was followed by the Queen herself, Collette Dinnigan.

Everyone had heard of the hype that Collette had caused in Paris when she showed for the first time the previous season. Now she was on home turf where we could actually see what the fuss was all about. The fuss was worth it in every sense. Collette, having already worked with Marco and Jennifer, presented a beautiful collection that let the clothes be the stars and set a very high benchmark for many to follow.

The last day of Fashion Week was Saturday, 11 May, and it kicked off with Leonie Levy, followed by Jodie Boffa and Scanlan Theodore, who closed the week. It was wonderful to have Scanlan Theodore in our first year but I spent the next decade chasing them to participate again and was only successful on the rare occasion. Gary Theodore has always marched to the beat of his own drum and it's still working for him today.

That last day also heralded the arrival of one of my finest achievements, the establishment of the New Generation Collections. Each year Fashion Week invites a group of new and aspiring designers to be involved. It has launched the careers of a number of Australian fashion's biggest stars, none bigger than that first year in the form of Akira Isogawa. His moment would not have happened if it hadn't been for his boyfriend at the time, Jac Vidgen, who organised the Sydney RAT dance parties of the 1980s. I had met Jac when I was touring Boy George in 1990. (I'd had a momentary lapse of reason and tried my hand at being a rock 'n' roll promoter.) A decade later, when I was running Australian Fashion Week, Jac got in contact about this amazing guy from Japan who was making beautiful dresses from the remnants of Japanese kimonos. He wouldn't give up hounding me until he dragged me around to meet Akira. He was a late entrant into the New Generation show and was struggling at the time. He couldn't even afford shoes for the models, so he sent them out in red Holeproof socks. The rest, as they say, is history.

There was also another Fashion Week star of the future making his debut that day, the label Miss Gladys Sym Choon from Adelaide. The designer was Ray Costarella, or Aurelio Costarella as he is known today.

*

The week wrapped up with two very special and different events. Nancy Pilcher felt that she would like to host a thank you party from *Vogue* following the Scanlan Theodore show. We all went to La Mensa in Paddington, where a classy soiree was held that *Vogue* would continue to top over the next few years. As a surprise, courtesy of the wonderful emerging jewellery designer Stefano Canturi, I presented both Nancy and Jane de Teliga with a beautiful diamond stickpin as a personal thank you for the years of support they had given me.

During the week, among about a thousand telephone calls I received, one came in out of the blue from Justin Hemmes. He was in the process of taking over and building what is now the Merivale empire of the best restaurants and clubs in Sydney. At the time he was running Slip Inn and CBD. He asked if I'd done anything about organising a huge after-party for everyone who'd worked on the event—as it turned out about six hundred and fifty people! Of course I took him up on his offer.

'What a brilliant idea,' was my response, and Justin, off his own bat, put together what was to become an institution at Fashion Week over the next decade, the official Wrap Party. The first one was off the Richter scale. Justin gave us his personal penthouse apartment on top of CBD as our VIP suite. Hundreds of us piled in for just the best time ever. Everyone was on a high. Designers hung out with production crew, models partied with the media, retailers danced with whoever they wanted, and internationals pledged never-ending allegiance to Australia. Justin just kept the champagne flowing. It was such a generous act and was greatly appreciated by all of us at the time.

The night for me ended at Goodbar on Oxford Street with the last of the Spinners and Fashion Week crew. As the sun came up I went where I had been going for most of my life in Sydney in the mornings, Coluzzi's in Victoria Street, Darlinghurst. I remember sitting there in my glittery Morrissey jacket, coffee in hand, among the early morning cyclists. I'm sure I looked like something left over from Mardi Gras. I was beyond exhausted but I just sat there for a reflective moment thinking, ever so quietly to myself, *we did it*.

5

A Star is Born

W HAT A DIFFERENCE it makes when you are trying to sell
reality and not just a dream. This week in London, the first
week after ORDRE has gone live, we can actually show designers
how the site looks and works. Similarly, when I went back out
on the road after the inaugural MAFW in 1996, I had video and
catwalk images of the first event. I wasn't selling a dream anymore—
Mercedes Australian Fashion Week was real! Designers who had
been sitting on the fence changed their minds and jumped on
board. Media saw the tremendous amount of content the event
produced. Most importantly, retailers saw there was great product
to buy. Not everyone can sell a dream and not many dreams become
real. However, the combination of one dreamer and an incredible
team had brought MAFW to life.

*

Sunday, 12 May 1996, was another defining moment in the history
of MAFW. It should have been a day spent suffering from hangovers,

post-event trauma and to a certain extent basking in our own self-congratulations. There was time for none of this. I was woken by a call from Christine, who had all the Sunday papers, and there was a major problem. Sydney's *Sunday Telegraph* had led with a story that read, 'Fashion Weak: How 25 Young Australian Designers' Hearts Were Broken'. It was a headline that was going to haunt me for years to come. British fashion writer Susan Owens had taken it upon herself to look at the event from the most negative perspective possible. She criticised the amount of internationals who attended rather than applauding or recognising those that came. She complained about the costs directed to designers rather than recognising the underwriting support received from sponsors and government. She laid into me for being self-centred and self-interested and single-handedly responsible for crushing the dreams of Australian designers. I think what she did that day was despicable. It was completely unbalanced, plain mean, and in a great many parts untrue. Above all it hurt a lot of people who had cautiously lent their support to this very ambitious event and were now questioning whether they had done the right thing. Something printed in black and white in one of the country's biggest circulating newspapers is very powerful.

Following Christine's call I had to wait at home for a call from the premier's office. It was worst fifteen minutes of my life and, as I expected, I got hauled over the coals by the premier's advisors on the PR disaster I had created for them. No one seemed to care that the facts were incorrect. This article had somehow turned from an opinion piece into a factual statement. The industry then wasn't what it is today, full of self-confidence and a never-ending list of success stories. It was completely insecure, regardless of its recent four days in the spotlight. I was beyond dejected. I jumped into the car and went around to Fox Studios to see how the bump-out was going. Everyone had seen the article. They were just so disheartened and overcome by exhaustion and emotion. I can remember Iain coming up to me and saying, 'But didn't we do the best job we could? What happened, wasn't it enough?'

My despondency then turned to anger. My anger to determination. My determination into action. There was no way I was about to let this get the better of me, our event or the industry I had grown to love. If I had been driven in the lead-up to the first event, the world had seen nothing yet. Game On!

I immediately got up on my soapbox and announced our plans for the following year. We would expand from thirteen shows to twenty and push the exhibitors from fifteen to sixty-five. We announced that we had generated $40 million worth of positive media for the industry—the sort of coverage that a major concert tour or sporting event would generate—and that that was just the tip of the iceberg. I promised more international and domestic delegates, bigger stars, more parties, more sponsors—basically more, bigger, best!! But first I had a little problem to attend to: I was going broke.

The Italians had not only left a Mercedes-Benz littered with cigarette butts but also a glove box full of speeding and parking fines equivalent to the national debt of their not-so-insignificant country. This was just a drop in the ocean. While we had negotiated toughly but fairly with all our contractors, all the extras I had approved in the lead-up came flooding in. The overrun in costs was beyond belief. We hadn't come in on budget in any area. I had basically spent about half a million more than I had. I owed a lot of money to a lot of people. The real position came to light about a month after the event. I was wringing every profit I could out of Spin, all my savings were invested in the event and we had pushed our bank to breaking point. My business partners were beyond worried, not just for the future of the event but the fact that it might go down and take the rest of The Lock Group and them along with it. MJ in particular was very nervous but held firm.

I actually had nowhere to turn than back to the industry itself. The biggest bill we had at the time was from the big four modelling agencies: Vivien's, Chadwick, Chic and Priscillas. Our Australian Fashion Innovators had booked every model who was involved in

Fashion Week as these costs were included in the package we sold to designers, as was hair and make-up in that first year. We owed about $300,000 and the agencies had already paid most of the girls and were now chasing me. Any one of these agencies could have pulled the plug on me and, ultimately, Fashion Week. I went and met individually with Peter Chadwick, Ursula Hufnagl (Chic), Kevin Smith (Vivien's) and Priscilla Leighton Clark. I proposed that, if they could wait a short while, I would soon be getting money from sponsorship for the next year's budget and could afford to progressively pay them. They all spoke independently to each other and agreed as a group that if I treated them all the same they would bankroll me. All they had was my word that they would eventually be paid and they accepted it. The most difficult conversation was with Meri Took of Staging Rentals, who decided not to break my legs but hold out for payment. Other creditors followed suit and agreed to wait in the hope that I could continue to pull off the government funding and sponsorship deals.

This whole situation, though, then created a snowball effect that in a few years' time was going to put even more strain on every aspect of the event and The Lock Group as I continued to put more and more money into Fashion Week. It was Greg Gleeson who was left with the day-to-day responsibility of managing the cash flow of Fashion Week and he continually chased late-paying designers and dealt with frustrated contractors. He had at the time, no doubt, the hardest job in the industry.

Many in the fashion trade had been outraged by Susan Owens' article, including Maggie Alderson, who was then the fashion editor at *The Sydney Morning Herald*. In an unbiased professional piece of journalism she correctly analysed the results the event had generated for the local fashion industry. While she recognised that obviously we had a long way to go she detailed early successes that had been made in terms of generating orders for designers and the media coverage the industry had received. The industry, sponsors and the government took a collective sigh of relief.

I let loose 'Simon everywhere'. Armed with a report on the event, including an appraisal of the media coverage, I hit the road. I went to the federal government first, to the office of Industry Minister John Moore, to get funding from them to support what we had received from New South Wales. Mercedes-Benz had set a real precedent in establishing a first in fashion sponsorships and it didn't go unrecognised by other corporate sponsors as they now responded with interest. We also organised a series of industry briefings and went on a national road show, including to Sydney, Melbourne, Brisbane, Perth and Adelaide, inviting every designer, every potential exhibitor, all the media, retailers and possible sponsors to come along and hear of our plans for the future and what we had achieved in our first year. Everyone had experienced the media the event had generated around the country and was interested to see what all the fuss was about. Apart from *The Sunday Telegraph* article, the coverage had actually been phenomenal and in most parts extremely positive. It meant that nationally every person in Australia was aware that MAFW had been on. This was a brilliant start, as these industry briefings were successful and generated even more interest.

There were murmurs in the industry, though, that Australian Fashion Innovators and I had had too much power over the event and the industry, with many pointing to the designer associations that controlled fashion weeks overseas. I knew what it had taken to get the first MAFW off the ground and there was no way an industry association could have had the single-minded vision or fortitude to do what we had been able to do. While the manufacturing industry had their own representative body—Textile and Fashion Industries of Australia—the ready-to-wear industry did not, and there was no way I was going to let industry politics stop the roll-out of MAFW into its second year. Nineteen years later, when the Australian Fashion Chamber finally did get off the ground, it generated enough politics in an industry that was now well established that I can't imagine the road blocks it could have created back in the mid 1990s.

However, in light of the criticism and of Fashion Week's initial success I set about trying to be more inclusive. I had already appointed Steve Bennett of Country Road as honorary chairman of MAFW to help guide me through all the politics, and I then expanded the selection committee to include a powerful cross section of industry players. This was to both support the vetting process to only invite the most appropriate designers to show at Fashion Week and ensure that key industry captains had the event's best interests at heart. The initial selection committee included Nancy Pilcher (*Vogue*), Marion Hume (*The Financial Times*), Jackie Frank (*marie claire*), Karin Upton Baker (*Mode*), Deborah Thomas (*Elle*), Michelle Graham (*Ragtrader*), Jenny White (Woolmark), Lindsay Bennett (Cotton), Christine Robertson (TFIA), Jessica Finch (Myer Grace Bros), David Bush (David Jones), Belinda Seper (Belinda's), Melissa Hoyer (*The Sunday Telegraph*), Charlotte Dawson (Channel Nine), Kellie Alderman (*The Courier Mail*), Jane de Teliga, Maggie Alderson (*The Sydney Morning Herald*), Carolyn Palliardi (*The Herald Sun*) and Anthea Loucas (*The Age*).

I also made another important strategic decision after the success of the first event: to open MAFW up to other designers from around the Asia Pacific region. There were two main reasons for this move. First, I was a fan of recently deposed Prime Minister Paul Keating, and I was totally in agreement with his and Annita's philosophy that Australia needed to be more engaged in the Asia Pacific and turn to our immediate neighbours for cooperation and trade. With this in mind, I made my first trip to New Zealand and held a number of town hall events to invite the best designers to participate. Over the next few years, New Zealand designers were to become a force at MAFW. In later years I invited designers from Singapore and Hong Kong to participate. It was a strategy that over time was going to strengthen the event enormously and truly position us as the most important industry fashion event in the region.

Things were progressing in both Australia and New Zealand towards the end of 1996 and it was time for me to go back on the road again to garner international support for the 1997 event. I had promised a huge increase in international media and buyers and I needed to deliver. I set off armed with my video of the first event, which made an enormous difference, the press clippings report, which was the size of a telephone book—minus Susan Owens' article, of course—and Karyn Westren, who had come on board to help out with international marketing. Together we embarked on a gruelling eight-week road show that took in Los Angeles, New York, London, Paris, Milan, Hong Kong and Singapore. We met with buyers and the media. Our target was to make six appointments a day, which was thirty every week and over two hundred and forty for the entire trip. The team in Sydney set up the meetings via fax—there was no internet, no international mobile phones and no Uber. Looking back now, I wonder how we ever did it!

Each day I carried our flip-chart presentation of everything you would ever want to know about MAFW from both a buyer and a media perspective. For buyers it was all about how efficient the event was in order to source new and exciting designers. For media it was about the new talent and stories on designers and models, combined with the interesting celebrities and supermodels attending. I constantly pushed the angle of Sydney being one of the coolest and most sophisticated cities in the world—it had been announced by then that we were to host the Olympics, which was helping to build the city's profile.

Regardless of what I thought about the talent of our designers and our beautiful harbour city it was still a very hard sell, especially in New York and Paris, where the thought of Australian fashion was actually laughed at. Literally. There was no international perception at all that Australia had any value to contribute to the fashion industry globally in any way, least of all the new ready-to-wear designers. The overall view of our country, particularly in the United States, was of a very casual-oriented nation that had great beaches, a wild outback, extensive minerals and energies and not a lot else. Oh, and Paul Hogan, Barry McKenzie and Dame Edna—not exactly shining lights when it came to the fashion stakes. The style and creativity of the Cate Blanchetts and Baz Luhrmanns was still in the making, and the Bill Grangers and Neil Perrys opening cool restaurants hadn't quite registered, and there was definitely no sass & bide or Zimmermann taking New York Fashion Week by storm. Any thought of Australia as a creative fashion nation just didn't exist.

Still, I was able to meet with the likes of Julie Gilhart at Barneys, Kalman Ruttenstein at Bloomingdales, Joan Burstein at Browns, of course, and Nicole Fischelis at Saks Fifth Avenue. To get an appointment with these industry legends you had to have something to offer and in their minds the only thing I had going for me was intrigue. The one angle I pushed was that their business was based on finding and discovering the next new thing. Fashion retailers always like to lead from the front; they want to be the ones to find the new talent and represent them on an exclusive basis for the first few seasons. This was the sliver of hope I had to get in their doors—that, and the fact that I just wouldn't take no for an answer.

In some instances it took years and years to get in to see the right people. After a few years of trying to see Joan Kaner at Neiman Marcus I dedicated a whole day to just sitting in her reception with my video and flip chart until she had five minutes to talk to me. I was like the annoying but nice travelling salesman who was prepared to wait. When I did eventually see Joan that day she was lovely and we started to make headway with Neiman.

The biggest advantage I had in those days, quite frankly, was my passion. I absolutely believed wholeheartedly in the talent of the Australian designers and still do. I knew their collections inside out. I knew them and their personalities and their design DNA. I wore their clothes. I was the ultimate ambassador for the industry. I presented well, was articulate, was educated in the business of fashion and could sell. Man, could I sell! Through these meetings I was able in many cases to get these buyers excited about what I was showing them: a group of undiscovered major talents with incredible use of fabrications, cool modern silhouettes, a great sense of style. With this vision I was also able to paint a picture of the allure of Sydney: its great weather, beautiful harbour, stylish shopping precincts and incredible food and wine. The Olympic City. Then, on top of this, I told them about the support the event would provide: airfares, hotels, courtesy car and an individual host. The picture started to form in many of their minds that perhaps a trip to MAFW would be worthwhile.

It was often thought that the only reason I got internationals to come was that I was giving away free holidays to Australia. Let me tell you, free airfares and accommodation to this crew are nothing. They are constantly travelling and the thought of what is often a nineteen-hour trip to the other side of the world was one they just didn't really want to entertain. The most difficult thing to get from them was their executive time. Whichever way you looked at it, it was a week out of the office, a week they could spend focusing on some other tried-and-tested market. I know in the early years that it was not the free trip, but the passion and the enthusiasm I was able to portray that got their interest.

By the time the 1997 event rolled around we had secured some huge names, including Galeries Lafayette from Paris, Browns and House of Fraser from London, Seibu from Japan and CK Tangs from Singapore. We had even more media than buyers coming, led by four huge names in the industry: Elsa Klensch from CNN, Jeanne Beker from *Fashion File*, Hilary Alexander from the UK's *Daily Telegraph* and the one and only Anna Piaggi from *Vogue Italia*. Although she has since passed away, Anna was a very important fashion icon and muse to no less than Karl Lagerfeld, among many others. It was Marco who introduced me to her in Milan and she graciously agreed to come. She was on the lookout for the next new thing. One of my fondest fashion memories is having dinner with her at her favourite local restaurant in Milan. It was like accompanying the Queen, she was so loved and adored.

The Australian industry was also responding well in the lead-up to the 1997 event. The three big magazine publishing houses—ACP

(*Mode*), Condé Nast (*Vogue*) and Murdoch Magazines (*marie claire*)—
had all decided to step up their involvement in the event. We offered
each of them an exclusive element on the official schedule. *marie
claire*, through Matt Handbury and Mark Kelly, had pledged support to take over the Opening Ceremony and turn it into something
spectacular. *Vogue* was to cement itself at the end of the week with
the stylish wrap party and *Mode* was going to have a presence during
the week with an invitation-only VIP lounge under the watchful and
stylish eye of the new editor, Karin Upton Baker.

Our industry briefing around the region had really helped to
drive huge growth in the schedule. The number of shows increased
to nineteen, involving now some forty-two designers, with another
sixty-five designers in the exhibition. This time the Australian designers closely monitored what was happening in London, Paris, Milan
and New York—as we did—and noticed a trend emerging in the way
collections were presented on a catwalk. They were being done in
a more theatrical way, leading in some instances to very elaborate
shows in settings ranging from jungle scenes through to a French
chateau. With their huge dimensions, the stages that Marco and his
team had built at Fox Studios were perfect for this sort of expression.

The 1997 MAFW kicked off with the most amazing Opening
Ceremony, and it upped the ante from day one. The event was held
at the Overseas Passenger Terminal at Circular Quay and everyone
entered through a mock backstage and then arrived at the party
by walking a catwalk the entire length of the venue. They had a
chance to be a supermodel. It was a great statement and everyone
really enjoyed the lavish night. That day we had also held our
second MAFW conference with industry leaders, the government
and invited international delegates. Again it had grown substantially
from the first year, attracting about three hundred and fifty delegates.

The first day of collection showings kicked off with MAFW's
first supermodel moment. Charlie Brown, a San Franciscan by birth
and a whirlwind of ambition and talent, had hooked up with Danny
Avidan, the head of big manufacturing outfit Discovery Group, and

together they had launched the Charlie Brown label. Charlie and Danny always thought big and over the years we worked with them to bring some amazing big stars to MAFW. This year we were able to do so with the help of Alex Zotos. He was one of the few Australian photographers involved in the international fashion week circuit. He had an amazing way about him and made every model he shot feel like a real superstar. He was also a gentleman and as such had become a favourite and friend of all the supermodels, including Elle, Naomi, Stephanie and Kristy. He had a direct line into the management of many models and we worked with him to bring one of the biggest to this year's event: Linda Evangelista.

Linda, who is famous for the line that she wouldn't get out of bed for less than $10,000 a day, did exactly that on 7 May 1997 at 10 a.m. The crowd and the media went into meltdown. Her runway entrance heralded the fact that MAFW was an international event. She also featured in Wayne Cooper's show to great effect and then Alex Perry took her on and created the first big 'media moment' of MAFW. Linda arrived late for the Alex Perry pre-show dressing—she had also insisted on her own change room, which cost us a fortune—and then proceeded to put on some sort of diva-ish 'go slow' as she got into her outfit. As the dress was too big for her she had to be sewn into it, causing further delay. At one stage Alex was so exasperated about how late she was running that he told her he didn't think she was that beautiful and to 'just get out there'. When she arrived on the catwalk the room took a collective gasp and just looked at her. Thank heavens she saw the funny side and cracked a smile when she finally made her entrance, which is still one of the most enduring images of Fashion Week to this day.

The week continued with some strong showings from Carla Zampatti, Country Road, Jodie Boffa, MARCS, Tea Rose and Third Millennium. The first designer to really embrace the theatrical mode of MAFW was Lisa Ho. Her collection was inspired by a garden party and that is exactly the setting she wanted to create. She and her team, including long-time PR collaborator Adam Worling, came up with the idea to cover the catwalk in freshly laid turf. It seemed like a simple enough request at the time, but it took Marco, Jarrad, Iain and a cast of hundreds many hours to bump it in and out. At the end of the show confetti cannons blew flowers across the catwalk and petals floated down from the ceiling above. It perfectly reflected Lisa's pretty collection and set a great standard for what was to follow.

The most beautiful image from that year was one of star model Julie Healy. One of the best walkers to grace MAFW, she—along with a whole host of Australian girls—was now getting her moment in the spotlight alongside Sarah O'Hare, Emma Balfour and Anneliese Seubert, who had all returned home again for Fashion Week. Over the next few years MAFW was not only going to create frock stars, it was also going to create our own supermodels, the best known today being Miranda Kerr.

The following day was the turn of Collette Dinnigan, who had shown in Paris again the previous year. She certainly gave the entire fashion industry a lesson in theatrics. In collaboration with her then husband Bernie Lynch, the Bazmark team of close friends Baz Luhrmann and Catherine Martin, Marco, Jarrad and our team, Collette took over the Byron Kennedy Hall at Fox Studios and took away the breath of the entire Australian fashion industry with her gorgeous lace creations set among the chaise longues of a stunning re-creation of a Parisian boudoir. The styling, hair, make-up and dance performance were absolutely beautiful.

Not to be outdone on the theatrics stage, Simon B was again creative director of the Saba show and he and Joe wanted to make a statement that Saba was as relevant to a younger market as it was to their traditional customers. Simon designed an amazing high-tech stage setting with the help of Marco, Jarrad and Iain. The complex backdrop comprised sixty-four huge television sets all linked to each other. The screens rose about 4 metres high and spread the entire 20-metre width of the backdrop. They had been programmed with special videos created by Simon B and Spin. It was a creatively stunning backdrop but technically, at the time, stretched the boundaries of what was possible. To repeat it now with flat screen technology would be a walk in the park but back then it took Iain and his team every bit of their know-how and patience to pull it off. It was simply amazing.

Later in the week Morrissey Edmiston took to the catwalk with their sexy rock 'n' roll aesthetic in full flight. Peter insisted on a shiny black catwalk surface and backdrop and for years to come this was his signature. Morrissey Edmiston again broke new ground with the hype they generated around their evening time slot, which was the envy of every designer on the schedule. Being later in the day, most of the industry delegates could attend, as well as many of Morrissey Edmiston's VIP clients. Well, clients and freaks. They had the most eccentric group of fans, from nightclub girls to gym junkies, drag queens, cool-cat executives, ladies who lunch and every guy who has ever been to The Taxi Club, and they all came out to play for Peter and Leona's show. The ensuing crush turned MAFW into a madhouse. All the bars were full to overflowing, queues formed around the block, John and I were going mad trying to seat everyone and backstage looked like the circus had taken over. I loved it! MAFW was fast becoming the hottest ticket in Australia.

While a number of designers had created attention through theatrics, supermodels or celebrities, the class act in many ways in 1997 was Zimmermann. Letting the clothes speak for themselves, Nicky and Simone presented a tour de force by showing for the first time both their ready-to-wear and swimwear on the catwalk. The styling just blew everyone away, with beautiful fedora hats and incredible make-up and hair to perfectly complement their collections. It was the year they started in earnest on their global expansion.

This was also an important year because we had started on our mission to become *the* Asia Pacific fashion week. Long-established New Zealand designers Neville and Elisabeth Findlay showed their incredible label Zambesi alongside the beautiful Song & Kelly from Singapore. The avant-garde designers World from New Zealand also made their first appearance.

Joan Burstein, the doyenne and owner of Browns, affectionately known throughout the world as Mrs B, was in attendance again. Mrs B had always been a huge supporter of young talent and had bought John Galliano's entire collection when he was a Central St Martins graduate. Little did we know that, on the last day of the 1997 event, we were to experience a similar design moment.

The previous year, thanks to my friend Jac Vidgen, Akira Isogawa had been a late entry into the New Generation show but had been hailed a star to watch. In the early years of Fashion Week I took lots of risks and often a lot of criticism for pushing young talent into the spotlight. I knew instinctively with Akira that we had a huge star in the making and after his first showing I took him aside and said I was prepared to give him his own show the following year. Underfunded and under-resourced, Akira used everything he had in preparing his solo collection for 1997 MAFW. There was certainly a high level of expectation around his show and a few of the editors even took sneak peeks backstage as the buzz built up around the room.

His tour de force collection in 1997 would come to define the Akira look: ethereal shapes, beautiful fabrication reinvented and new draping techniques. As amazing outfit after outfit came down the runway you could literally feel the collective adoration and respect growing in the room. Mercedes Australian Fashion Week's first home-grown star was born right before our eyes. As the last of the models took their lap of the runway to an ever-building applause, Akira very shyly came out to take his bow. The room fell into an almost surreal state of creative shock. Then it happened.

From her seat at the end of the runway, Mrs B rose, walked straight onto the runway and in front of the stunned crowd basically ran the full length of the catwalk to be the first backstage to congratulate Akira. She has only ever done this on a handful of occasions to a number of greats and they include both Galliano and McQueen. Mrs B then bought the entire collection.

6

Dancing Divas, the Love Boat and the Bottom of the Harbour

To this day, Paris remains one of the most impenetrable fortresses of fashion. Its enduring success as the global centre of presenting fashion has instilled a sense of righteousness—some might say arrogance—in this very tight-knit community. As a result it is not necessarily open to new ideas. Australian Fashion Week was dismissed as an aberration and today ORDRE is, to a certain extent, being received the same way. However, twenty-five years of experience have provided me with the skills to find a way to get my message across. No longer do I have to rely on somehow getting past the fashion elite's all-powerful personal assistants with my well-meaning faxes, in English, and my never-ending phone calls, also in English. We now have a 'French Fashion Whisperer', having convinced one of the inner sanctum and most respected fashion leaders of our vision for ORDRE. A quiet word by them to the right people and all the doors to the best designers and most influential retailers are opened.

If only we'd had our fashion week insider in Paris all those years ago. Instead it took us years to get the attention of French

retailers and media and it was only after the United States and the
United Kingdom had embraced us as an event. I can still remember
a comment from the fashion director of Galeries Lafayette, which
epitomised the attitude at the time: '*Excusez-moi*, Simone, don't you
have an expression in Australia, "It is like taking coal to Newcastle"?
Why would I want to fly halfway around the world to try to bring
new fashion to Paris when the best in the world is here?' What she
didn't realise was that it was impossible for our industry to come to
Paris en masse. Only one designer at this stage had ever been brave
enough to come and show, and that was Collette Dinnigan, and she
was only one of a number of shining stars.

*

After 1997 the industry realised that the first year hadn't been a fluke
and perhaps MAFW was really going to cement itself on the international fashion week circuit. For our little organisation, Australian
Fashion Innovators, it also built our confidence in that we could now
start to establish the permanent foundations of a proper company to
really manage and develop the event on an ongoing basis. Up until
this stage AFI had been a shell and we had relied on the financial
support of The Lock Group, the staff at Spin and a huge team of
contractors to manage the event. It was time to establish a company
that could over time run and develop an international fashion week.
This had never been done before and from a business perspective
I found the challenge exciting.

The big four—New York, London, Paris and Milan—were run
by industry associations which, at that stage, only managed a schedule and, in the case of New York and London, a central venue. These
organisations left a lot of the logistics in the hands of the designers.
Our designers weren't experienced enough yet so AFI took on the
entire role of running and producing MAFW. This included managing designer sales from both individual and group shows; managing
all the exhibition sales; lobbying federal and state governments for

funding; promoting and managing commercial sponsorships; designing and developing an international marketing program for media and buyers; establishing a national marketing program for buyers and media; implementing an integrated marketing communications program, including both a national and international publicity program; managing the delegate registration and seating program; overseeing an enormous event program ... the list goes on and on.

A number of clear department divisions were forming within AFI: designer management, sponsor management, event production and marketing communications. People were starting to gravitate towards key roles. We only had one year left of our contract with Marco and his team and Jarrad was clearly stepping into the role of managing all event production. Over the first few years Jarrad and I had become very close and over time he understood more and more what I had in my head and how I wanted things to look. In the years to come our partnership in designing live fashion events was going to help define the events industry in Australia through both AFI and Spin Events. Add to this partnership the creative direction of Simon B and we had evolved into a very creative and tight team.

Christine Bookallil recommended that we also bring Louise Di Francesco on board. Louise was an ex-journalist who had a take-no-prisoners approach to publicity and had had nothing to do with the fashion industry. She was perfect. She had a great nose for news and didn't care about the petty politics of the industry. She was going to be hugely influential in continuing our drive for important media coverage of the event.

During these next years, however, the person who was to become the core and backbone of the team was Jodi Pritchard, our general manager at Spin. Early on she had established herself as a dedicated consultant and, more importantly, an amazing manager of both processes and people. She was my go-to person in every venture on our fashion journey together. Often, much to her frustration, I provided the inspiration and the vision and Jodi had to find the way to deliver on the promises. She continuously did so through her enthusiasm, dedication and loyalty. She worked on the first few fashion weeks, looking after international delegates, and this is how she met the famous Mrs B. Always adept at spotting talent Mrs B whisked Jodi away to London for a period of time to be the general manager of Browns. When it came to the role of running AFI, when we were finally able to set up the right structure, I knew there was only one person to do it. I flew to London and convinced Jodi to return. At the time having the ex-GM from Browns running MAFW was a bit of an industry coup but it was nothing compared to knowing I had the right person in place and that it was someone who was always going to have my back—boy was I going to need that!

The rest of the AFI team was also coming together, with Greg Gleeson always trying to stop us from going broke, Lucia Labbate saved from the Spin reception to be my personal assistant and John Flower slowly becoming the seating king.

While the 1998 event was full of expectation, the reality was that AFI was still up to its eyeballs in debt. We had just managed to pay off the model bills and contractors from 1996 before the 1997 event got underway, and that year I again spent way above our budget. Now I had also made commitments to staff structuring at AFI to grow the event. The debt was huge, somewhere north of half a million, which represented about 40 per cent of the total budget. However, rather than cut back and try to create a balanced budget I took the opposite approach. I decided to grow the event to double its size in twelve months. It was going to be a huge risk but if I could do it the new revenue streams would eventually cash-flow us out of debt. The roulette table was delivered in the form of the completed and newly renovated Royal Hall of Industries and Hordern Pavilion at Fox Studios Australia. I now had the venues and the space I needed to take the event to the next level.

Three new runways needed to be designed and created in the Hordern: the Blue Room, with a capacity of close to eight hundred; the Yellow Room, with a capacity of five hundred; and a more intimate space, the White Room, able to take up to two hundred and fifty. Marco and Angelo, in their last year with us, worked with Jarrad and our local crew to design three amazing and flexible new catwalks. It would be Marco's legacy to the event.

I knew exactly what I was going to do with the Hordern. I had already expanded the schedule to five days and now, with three showrooms, I could double the number of collection shows. This was going to be imperative to generate the increase in revenue that I needed to pay down what we owed. Our debt wasn't with some huge bank that we didn't care about, it was with the model agents and our contractors, who had agreed to bankroll us again. I owed it to them in more ways than one.

The RHI has a floor space of 700 square metres and this presented both a huge challenge and a huge risk. We needed to grow our exhibitors from about sixty to one hundred and fifty in order to fill the space. In other words, as with the collection shows, we needed to double the size of the exhibition in one year. Rather than invest further in sales and exhibition staff, we structured a deal with Daryl Herbert of APN Miller Freeman, a new international exhibition organisation who had approached us the previous year. APN Miller Freeman operated under licence to manage the sales and execution of the event. Daryl brought in his trusty salesperson, Phillipa Scott, who would eventually work directly for AFI. She was the gun we needed at the time to take on this enormous and risky sales job.

We had six months to fill the event. As usual I got up on my soapbox and told the industry and media we were doubling the size of the event in just one year as a result of demand—well, demand we hadn't yet created! Jodi, Jarrad and I worked on the designers; Phillipa and everyone else set about selling the exhibition. On the side we had to undertake all the overseas marketing visits to grow our international delegate attendance, try to double our sponsorship revenue, lobby both the federal and state governments for more money as our initial grants were running out, refine the delegate registration and seating program to cope with the expanded schedule, and keep the Australian media happy with a thousand and one stories on MAFW. From 1998 onwards, MAFW gave the Australian fashion industry the most incredible sandpit in which to play. We had the space to expand and physically flex our creative and commercial muscles. The number of designers involved grew from seventy-five in 1998 to over two hundred in 2000. Media coverage tripled and wholesale orders went through the roof.

A funny thing happened, though, on the way to MAFW 1998. The previous year the enduring partnership of Morrissey Edmiston had blown up. Leona went off to sort out her personal life and Peter at first lived up to his name 'Party Pete'—and then the crash happened. Word reached us through creative director Jayson Brunsdon that Peter had taken to his bed in his home in Paddington and had become a hermit. I was incensed that he was not rising to the challenge of launching his own label. Over the next few days I dragged Peter out of bed, slapped him around and convinced him it was what he had to do. Within another few days Simon B had created the logo for Morrissey and I had booked the ballroom at the InterContinental Hotel for a media conference that convinced the nation that Morrissey was back and planning the MAFW fashion show from hell ... just as soon as we found a backer! The fact of the matter was that all we had was a banner with his name on it.

The day after the conference I got a call from the most unlikely fashion impresario ever, Rene Rivkin. Rene was a stockbroker of legendary status in Sydney. He was a Rolls Royce–driving, cigar-chewing, worry bead–wearing enigma whose bravado was matched only by his heart of gold. A few days later I found myself with Peter at my side aboard Rene's floating gin palace on Sydney Harbour, presenting the five-year business plan I had developed for Morrissey. We were surrounded by a ship crew who looked like they had escaped from the cast of *The Love Boat*, enough Dom Pérignon to sink the boat, and gold-plated everything. The next day I received a box of cigars worth a small fortune from Rene and Peter had his bankroll and a brand new black BMW convertible. Until Rene sold the Morrissey business to The Oroton Group for a small fortune

In the front row with Helena Christensen at the Morrissey collection, 2004
(*Robert Rosen*)

Above: Jarrad Clark backstage at the first Fashion Week, 1996 (*MAFW Archive*)

Left: Marco Maccapani, the Italian production maestro (*MAFW Archive*)

Wayne Cooper and Peter Morrissey with Elle Macpherson at the 2002 Opening Ceremony (*Robert Rosen*)

Creative guru Simon Bookallil with his then wife Kirsten (*Robert Rosen*)

Backstage manager Deb Kirkwood with supermodel Linda Evangelista before the Wayne Cooper show, 1997 (*Robert Rosen*)

Nicky Zimmermann backstage before the show that really put her and sister Simone on the global fashion map, 1997 (*Robert Rosen*)

Good friends Jodhi Meares and Kristy Hinze at the debut of Tigerlily at Fashion Week, 1999 (*Robert Rosen*)

Alannah Hill and her dancing divas, 2002 (*Robert Rosen*)

The scale of our collection showrooms at Fox Studios really gave the designers huge creative flexibility (*MAFW Archive*)

Right: John Flower in full flight directing the front row (*Robert Rosen*)

Above: Cate Blanchett and Jerry Hall backstage at the Charlie Brown show (*Robert Rosen*)

Left: Designer Akira Isogawa and Anna Piaggi from Italian *Vogue* (*Robert Rosen*)

The Tsubi posse at the end of the
infamous rat show (*Robert Rosen*)

Designing duo Heidi Middleton and
Sarah-Jane Clark from sass & bide
(*Robert Rosen*)

Lucia Labbate (in red) sorting out seating at the Akira show (*Simon P Lock*)

Jayson Brunsdon's debut collection at MAFW (*Getty Images*)

Jodi Pritchard, general manager and
international marketing director for
MAFW and RAFW (*Robert Rosen*)

Lorraine Lock, founding team member
and designer liaison manager for
RAFW (*Robert Rosen*)

Leona Edmiston and Peter Morrissey just before their split (*MAFW Archive*)

a few years later, he was to become a regular in the front row at MAFW and an amazing host, particularly to the international buyers. At one outlandish event hosted on his flamboyant yacht, Rivkin greeted guests from the spa on the pool deck surrounded by Morrissey-clad pool boys. He then proceeded to offer all the international buyers joy flights around Sydney Harbour on his private helicopter—which just happened to be sitting on the helipad behind him on the boat—if they wrote a Morrissey order for $100,000.

The expectation around the debut of Morrissey that year at MAFW was huge. Luckily, the collection proved to be an immediate hit. Rivkin's helicopter certainly got a bit of a workout. However, Morrissey wasn't the only designer creating headlines at MAFW that year. It proved to be a year of great expectations as more and more designers embarked on presenting an individual show as well as participating in the expanded group shows format.

Akira presented his collection following his stunning debut the year before. He further established his flowing silhouettes and amazing use of embellishments and remnant fabrics. Alex Perry flexed his muscles in presenting his individual show and then went on to have the longest run of showings, year after year, of any designer at MAFW. Rebecca Davies, an industry model booker turned designer, launched her Bare label, which became a favourite with stores like Selfridges and David Jones. She also introduced a new face to MAFW: Kristy Hinze. Years later I was to join Kristy as a judge on *Project Runway* on Foxtel and, following a stellar international modelling career, she went on to marry one of the richest men in the world, the founder of Netscape, Jim Clark. This introduction to MAFW wasn't the first time she was to steal headlines around the country.

All the MAFW regulars were back, including Wayne Cooper, Lisa Ho, Collette Dinnigan, Saba and Charlie Brown. They had a renewed confidence and were pushing the boundaries in the way they presented their collections. Collette was again influential in 1998 following her theatrical show in the Byron Kennedy Hall at

Fox Studios the previous year. She insisted that her new show be
'off site', meaning away from the central venues at Fox Studios. I was
keen to make sure all the shows remained at the studios to make it
easy for buyers and media to see every collection and to not have
to travel from venue to venue as they did in Paris or Milan. Collette
was insistent, however, and had secured the beautiful waterside
mansion *Boomerang* in Elizabeth Bay as a site.

I thought long and hard about extending the schedule to include
off-site shows and in the end decided that once the main shows had
finished at Fox I would allow one show later in the evening each day
if the designers wanted to do it. In the end it actually worked a treat
because it allowed over the next few years some of the most iconic
venues in Sydney to be used as stages. Collette conceived an incredible show to be held over dinner in the foreshore gardens with a
pièce de résistance for dessert. She broke new ground and presented
one of her best collections to date, followed by a glamorous supper
around one incredible, opulently decorated dining table. The dinner
culminated with Kate Ceberano walking down the table through the
decorations as she sang, much to the VIP crowd's delight.

MAFW also introduced another Australian supermodel star in
1998, Alyssa Sutherland. Discovered by Ursula Hufnagl at Chic and
sent straight to New York, Alyssa captured the attention of some
of the biggest photographers and designers in the world, including
Ralph Lauren. Alyssa made a stunning MAFW debut. She walked
in just about every show and, given her international success, was
soon catapulted into the media spotlight. She was a natural in every
sense, gliding easily between the catwalk and the media conferences
held afterwards with me. In the following years our film and television company, Propeller Productions, was to take her on as a key
presenter for our fashion series.

In 1998 we also introduced two designers who over the next few
years were going to grow to national prominence. I knew Alannah
Hill from my days living in Melbourne, and through fierce negotiations with her funding partner she was eventually allowed to

participate in a group show. The internal tensions at her company were eventually to be her undoing as she had transferred ownership of her name to her business partner. Only recently the culmination of this was Alannah's launch of a new label called Louise Love. It's often a bitter lesson for a young designer to learn when, in the hope of financial security and funding for growth, they sign over their name to someone else. Many have fallen victim to these deals with the financing devils—not just Alannah but Kit Willow (Willow) and Morrissey to name a few.

The other impressive designer introduced in a group show that year was Easton Pearson from Brisbane. Having heard the buzz on the street I flew to Brisbane especially to meet with Pamela Easton and Lydia Pearson. I have never met more humble yet incredibly talented designers in my life. They spent an afternoon taking me through their take on design and fabrication and their ethical approach to manufacturing, long before ethics was fashionable. It was amazing to me that I had to literally beg them to do MAFW, as they considered themselves not ready or good enough. They became one of the biggest and most loved designers MAFW produced … and perhaps the nicest.

In 1998 our hard work and market visits in New Zealand paid off and four designers from across the ditch showed that year. Neville and Elisabeth Findlay from Zambesi presented an individual show to absolute critical acclaim, which it needed to be as anyone who knows Neville will tell you what a hard taskmaster he is. Over the coming years Neville and I were to have many ongoing battles about what Zambesi did and didn't want at MAFW and Neville always held me accountable like no other. I can truly say, though, that he is a tough but fair man and I always enjoyed working with him. Two New Zealand designers also debuted that year, Karen Walker and Kate Sylvester, both of whom were alumni of the New Generation Collections show. Karen's collection was memorable for the electric extension cords the models dragged behind them in a comment on New Zealand's power storages at the time.

In 1998 *Mode* was renamed *Harper's Bazaar* with editor Karin Upton Baker at the helm, and the infamous Bar Bazaar was born. This exclusive invitation-only VIP lounge perched high above the MAFW Exhibition was the coolest place to hang at MAFW. With a constant supply of Moët between shows this was where celebrities met the designers, international delegates met the local media and, more often than not, the top models would just hang. Finally we had a place to host the stream of VIPs who were now coming to attend shows as our guests.

*

Heading into 1999 the momentum from the new venues continued but it was the year that our training wheels finally came off. No more Marco and his team. After three years we were on our own. Jarrad Clark was now the production director and he was responsible for developing all the producers who eventually worked on the event.

The MAFW Exhibition under the direction of APN Miller Freeman took another giant leap forward and group shows were expanded to include Ready-to-Wear Women's, Ready-to-Wear Men's and Swim and Resortwear. The now highly anticipated New Generation Collections that had discovered Akira and Karen Walker was about to launch sass & bide and Tsubi. The group shows were a great way for a designer to grow their business in considered steps. We had established a pathway for designers to start with a showing at the MAFW Exhibition, followed the next year by a debut in the New Generation Collections to showcase eight to twelve outfits, followed in turn by a show in the Ready-to-Wear Collections to present twelve to sixteen outfits, and then finally an individual collection show. The hope was that from one year to the next a designer could manage the growth in production and the cash flow required as well as increasing their media profile year on year.

In 1999 our little industry seminar had grown into a day-long event now hosted in the new IMAX theatre at Darling Harbour and starring a fabulous line-up of speakers, including Tyler Brûlé, the founding editor of *Wallpaper*. *marie claire* again hosted the must-attend Opening Ceremony, with Matt Handbury, Mark Kelly and Jackie Frank trying to outdo themselves year on year. Matt and his then wife Fiona had also started hosting dinner parties on our behalf at their harbourside mansion, *Altona*. These private affairs of hand-picked international delegates were an incredible way to introduce some of the most sophisticated fashion professionals in the world to the finer side of Sydney and Australian culture, and no one did it better than Matt and Fiona. I will always remember that only after all the guests had arrived and were very happily sipping champagne in the drawing room would Fiona then descend the very *Gone With the Wind* staircase in *Altona*, looking absolutely stunning. For many key buyers and media who thought they were coming to a fashion week for beginners this start to proceedings was impressive indeed. I will be eternally grateful to Matt and Fiona for their support in those early days.

As if my vision for MAFW wasn't enough I had also become obsessed with creating a televised version of the Australian Fashion Awards. The manufacturing industry body TFIA had been running the industry awards for years and it showed. I knew I could produce an amazing live televised event from MAFW using all the production infrastructure we had at Fox. After months of negotiations I was able to secure Channel Ten as the broadcaster and they assigned one of their most experienced television directors to work with us. I had struck an agreement with the TFIA that gave us creative control over the event while they managed the industry nomination and voting process. The awards were produced as the finale of the week and we turned the enormous Blue Room into the ceremony venue with the runway acting as the stage.

The hilarious Julia Morris was MC and a who's who of the Australian fashion industry were either presenters or recipients. Jackie Frank from *marie claire*, Kirstie Clements from *Vogue*, Marina Go from *Elle* and Karin Upton Baker all had equal billing in handing out the gongs along with a number of MAFW celebrities, including Donald Trump's model daughter Ivanka Trump and the premier of Victoria's model son Angus Kennett, a great public performer whose almost stand-up comedy routine with Ivanka brought the house down. Standout awards that night included Best Designer for Akira and Best Model for Alyssa Sutherland. After only four years of MAFW there were enough well-known names in the Australian fashion industry to hold the attention of a national television audience. It didn't break any ratings records but it certainly provided what I was hoping would be an annual broadcasting platform for the industry. Unfortunately the commercial realities of television just couldn't sustain my vision and this event was the first and last.

For many others and me the highlight that night was the after-party. We had transformed the Yellow Room into our version of New York's Studio 54, removing all the seating and placing café tables with lamps on the tiers. The catwalk became the dance floor. The vibe in the room was electrifying. Everyone was in a party mood. One of the best images of any Fashion Week for me will always be that of Ivanka Trump slow dancing with beautiful Australian model Cleo Maxwell on top of a table under a moody spotlight in the middle of the room. It was such a sexy and sophisticated fashion image. I can also remember party boys Peter Morrissey and Wayne Cooper trying to outdo each other. What a night!

That week was also memorable for a number of standout shows. Charlie Brown and her business partner and husband Danny Avidan were always keen to add a wow factor to their shows and in 1999 it came in the form of a double whammy when they booked both Ivanka Trump and English superstar Sophie Dahl to walk in Charlie's show. It was going to establish a precedent that for the next few years Charlie and Danny would top time and time again. Danny was always the driving business force behind these deals and the fees paid to the models hadn't been seen in Australia before. Each year there was an intense period of negotiation between Danny and me, with him insisting that the still-broke MAFW pay for airfares, accommodation and contribute to the fee. As the vibe around Charlie's show each year got bigger and bigger and became a drawcard for media attention around MAFW, Danny got harder and harder to negotiate with. At times it was not the most pleasant experience going head to head with Mr Avidan but looking back there is no doubt his and Charlie's passion about superstars and supermodels really did help the media profile of the event and had a flow-on effect to everybody involved.

Wayne Cooper and Peter Morrissey also went head to head that year, with Peter presenting his version of a new Australian flag that paid tribute to Indigenous culture. It created a number of headlines around the country. Wayne perpetuated his bad-boy image when at the end of his show he proceeded to destroy a number of what appeared to be glass boxes at the end of the runway with a baseball bat. The glass boxes were actually made from confectionary and everyone in the front row was provided with ski goggles to don while Wayne did his best Pete Townshend impersonation on stage. Fabulous fashion frivolity that created great images.

Alannah Hill, who the previous year had demurely presented her first collection in a group show, returned with an individual show that was the popular hit of the week. Alannah had spent time both as a circus performer and a dancer in a previous life and her vision was to bring both elements together in an all-singing, all-dancing spectacle. In addition to models she used a choreographed troupe of dancers to present certain sections of the collection. A legend and a whole brand image was born that year when Alannah's girly, frilly creations were presented in such a unique way. Both the extravagance of her shows and the size of her business were going to skyrocket over the coming years.

Like the year before, when Morrissey took to his bed after the demise of Morrissey Edmiston, there was another designer meltdown leading into 1999. Alex Perry had been slowly growing his business from group shows to an individual show at MAFW and was finding his way to becoming the powerhouse he is today. The initial miles of tulle and *froufrou* were being replaced by the sophisticated lines and shapes that thousands of women have now come to love. However, behind the scenes everything was unravelling. A few months before the event Alex ended up in my office in a state of combined dismay and terror. He had been given some bad business advice and taken a loan from some very dodgy individuals—the sort who aren't that patient when it comes to defaulting on loan payments. From what Alex told me he had been physically threatened. The only way he was going to dig himself out of this situation was for his next show to be a success, as the cash flow from orders would enable him to pay off his debts. The problem was that he had no money to pay for his show. It was a catch-22 of the worst sort. With Alex in tears I agreed to pay for his show myself. The MAFW hole is so deep at this point what difference will it make? I thought. Maybe Alex and I could end up at the bottom of the harbour together. Alex was hugely appreciative and has basically never looked back since. The show was a massive success and as I understand it he was able to attract other backers and the thugs were sent packing.

MAFW was making our company the go-to place for any fashion event and 1999 was to see our first foray into the realm of such events for consumers rather than the industry. Back in 1996 I had been invited by the Kennett Government, in power in Victoria at the time, to contribute to a research project that later became the L'Oréal Melbourne Fashion Festival. Our agency in Melbourne had also been asked to become the producers of another public fashion event called Spring Fashion Week, underwritten by the City of Melbourne—we ended up running this event for nearly nine years. Both of these were about showing clothes that were already in-store and available for immediate purchase to the public. We also worked again with Alex Zotos, who had developed his own consumer fashion event, a one-night spectacular known as the Australian Designer Collections or ADC. Alex had the idea of bringing a version of ADC to Sydney and allowing the public to experience a 'best of' MAFW collection on the Saturday at Fox Studios Australia after the industry had finished its job for the week. In 1999 we collaborated together to great effect and the fashion-consuming public in Sydney got its first taste of MAFW. It wasn't to be the last.

Hong Kong designers also joined MAFW for the first time in 1999. As we had done in New Zealand, our visits to Hong Kong resulted not only in retailers such as Lane Crawford coming to the event but had also secured the support of the Hong Kong Trade Development Corporation and their sponsorship of a number of leading Hong Kong designers, including Barney Cheng and Pacino Wan. In 1999 I also introduced the first graduate student collections. During a visit to London Fashion Week I had seen the success of the show presented by leading fashion design school Central St Martins, and replicated this back at MAFW to provide a platform for show-casing recent graduate talent. It was to prove a great success and would ultimately inspire Nicholas Huxley, of what was then East Sydney Design Studio, to mount his own show each year. It is now a fixture on the schedule.

Both 1996 and 1997 had created some very wobbly foundations for MAFW but the weight of two solid years in 1998 and 1999 laid a very firm platform for what was to become a seminal year in 2000. It was going to be our make-or-break year in more ways than one.

7

Going Global with Mercedes-Benz

DESIGNERS TAKE PRIDE in their individual sense of self, unique aesthetic and the fact that they walk their own path without considering what others are or aren't doing—providing everyone else is doing exactly the same thing! As I travel the world inviting designers into the ORDRE portfolio often the first question asked yet again is, 'Who else is in?' It never ceases to amaze me that the biggest and most successful designers in the world only want to travel as a pack regardless of whether it is in a shopping centre, at international fashion weeks or on an online wholesale platform.

In the lead-up to the fifth MAFW in 2000 we had finally gathered the momentum we needed to attract the fashion pack. Every designer wanted in and it was going to be a milestone year in more ways than one.

*

In between fashion weeks, we faxed, emailed and called the world for appointments. It was still not easy. MAFW continued to be a hard sell. The hype leading up to the 2000 Olympics, however, was helping attract interest in our host city. For buyers and media from the northern hemisphere it was a nine-day proposition: the four- or five-day schedule of MAFW and two days of travel and/or recovery on either side. Where budget would allow we provided airfares and hotel accommodation from our sponsors. This helped, but the hardest part was to get approval from senior executives of retail or media organisations to allow buyers or journalists to spend that much time out of the office exploring an untried market. Our strategy was to support new buyers, in particular, until hopefully they were buying enough Australian designers that we could wean them off the sponsorship. This worked time and time again. There were, however, those that saw the opportunity as a junket and a good way to have that holiday in Queensland they'd always wanted. This type of guest was seldom invited to return.

Another important strategy that assisted greater engagement between international buyers and media and Australian designers was the MAFW International Host Program. The program took off when Mariela Demetriou came on board to run it after the first few years. We'd recruit switched-on fashionistas, graduate students and industry professionals to host international delegates. In some years we had up to fifty hosts managing nearly two hundred and fifty internationals. We set up a whole training program for the hosts and they had a range of services at their disposal, including Mercedes-Benz courtesy cars, an exclusive Media/Buyers Lounge at the event to work from, as well as 24/7 access to the VIP bar or Bar Bazaar. The program helped build our reputation globally as we were the only fashion week on the circuit providing this sort of support. In reality it was a very calculated plan to squeeze every last order out of the buyers. Before they arrived in the country individual buyers would be profiled and matched with specific designers to try to maximise their time and buying focus. Hosts ensured the buyers attended all the right shows, arranged schedules at showrooms and followed up to ensure orders were placed. On a nightly basis each host would report back on what was hot and what was selling. This is where we got our sales figures.

Many local buyers in the beginning were critical of the focus we put on the internationals, seeing only the VIP passes and access they were being provided. Little did they know it came at a price and many a poor international buyer was packed back onto a Qantas jet feeling as though they had been put through the wringer—and they had. All the time, however, international orders for Australian designers grew each year.

My trips to Parliament House in Canberra and to Macquarie Street had also been slowly paying off. The NSW Department of State and Regional Development had now stepped up to be the lead government agency. Paul Judge in particular was instrumental in helping us establish a host of valuable MAFW programs for the industry. We also built a strong partnership with Austrade, whose offices around the world actively promoted MAFW. They also assisted as hosts for the internationals and were as adept as we were at twisting arms to get orders. Through lobbying we had also been able to access Tourism Australia's Visiting Journalist Program, through which, in association with Destination NSW, we were able to support hundreds of fashion media over the years to come to Sydney to cover MAFW. All this was combined with Austrade's Export Market Development Grant Scheme, which gave rebates to design-ers for international marketing expenditures, various industry grant programs available through AusIndustries, and the support of and appearances at the event by prime ministers, premiers, government ministers and departmental heads. This really was Team Australia.

Even though 1998 and 1999 had been huge years both in terms of the expansion of the schedule and the exhibition, and the growing list of fashion superstars who were now attending the event, their scale was going to be nothing compared to 2000. The schedule alone expanded from fifteen individual shows in 1999 to twenty-seven the following year. And the whole industry seemed to undertake a mission to outdo each other on the catwalk. Shows would make new stars overnight and reinforce the best. For many others, it was to be the highest they would ever climb in the industry before their spiral into oblivion. The process was going to stretch our production capabilities to breaking point.

We had dedicated the MAFW seminar that year to discussing this newfangled thing called online shopping. How hilarious it is now to think it was a subject for the future, and how far we have come in the fifteen years since. The Lock Group had also entered into the digital era with the launch of Spin New Media under the direction of Karson Stimson and my first efforts to create a blog called Stylebyte, which reported on the goings-on in the Australian fashion industry. Linlee Allen was our first editor and later that year we launched a television series on Foxtel's Arena called *Stylebyte TV.* The plan was to also have radio spots as well as a regular column in the Sunday papers, with advertisers going across all four mediums. Unfortunately MAFW was chewing up all available cash flow and the Lock Group just didn't have the ability in the end to provide the development funding required. This would have to be one of my biggest business regrets. Stylebyte could have been an industry changer long before its time.

In the lead-up to the 2000 event buzz had been building around the fact that Karin Upton Baker at *Harper's Bazaar* was bringing a guest editor to MAFW: Cate Blanchett, whose career had sky-rocketed internationally. Cate made it very clear from day one she wasn't going to be a fashion princess permanently glued to the front row. She wanted to experience the event and the creative forces it encompassed. She was, though, going to need a guide, a host who could show her the ropes and introduce her to the players. It had to be someone from within our MAFW family and who better than Mrs Fashion Week, Lorraine Lock.

In the lead-up to MAFW each year Lorraine played host at cocktail parties at our home at Elizabeth Bay, where I was always trying my sales pitch on designers or sponsors or media or buyers. We used our home and these parties to get to know the people we didn't and influence the ones we had to. Lorraine was also at the event 24/7, one minute greeting people at the Opening Ceremony, the next helping Jarrad calm a designer or assisting Louise Di Francesco to pitch a story. For the rest of the year, often months at a time, she was left home alone to look after our two small children, Hannah and Jules, and all the time support me to prevent a mental breakdown because of the finances of the business. In fact, she was the one who had to rush me to hospital when an anxiety attack closed my system down and I passed out. She was there for all of it, and she wasn't just there for me. There was hardly a person in the whole of The Lock Group at the time who wouldn't turn to her for help or advice. In later years, when the children were a little older, Lorraine worked full-time on the event, managing designer relations. So who better to look after Cate Blanchett than Lorraine.

Cate was so cool, often choosing to sit cross-legged at the end of the runway with her camera in the photographer's pit rather than in her designated front-row seat or backstage. The stars that year, though, didn't stop with Cate. An equally forthright vision of feminine charm was to arrive in the form of Texan model Jerry Hall. She made a show-stealing entrance at the Charlie Brown collection, complete with a chihuahua tucked inside her Kelly bag. Danny and Charlie had hosted a dinner for Jerry a few days before the event and I had never seen anything like her effect on men. One certain man about town, who had a reputation for being a bit of a ladies' man with all the smooth moves, was invited to said dinner. He didn't have a chance to even deliver his best chat-up line. Jerry was all over him, controlling his every thought and manipulating him as though he was a puppet. The only difference is that puppets don't drool. I was absolutely mesmerised by it all. She was a smooth as silk cheetah stalking her prey. It made me think about Mick Jagger in a whole new way.

If one leggy Amazonian wasn't enough, that year Wayne Cooper had done a deal with me and a few other sponsors to have Eva

Herzigová walk in his show. She was amazing, all blonde hair and curves, and she set the catwalk alight.

One designer who I always really enjoyed being around was Mark Keighery from MARCS. I had been pleading with him since day one to participate in MAFW but he, along with Peter Metzner, his PR manager, were only going to do it on their terms, when the time was right. Well, that time again came in 2000 and I must say that Mark and Peter came up with the most brilliant concept for a show. It fully embraced the style and culture of MARCS. Kept expertly under a cloud of mystery, guests arrived at the show to be confronted by a huge stage curtain at the rear of the catwalk in the Blue Room. The lights went down and the stage curtain opened to reveal none other than Macy Gray. With her full band she performed her hit, 'I Try'. It produced huge media coverage for MARCS nationally and put the brand among the major players in Australia. Many years later, after Mark's untimely passing, I was able to present his wife Lisa with Mark's plaque on the Australian Fashion Walk of Style at The Intersection on Oxford Street. It was a real honour.

Mark's business partner was James Packer and the Packers were also to feature heavily in 2000 through James's first wife and the founder of Tigerlily Swimwear, Jodhi Meares. She was a swimwear model and had been involved in some earlier Fashion Week shows, and was also a host on a Foxtel TV series. Jodhi had emerged as a very astute businesswoman, putting together her successful collection, which was taking Australia by storm. She had a number of not-so-secret weapons, the first obviously her husband. But his liquid assets alone weren't capable of delivering the creative and commercial success that Tigerlily was to become. I had the good fortune to conduct an exclusive interview with Jodhi for *Stylebyte TV* in the lead-up to MAFW that year and she completely impressed me. Her partner in crime in all things marketing was Victoria Fisher. Victoria had worked in magazines and with her husband Robert

'Fish' Fish, of Cointreau Balls fame, had established Mr & Mrs Fish, an events and PR company.

Jodhi, Vic and Fish, and I think creative director Tony Assness, had come up with an out-there concept for the show, one that wasn't actually going to work in Fox Studios because of the extended bump-in required. As such we came to an agreement to give Jodhi in her first year at MAFW one of the highly coveted off-site evening shows. Over a number of days in a huge warehouse in Alexandria the team built an incredible set: the entrance to the catwalk was through a wall of water and the catwalk itself was a few centimetres deep in water. When the water was first turned on and a smoking-hot Megan Gale broke through the waterfall and proceeded to strut her stuff, dripping wet from head to toe, jaws collectively hit the floor. None more so than Kerry Packer, sitting with James in the front row in their regulation attire of plastic ponchos. The highlight of the show, apart from the cool and sexy swimwear, was when Megan again stopped front and centre on the catwalk in front of Mr Packer senior and playfully kicked water all over him, to the crowd's and I think his great delight. The pièce de résistance was at the very end when a $500,000 bikini made of Paspaley pearls graced the catwalk.

The amazing shows that year just kept coming. Joe Saba and Simon B again collaborated to present a live art installation rather than a catwalk show. Scanlan Theodore added to production values by introducing an all-copper runway that took the production crew endless hours to erect. Two New Zealanders—Karen Walker and Kate Sylvester—stepped out of the group show to present individually in 2000. Both showed an eclectic mix of fashion, art and substance. Kate presented her pretty girl-gone-bad collection by elevating the catwalk to dining table height and having the girls walk between white china plates and doilies that were eventually trampled. Karen Walker and her creative director husband Mikhail Gherman gave everyone personal CD players, headphones and an individualised soundtrack for the runway. The end result was seamless from an audience-participation point of view but for me and the boys in the media pit it was hilarious to hear all the photographers' comments, clearly audible, as there was no music actually playing in the room. Many models just cracked up laughing on the runway as for the first time they could hear what the snappers were saying and yelling at them!

Morrissey in 2000 presented his famous Aboriginal collection, a collaboration with a number of Indigenous artists. Qantas was so inspired Peter was asked to design their new uniforms. It was a memorable moment backstage that night as the industry celebrated another Morrissey masterpiece. I can remember leaping onto a crate at the height of the party to toast Peter, declaring to all that this was why I built Fashion Week—to truly show the world the essence of unique Australian style. A style that Morrissey had captured.

Another memorable moment was delivered by Betty Fong and Wayne Homschek of label Paablo Nevada. Wayne was a huge fan of Roy and HG, the iconic sports presenters from radio station Triple J, and he convinced the duo to call a live commentary of the show as the models took to the runway. The production team helped Wayne and Betty re-create a 1950s-inspired cricket pitch, along with a score box from which Roy and HG, perched high above the models, called the show: 'Well, that's a lovely lassy coming down the leg side … how would you describe that ruffle she's wearing, HG?' The end result was pure fashion and comic magic.

This year also introduced Michelle Jank to the world. She was in her final year at East Sydney under the tutelage of Nicholas Huxley. Nicholas rang me enthusiastically to tell me he had unearthed this amazing new talent and I had to do something to help. I went down to the college, fully expecting to find a jewel in the rough destined for the New Generation show. What I came across was much more astounding: a new designer with very much her own handwriting, bringing together fabric and patterns in ways that hadn't been seen before. Her work was a cross between a magpie's nest and a couture dress. It was different and exciting and I wanted to show the world.

Between Nicholas, myself and Michelle's extended family of fashion friends a team was built around her to support her debut collection as an individual designer. She is still the first and only graduate student to be offered an individual show at Fashion Week. The result was everything everyone had hoped for.

Michelle, in her very unassuming way, was completely over-whelmed by the immediate reaction to her show. Cate Blanchett was the first to congratulate her backstage, and Mrs B staged yet another runway sprint to be the first buyer out the back to snap up as much of the collection as she could. In every sense—as it is clearly evident today in the creative work that Michelle continues to do—a star was born. However, the mantle rested uncomfortably on Michelle's shoulders and in the following years it was to be both a blessing and a curse.

There were three significant events in 2000 that broke new ground for us. In the lead-up to the fifth year I was keen to publish a book on our journey to date and also preview the 2000 collec-tion. I was fortunate to have the opportunity to work with Alex Smart, a publisher at ACP at the time and now, along with her sister Genevieve, one half of design duo Ginger & Smart. The result was *Catwalk*, a hardcover coffee table book and brilliant showcase of the work that had been generated out of MAFW by the designers. I wrote the foreword and Lee Tulloch worked on the copy and art direction with Alex. A glamorous launch party for the book was held in the brand-new penthouse apartment at the newly developed complex at 28 Billyard Avenue on Sydney Harbour. It was a very stylish event.

Proceedings were capped off by an official launch speech by premier of New South Wales Bob Carr. It was only after Bob com-pleted his duties that I got up the courage to tell him about sneaking into his office at Macquarie Street. In 1998 our grant from the NSW Government was up for renewal and after months and months of meetings with this minister and that minister and department heads from the Department of Arts, Industry and Trade—the fashion industry is usually without a government portfolio as no one knows quite where to slot us—I was still no closer to getting a commitment. I had finally secured a meeting with the tourism minister and been granted a security pass to be taken to a certain floor. Unfortunately the minister never turned up and the meeting was cancelled. I was completely exasperated and at the end of my tether in dealing with the government on behalf of the industry. I returned to the lift, got in, but it went up instead of down, and I found the doors opening on the floor of the offices of the premier.

I made a decision on the spot to take my chance and arrive unannounced at the premier's office to make my bid directly to him. The security at the entrance reception presumed the pass around my neck had me in the right place and I simply walked in. I got within a few metres of the office before someone finally asked me if they could help me. I nonchalantly told him I had a meeting with the premier. He instructed me to sit and wait in reception while the personal secretary was summoned. My brief gig was up. No amount of explaining my situation was going to get me an audience with him that day. I did try staging a personal sit-in until the premier was available, but that was when I crossed the line and security was called. I was escorted from the building. A few days later I got the call from the Department of State and Regional Development and things were back on track. I have a suspicion that a very empathetic but protocol-entrenched private secretary had taken matters into her own hands.

MAFW in 2000 also introduced the next incarnation of public fashion events in the form of the *marie claire* Fashion Show Live. In London the previous year I had seen the hugely successful BBC TV program *The Clothes Show*. Event organisers took the content from the TV program and turned it into a live event incorporating a public exhibition of runway shows, beauty promotions, makeovers and designer sales direct to the public. Our version was held the weekend after Fashion Week and featured hourly fashion shows of designers from MAFW, interviews with fashion celebs by myself and *marie claire* editor Jackie Frank, designer clearance sales, an array of fashion exhibitors—many of whom had also been in the MAFW Exhibition—and a performance by the new girl band called Bardot. It was a girl's shopping day out. That first year we had over fifteen thousand people attend.

Another special happening in the lead-up to the 2000 event was when I was invited to the Mercedes-Benz global headquarters in Stuttgart. Horst von Sanden, who was then the marketing director in Australia and would eventually become CEO, and I created a strategy to engage Mercedes-Benz even more significantly in fashion internationally. Our strategy was twofold: we had a good sponsorship case study that Mercedes-Benz could embrace globally to start sponsoring other international fashion weeks, and we proposed that this could happen through the combination of both country-based and international marketing funds. Our hope was to get headquarters to buy into a global strategy and in the process we would get a contribution from headquarters to assist Mercedes-Benz Australia to pay for the next sponsorship contract. Our first five-year sponsorship contract was coming to an end and I had set ambitious goals to get a five-year renewal.

Professionally this was an amazing opportunity. I was able to present our case study and strategy to every marketing director of Mercedes-Benz from around the globe, who had all gathered in Stuttgart for one of their regular conferences. My presentation extended to over two hours and everyone in the room saw the merit in creating a global sponsorship strategy around the international fashion week circuit. Mercedes in some markets had already dabbled in promotions with the fashion industry but nothing was as structured or had had the impact we had created in Australia. This presentation was to be a major catalyst for Mercedes-Benz, which now sponsors over twenty international fashion weeks around the world. I'm proud that the combined team of Australian Fashion Innovators and Mercedes-Benz in Australia can lay claim to a strategy that has been the most enduring and impactful in the fashion industry globally.

8

Store Wars,
4 cm Zips and Rats

THIS WEEK I am in Tokyo doing all I can to try to secure Japanese designers to become part of the ORDRE portfolio. In the early days of promoting MAFW in Tokyo to various department stores and boutiques someone said to me that after he had been in Japan for ten years he felt he was slowly starting to understand the place. But after he had been there for twenty years he knew he never would! Never a truer word spoken. That is exactly how I feel and why I love the place. For years I have stared across the desks of buyers and through interpreters espoused the virtues of MAFW to be met with all-knowing nods and 'Yes, yes, yes, we will come.' However, 'yes' doesn't always mean 'yes' in Japan; it can mean, 'Yes, I'm disappointed that I can't come but I will say "yes" so as not to disappoint you.'

In my early years I was arrogant enough to think I was the one doing business the right way in Japan and why wasn't everyone doing what I wanted?! Today I realise the art of making the correct approach is to target the right person, someone of similar seniority in the business community. When dealing with established and legendary Japanese designers for ORDRE we have had to secure respected Japanese industry figures who can be our ambassadors to help make the right impression first. Experience is great, if you learn from it.

*

The celebration of our fifth MAFW in 2000 had been a triumphant occasion for the industry. Designers participating in both the shows and the exhibition reported strong sales. Our consistent marketing overseas had paid off and the event and our designers were starting to gain more and more international recognition. Locally the multi-label boutiques were quietly beginning to support Australian designers with bigger orders. The stores owned by the designers were now attracting new and loyal customers. A lot of this had to do with the fact that maybe for the first time Australian consumers were recognising the value of Australian designer brands and were willing to pay good money for them. They were seeing more of Australian designers in newspapers, magazines and on television. They were hearing about Akira Isogawa's or Zimmermann's success overseas.

For Australian consumers that global recognition had become an important part of buying into Australian brands. Once a year, they were bombarded with an extraordinary amount of media coverage. By 2000, MAFW was annually getting $25 to $30 million worth of media coverage across all sectors. This was more than what a major car brand would spend on an advertising campaign and was on par with other major national events, including the various football finals and horse racing festivals. When MAFW was on there was not a man, woman or child in Australia who didn't know it. Well, unless they lived under a rock in the desert.

After the 2000 event the NSW Department of State and Regional Development conducted an independently verified audit on the outcomes of MAFW. It was presented to state parliament, citing the fact that the event had contributed $101 million in economic development to the state and was responsible for generating 191 new jobs. My plan of growing the event in a rapid manner over the three years from 1998 had paid off. We had managed to pay down our debt while maintaining enough cash flow to sustain our growth. A major factor in this was the growth and development of Spin. As the major shareholder I was able to take all the profits I was due and channel them back into MAFW. We did have one casualty during this period and that was the wonderful Marguerite Julian. I think in the end the constant pressure I was putting on the business and my partners was too much for her and she opted for an easier life without me. I can't really blame her. MJ went off and set up Stella and it has become one of Australia's leading and most enduring PR agencies. In years to come Stella would work on our event for various sponsors.

The media impact made by MAFW had a number of different outcomes. I was getting the best tables at every restaurant I was going to and my media profile had gone through the roof. I was on everything from *60 Minutes* to ABC programs and in every fashion magazine and newspaper in the country. I was being asked to speak at conferences, attend events and sit on government advisory boards. To be honest, I enjoyed the notoriety. This media coverage had an impact in a couple of other areas. The first was marvellous, the second insidious.

At the very beginning of MAFW the department stores Myer Grace Bros and David Jones weren't interested. They were both doing quite well with their designer imports and house brands and didn't have much time or energy for Australian designers. In essence they were reflecting their customers' attitudes. But those attitudes were changing by 2000 as MAFW drove up the profiles of Australian designers and the public started to show a real interest. For years I had been treating the department stores equally, likening MAFW to the United Nations in that we needed to love all countries/retailers equally. This was not working and no matter how we encouraged them to attend MAFW and buy the collections they resisted.

Around this time I had a seminal meeting with Colette Garnsey, who—along with David Bush, who now works with me on ORDRE, and Damian Burke—was a key figure in making all designer purchasing decisions at DJs. There was an inkling of interest from them for the first time in designers at MAFW and we discussed how I might be able to help them. Immediately I developed a strategy that over the next few years was going to make David Jones the home of the Australian designer, much to the annoyance of Myer.

In 2001, I quietly provided DJs with a buying office backstage where they could review collections and hold meetings with designers. At the same time I worked with John Flower, our seating director, to seat all DJs' buyers together in one block in every front row. Everybody in the industry took notice of this. We then started to steer all our media inquiries for buying to Colette. DJs was everywhere. Backstage I led a constant procession of Australian designers to meet the DJs buying team. We basically gave them the inside running on every collection and every hot new designer we could. It is my understanding that in a single season DJs tripled their orders on Australian designers and then came back for more in the autumn/ winter season later that year. The good news was the sell-through rates. Australian consumers were ready and waiting. They wanted and expected their favourite department store to have their favourite Australian designers and now they did. DJs was hooked.

In January 2002 I then paid a visit to the buying team at Myer in Melbourne—sorry, Colette. My introduction went something like this: 'I can't believe that the DJs buying team thinks it owns the Australian fashion industry. The rightful home is here at Myer. What can I do to help?' That year, the whole Myer team miraculously found themselves seated in every front row, eye to eye with DJs. Gee, I wonder how that happened? The next thing, Myer had its own VIP lounge and were hosting an array of dinners and events on the official schedule.

Behind the scenes we were now actively introducing new designers to both department stores. The portfolios were building on either side. The media coverage kept coming, the customers kept buying and the phenomenon now known as 'Store Wars' was born. I'm not saying I was solely responsible for this happening but I must admit the role MAFW had to play was instrumental. Store Wars now involve huge advertising support by the respective department stores for their designer portfolios as well as millions of dollars spent on seasonal launch events. However, nothing gave me more pleasure than when DJs launched their Home of Australian Designers campaign back in 2004, featuring MAFW regulars Anthony Kendal, Sally Smith, Easton Pearson, Trelise Cooper, Zimmermann, Tanya Carlson, Morrissey, sass & bide, Akira Isogawa and Collette Dinnigan. For years people have said the big story around MAFW is the international opportunities it creates for Australian designers but I truly believe its biggest commercial success has been the support it provided our department stores to realise what they had in their own backyards.

With DJs' buying office tucked away backstage we headed straight into MAFW 2001, and it was shaping up to be a killer season. Market visits to New York, London, Paris, Milan, Singapore and Hong Kong had rounded up an international contingent of over two hundred delegates. Australian delegates now topped a thousand and, by the time we added the designers' guests, sponsors and their guests and VIPs to the list, we were seeing around five thousand people at the event.

Key internationals that year included the fashion history oracle himself, Colin McDowell from the *The Sunday Times*; ex-pat Yasmin Sewell from her boutique in London; Yasmin Cho, whom we are now working with at ORDRE; Harvey Lee Sutton from Selfridges; Armand Limnander from the then fledgling online site style.com; hugely influential Sarah Lerfel from Colette in Paris; and our regular Mrs B, whom we still loved and adored, among the hundreds of others. Star power was also present in 2001. Jodie Kidd had flown in courtesy of me and Danny Avidan to star in the Charlie Brown show; Sarah Wynter had taken over as *Harper's Bazaar* guest editor;

Shakira Caine, the actress/model and wife of actor Michael Caine, turned up; and one of my favourite models and soon-to-be fine actress Emma Booth took much of the spotlight on the catwalk. Halfway through the week I convinced her to radically change her hair colour overnight from blonde to bright red. It was a hit with the media and our sponsor L'Oréal loved it. The local stars were now turning out in force and actually hassling John and me for front-row seats: 'Yes, yes … we know who you are!'

The real stars in 2001 were definitely on the catwalk. The industry was gathering strength and confidence with each year. Akira kept pushing his talent and impressing Mrs B. Alannah Hill took her dancing girls to new heights and actually matched it with frilly clothes that girls just adored. Alex Perry was getting slicker and slicker and now had a red carpet rival in Aurelio Costarella, who staged his first individual show. Charlie Brown naturally got her due press. Easton Pearson were slowly and surely making their presence felt. Radical newbie Justine Taylor, with my support, had been plucked from the group shows and given her own stage. Kate Sylvester swapped her dining table for a boxing ring with a great take on sport chic before Alexander Wang in New York had ever heard of it. Morrissey outdid Morrissey. Paablo Nevada swapped the cricket pitch for the stables at Fox Studios. Nicola Finetti graced us with his presence for the second year in a row. Anthony Kendal and his Thys Collective collaborated with artist Mary Shackman. Tigerlily did it again thanks to Mrs Fish and her team. Wayne Cooper gave us his best bad-boy impression all afresh, combined with beautiful party frocks. Zambesi showed their mastery of the game and Zimmermann were going from strength to strength.

The two standout shows that year were S!X and Michelle Jank for very different reasons. Denise Sprynskyj and Peter Boyd from Melbourne label S!X showed for the first time. Currently these two creative dynamos are an integral part of the RMIT fashion design course in Melbourne but back in 2001 they gave a great lecture to the entire industry about how fashion can be a medium for art. While their clothes may not have always been the most wearable, the interpretation of traditional patterns and silhouettes was inspiring. There is no doubt S!X can sit very comfortably next to some of the great deconstructionists of our times, including Yohji Yamamoto, Dirk Bikkembergs and Martin Margiela.

Michelle Jank's collection in 2001 was beautiful and extraordinary but it was to be her last as a solo designer. I had felt in many ways I was a mentor for Michelle over the three years of her meteoric rise at MAFW but in the end I truly believe that it was our industry's infancy that let her down. She is a rare talent as is evident from the incredible body of styling work and accessories she has developed over the years. The fashion world is a poorer place for the fact that she is not producing ready-to-wear collections. Michelle at her core was always an artist, an artist who at the time was in need of a system that would nurture and guide her. Over the heady first three years the media spotlight on her was intense. Her collections were in fact *demi-couture*, not ready-to-wear at all, but everybody wanted a piece of Michelle and in the end there just wasn't enough to go around. Michelle walked away from what could have been a career as a ready-to-wear designer that would have put her in the league of Balenciaga or Alexander McQueen.

If only our industry had had a proper incubator program in the early 2000s or Michelle had had the good fortune to find the partner who could have been the balance of commerce to her art. Instead Michelle only had by her side a boyfriend with little industry experience, a well-meaning family and a few of us who were trying to help. In the end she got buried under a ton of publicity and expectation. She re-emerged, though, and now has a glorious career in a number of disciplines within the fashion industry and is one of our most credentialed international fashion artisans.

In 2001 we went on to deliver a never-ending procession of debut collections from brilliant talents, including Glen Rollason, Lorinda

Grant, Marnie Skillings, Rebecca Dawson, Saint Teresa, Vixen, Sabatini, Flora Cheong-Leen and Doris Lee. Our New Generation show also delivered three huge names to the Australian industry.

When I first met Sarah-Jane Clarke and Heidi Middleton from sass & bide they had just returned from London, where their hipster jeans were already the hottest thing at the Portobello Road market. We picked them up on our radar and I immediately asked them to come in so we could discuss how we could help them. I will always remember them both sitting on my couch in our office on the corner of Liverpool and Palmer streets in Darlinghurst and with all my best fashion-speak asking them to describe the 'creative essence and inspiration' behind sass & bide. They looked at each other and then Heidi said, 'Well, basically it is all about a 4-centimetre zip—it's that easy.' While it might have been a 4-centimetre zip that made their jeans the lowest cut in the world, it was a bustier that they presented in the New Generation Collections that year that caught the fashion pack's eye.

Lisa Gorman was another designer who eventually built a national and international presence from a debut at New Gen that year. And a tribe of boys from the Skull Cave in Manly will be remembered above everyone else in 2001 for one of the most audacious shows ever.

Sophie Miller had joined Australian Fashion Innovators as designer liaison and would eventually be based in Singapore with me as part of our Asian expansion, but it was a call she received from Dan Single from Tsubi at 3 a.m. the day before the New Gen show that had her wishing she could leave the country straightaway! The Tsubi crew, comprising founders Gareth Moody, Dan Single, George Gorrow, Paul Wilson and Oscar Wright, was a posse of skater/surfers turned street artists and jean makers. They had been creating waves with their customised denim jeans, turning patterns back to front, adding graffiti, patches and tears. Their deconstruction and derelict aesthetic had a cult following but the idea they had conjured up for the New Gen show was going to catapult them onto front pages around the world. Their models were to share the catwalk with two hundred and fifty RATS!

I think when Jarrad got the call from Sophie he thought it was a joke but he soon brought the problem to me. We had always taken pride in our attitude towards designer requests. Our view was to say 'yes' first and think about how to do it later. I think the Tsubi boys went into a panic when they realised we were actually up for it. Jarrad and I quickly came up with a production solution. The chaos that two hundred and fifty rats would cause backstage would totally disrupt the other New Gen designers so we decided to split the show in two. Everybody else in New Gen 1 and Tsubi and their rats in New Gen 2. Jarrad then came up with the ingenious idea of running a lip of Perspex about 30 centimetres high around the entire catwalk so the rats couldn't escape into the front row.

Meanwhile, Louise Di Francesco was in publicity heaven and packed the media pit to bursting point with the promise of an amazing spectacle. There was certainly a mood of expectation when the lights went down in the Blue Room. A huge red-velvet curtain hid the rats in their containers backstage. Then the curtain was drawn, the cages opened and the rats went mad. Like a scene from the Pied Piper a wave of them in all shapes, colours and teeth-length charged down the 30-metre-long catwalk. A wave of shrieks and screams followed them as the guests in the front row freaked out. There were people literally climbing over each other to get out of the front row and its eye-to-teeth view of the rats. Others tucked their feet up underneath themselves, fearing a stray rat was about to leap over the Perspex. The most outraged person was Mrs B. She was absolutely disgusted and let me know in no uncertain manner, as I was sitting very close to her in my usual seat at the very end of the runway with my son Jules, who was about five at the time, on my knee. It was his first MAFW show ever: 'Dad, this is so cool! Do you do this every day?'

After the rats had staked their claim down the catwalk out came the models. Some absolutely regretted the decision to do the show, trying not to step on a rat's tail with every tentative step they took. Others just went with it. Tione Hawkins was a country girl and she got right into it, standing at the end of the runway and picking up a group of the rodents, letting them scramble up her arms and neck and into her teased hair. The show ended in complete mayhem with all the Tsubi crew on stage dressed head to toe in their new collection—looking like crosses between *The Pirates of the Caribbean* and Jean Paul Gaultier—and models either dancing happily or screaming to leave the runway and two hundred and fifty rats climbing over each other as if it was a scene from a horror movie. It was beyond belief!

The television and pictorial images of that Tsubi show went around the world as fast as AAP could get them out. Front pages in London, page three everywhere else and the lead on every news station in Australia. Tsubi the legend was born and everyone knew they were MAFW's baby—well, impetuous teenagers at least! The media coverage we were receiving was good; however …

The fashion industry in general is aspirational to a lot of people. It portrays a glamorous and stylish lifestyle: beautiful models, fabulous parties, creative designers, inspiring shows. These images are alluring, especially to young women searching for their own identities and ways through life. This is the reason we had been so successful in attracting so many sponsors to MAFW, like Mercedes, of course, but also L'Oréal, MAC, Moët, San Pellegrino, Visa, Napoleon and many others. Unfortunately we were about to have a few unwelcome rats jump on our bandwagon.

Following the event in 2001 I was approached by a whistleblower from the cigarette industry. He gave me a number of video recordings that had been made in secret at an internal marketing meeting of one of the big international cigarette companies. We had long ago banned cigarette advertising and sponsorship in Australia. The video showed the Australian market being referred to as one of the 'darkest' in the world, where legislation had made it difficult to promote their product. It went on to showcase a new strategy that had been devised and was being trialled in Australia, targeting the fashion industry. To get around the law, the company paid for designers' after-parties, providing free cigarettes to anyone who wanted them and then placing as many images as they could from these events in the media. At the same time they were independently producing public fashion events at nightclubs. During these events they handed out free cigarettes and took photos of people smoking. Basically they were trying to photograph as many cool fashion people smoking as possible and place these images out there for all to see. The idea was that young girls in particular would see them, think smoking was cool and glamorous and take up the habit. At the same time many in the fashion media were actually helping this strategy by placing photos of models smoking in editorials without any encouragement at all. The whistleblower proceeded to tell me that MAFW had been a specific focus of this strategy and the idea was to expand to other markets. Apparently South Africa was next.

I was horrified and it didn't take me long to check the facts and find out that a few designers had taken money for their after-parties, not fully knowing the plans they were caught up in. Then we conducted a media audit and were astonished at just how many images there were of cool people smoking in fashion media. Then came the straw that broke the camel's back. An anonymous phone call was put through to me and I was offered $300,000 in cash to turn a blind eye to everything and not stop or comment on designer after-parties that were supported by cigarette companies. I slammed the phone down. How dare these companies think they could use me! No one was going to use my industry to give young people cancer if I could help it.

I got on my high horse and flew straight to Canberra with the tapes in hand. I handed them over to the parliamentary secretary for health at the time, the Honourable Trish Worth MP, and pledged my support to fight these creeps. In a matter of weeks in the lead-up to the 2002 event we came up with a dual strategy. Trish was going to lobby the House of Representatives for tighter legislation to stop big tobacco from securing email addresses for promotional use as well as paying outright for the parties. I had by then come up with what I thought was a brilliant initiative, even if I do say so myself, called SMOKE FREE FASHION.

Trish and I planned two major events: one in Sydney and the other in Canberra. Under the guise that I had a top-secret announcement to make about MAFW I invited all the leading designers, models and fashion editors to a luncheon at the Overseas Passenger Terminal in Sydney. The usual niceties and air kisses prevailed and then I took to the lectern. Without much fanfare I introduced a young lady from Kincoppal-Rose Bay, a private girls' school in Sydney. Her name was Sophie and she was in year 11. She was one of those inspiring young women who are forthright and not afraid to speak their minds and, thankfully, a great public speaker. I'm sure she was queen bee of the debating team. In her own words she told all those gathered about the perils of being a young woman, trying to find yourself and to fit in at the same time. She spoke of peer pressure and the general need to be accepted into various friendship groups. She spoke from the heart about wanting to be cool and liked. She spoke about her role models and the things she surrounded herself with. She spoke about what influenced her and where she turned to for inspiration. She then, to the great delight of a certain section of the room, picked up a copy of *Vogue*. Opening it to an editorial spread of a really cool fashion shoot with a hot model of the day dangling a cigarette nonchalantly from her bee-stung lips, she turned to the audience and said, 'This is why I smoke. *Vogue* and the fashion industry told me it was cool.'

No one in the room knew where to look. Sophie then went on to explain the key influences around her in school had all taken up smoking and now half the school population in years 11 and 12 was smoking to fit in and be like everyone else. I returned to the lectern and trotted out example after example of fashion people smoking in social media and fashion shoots. I told everyone what had happened with the whistleblower, the videos, the paid-for after-parties, the email promotions and the bribe. Trish then spoke on the government's behalf and told the fashion pack what she was going to try to do in Canberra. I then unveiled what I knew would stop this thing dead in its tracks.

Firstly I declared that every fashion event I would ever produce again in my life would be smoke free, starting with MAFW in a few months' time. Secondly I held up the SMOKE FREE FASHION pledge. It basically said that as a member of the fashion industry you would never knowingly have your photo taken while smoking and, if you worked in the creative services or media, you would not style cigarettes into photo shoots or publish any images with smoking in them. Over the next ten days one hundred and ten people signed the pledge. All the fashion editors signed, including those of *marie claire*, *Vogue* and *Harper's Bazaar*, and all the top models of the day and designers from Collette Dinnigan through to, you guessed it, Wayne Cooper signed as well.

Trish and I had what we needed and ten days later in Parliament House in Canberra we held a national press conference where we presented the SMOKE FREE FASHION initiative and its one hundred and ten pledges, including my signature at the top. Since then as far as I know no Australian designer has accepted money or had their after-party sponsored by big tobacco; very few smoking images have appeared in Australian publications and none to my knowledge of any model smoking at MAFW. Fashion industry one—Big Tobacco zero. KO'd in the first round!

Almost immediately following the launch of SMOKE FREE FASHION we went straight into MAFW 2002. It was shaping up to be another great season. A whirlwind tour of New York, Los Angeles, Paris, Milan, Seoul, Hong Kong, Tokyo and Singapore had delivered a new batch of international retailers and media. We were now getting close to two hundred and fifty international delegates a season.

The Opening Ceremony in 2002 was, I believe, the first time we crossed the line with our sponsors. We had up until then been able to ensure that our sponsors got the rewards they deserved without taking away from the fashion. Well, I went over the top with Mercedes-Benz at the Opening Ceremony. I had promised that at some time we would allow them to launch a new car at MAFW and with the arrival of the beautiful new C Class in Australia the timing seemed right. We produced an Opening Ceremony where the C Class was unveiled surrounded by our top models and as a backdrop to a live performance. Unfortunately it ended up looking like the showcase on *Sale of the Century*, complete with me as the host.

Alex Perry made the other sponsorship faux pas that year when he introduced his show with a voiceover from Emirates Airlines, his sponsor, and walked out with two hostesses either side of him for his finale. Between him and me the press had a field day, although they didn't seem to complain too much about the millions in advertising dollars our sponsors were pumping into their publications.

The industry may not remember the Mercedes launch that year but many will remember that Australia's biggest supermodel Elle Macpherson was in attendance. After months and months and months and then a few more months of negotiation with her and her manager Stuart Cameron, we eventually got a deal on the table for her to come to MAFW. It involved her being the guest editor of *Harper's Bazaar*, launching a new range of her lingerie on the schedule, and attending the Opening Ceremony as well as a charity event. It had taken us seven years to get her home for MAFW but it was worth the wait … in more ways than one for some!

We swung into action at Fox following the Opening Ceremony with a slightly expanded format. We had added another collection showroom in a tent down the side of the Hordern called the Red Room and all the other usual elements were in place, including the seminar, exhibition and *marie claire* Fashion Show Live on the week-end. Within the individual collection shows a number of designers who were going to make their mark both nationally and interna-tionally made their debuts in spectacularly different ways. First was the much-anticipated return of Leona Edmiston. She had found the

right partner for life and business in film producer Jeremy Ducker.
With him by her side she had someone to take care of the business
while she could focus on the design. Leona and Jeremy, much to
my frustration, had sat on the sidelines for a few seasons, timing
Leona's return to perfection. Her first collection at MAFW was a
huge hit, attracting orders from Browns in London to Villa Moda in
the Middle East. Jeremy was a hard but fair man to deal with and I
always enjoyed our negotiations over MAFW.

I should have seen the storm coming when Victoria Fisher
(Mrs Fish) again took one of her prized clients, Terry Biviano, off-
site for her debut in a disused glass factory in Alexandria. Terry's
installation was stunning and the Australian shoe queen had arrived.
Complete with hot local film star Alex Dimitriades as a partner,
Terry was to become a staple on the Sydney social scene and still
is to this day. Then my second inkling of a rising storm happened
when Mrs Fish tried to break all the rules at MAFW and present a
sneaky Kerry Grima show within Bar Bazaar at the same time as a
show in one of our main showrooms to an invitation-only audience
of our delegates. I was beyond furious, not only with her but with
the new editor of *Harper's Bazaar*, Alison Veness. In the end there was
a stand-off, with us agreeing to time Kerry's show in between other
shows so delegates could attend everything. But unbeknown to me
a ticking bomb had been ignited that threatened to blow MAFW
completely to pieces.

Other notable debuts that year included Toni Maticevski and
his beautiful silk-draped organza. I can still remember sharing his
tears of relief backstage after it had all gone so well and he'd been
applauded by none other than Ian Thorpe in the front row. Other
standouts included Gwendolynne, Melbourne bad-boy Roy and
Third Millennium.

Under the leadership of Andy Amos, initial general manager,
sass & bide took a huge leap forward in 2002 to mount their individual show in the disused Balmain Power Station. It was a stroke
of genius and helped to cement the designing duo's brand as a mix

of elegance and edginess. The designers presented an artful collection complete with make-up the likes of which hadn't been seen at MAFW. Collaborating with Swarovski, the make-up artist spent hours painstakingly gluing intricate designs of crystals all over the models' faces to complement the collection. It was beautiful.

Tsubi were back, causing mayhem as only they could. Karen Walker had now become a regular, and MARCS launched their Baby Doll range. Morrissey presented a collection inspired by the Caribbean complete with terry towelling shirts. Wayne Cooper continued to build his business, showing why he was one of the most important designers in Australia. Alannah Hill kept finding new ways to present dance routines with her collections. Nicola Finetti's star was on the rise. Zimmermann had now rapidly expanded, and Zambesi continued with their thousand shades of black and grey. A new entrant to MAFW was Tina Kalivas. Originally from Adelaide, Tina had taken her fashion talents to London, where she became part of the Alexander McQueen studio that worked on the runway editorial pieces for his elaborate collections. We were thrilled when she decided to launch her own collection at MAFW rather than at London Fashion Week, where she had had a standing invitation. Supported by a clever team, including Antonia Leigh, an ex-Spinner, her debut was an instant success and was supported by both department stores and boutiques.

The week was an action-packed one. From memory I attended seventy-five separate events and collections over six days that year. I always prided myself on attending every event that was on the official schedule, regardless of whether it was a collection show, media conference, sponsor event or envelope opening. My feeling was that if people had invested time and money to be part of MAFW, as the founding father I would attend their event. This sometimes meant that my day began with a live cross to *Sunrise* and finished at 2 or 3 a.m. at a designer after-party. The secret to my success was to never walk past a tray of canapés without taking one or two and to always hold a full glass of champagne but never drink it. This worked well until the official wrap party, when all bets were off and I really let loose. Which is what I did at the closing party of 2002, but not as much as some others.

In 2002, Christine Bookallil had again worked her magic and come up with the ultimate way to close MAFW. Christine had started to work with Autore South Sea Pearls and its owner Rosario Autore. Together the three of us formed a wonderful partnership and for several years, while the Autore brand grew in profile, many in the fashion industry benefited. As well as becoming an official sponsor of MAFW Autore supported up-and-coming designers. It was the only reason, for example, that Toni Maticevski could make his debut in 2002 in the way he did. Just about every time I ran out of my own money to support a new designer Rosario was there to help.

In 2002 we closed MAFW with a charity masked ball sponsored by Autore to launch the Ian Thorpe Foundation, with special guest Elle Macpherson, and staged at the Overseas Passenger Terminal. It was to be a night full of stars and surprises. Everyone looked amazing and had gone to extreme lengths to have stylish masks. Sarah O'Hare, who had recently married Lachlan Murdoch, accompanied Ian Thorpe on the head table along with myself, my then wife Lorraine, Elle Macpherson and Rosario Autore and his wife Jane. An auction was held to raise money for the foundation, with some amazing items sold, including a perfect strand of pearls that went for a fortune. Rosario bought a beautiful rose gold watch donated by Ian Thorpe and that raised another $35,000 for his foundation. One of the biggest donations of the night was to secure a chance to hear Ian Thorpe sing. While presented as a joke at first, the bidding took off and it looked as though Ian was going to have to deliver. What no one realised at the time was that Ian had secretly been rehearsing with Katie Underwood from Bardot fame. To the astounded audience later in the evening he fronted a live band and sang a duo with Katie, 'Kids Are Alright', made famous by Kylie Minogue and Robbie Williams. Ian rapping in the song was a highlight of the night and, while Kanye West is not about to invite him out on tour, it was a great effort.

Meanwhile, backstage a certain supermodel made her first acquaintance with the young son of a fashion publishing icon. Over the coming months the speculation around this supposed liaison grew to fever pitch. I was just excited to be part of it all.

9

The Fashion Hostage Saga

F OR THE PAST nine months Kirsten and I have been constantly
on the road locking in designers, retailers and market managers
for ORDRE. We have lived out of a suitcase and spent each week
in a different city. We have done three complete circuits of Hong
Kong, Shanghai, Seoul, Tokyo, Sydney, New York, London, Paris
and Milan. In between I somehow managed to write this book.
However, all this is nothing in comparison to the period between
May 2002 and May 2003. In some respects this was professionally
and personally one of the most intense periods of my life. MAFW
was to finally become a fully fledged fashion week and at the same
time it almost collapsed. All of this happened while I was summiting
a personal goal that had been a decade in the making.

*

The industry first knew I was up to something when the head of
Victorian Major Events Company, former television comedian Steve
Vizard, was seen casually getting a guided tour of MAFW at Fox

Studios in May 2002. The major events company had been set up by the Kennett Government to attract major events to Melbourne to support tourism and economic growth. They had already secured the Formula 1 Australian Grand Prix and with a big budget they were again on the hunt. In my grand plan for MAFW I always had ambitions of us becoming a fully fledged international fashion week. In other words, we would show annually a spring/summer collection in May and also hold an event to support the autumn/winter collections in October or November.

The spring/summer collections had already been going for seven years and the industry was growing strongly. More and more designers were launching themselves into the Australian and international markets, and the market share for Australian designers had grown enormously—some estimated by 400 per cent since the start of the event. The local department stores were now fighting over who had the most Australian designers in-store, multi-label boutiques supporting Australian designers were opening in every cool shopping mall or strip, the designers' own stores were multiplying, we were getting over two hundred and fifty international delegates to MAFW and exports were growing strongly. There was good reason to believe the industry was ready to take the next step.

A number of the more established designers like Wayne Cooper, Peter Morrissey and Carla Zampatti were already independently presenting their autumn/winter collections as well as using show-rooms to generate their wholesale orders. The initial thought was that if we could bring all these collection shows into a schedule, then we could establish an official autumn/winter collection event for MAFW. Following the 2001 event we organised, as a first step, an official autumn/winter schedule to help coordinate the timing of these shows so there was no conflict. My concern, though, was that the industry was going to need a lot of support until a strong sales momentum was established behind the autumn/winter collections. It was difficult enough to get international buyers to come to Australia once a year let alone twice to see collections. Nevertheless I was hell bent on ensuring MAFW came of age and stood up in the international fashion community.

My usual tactic was to create tension in these situations and I went back to the NSW Department of State and Regional Development to present them with a case to support a centralised venue option for the autumn/winter collections of MAFW in Sydney. I knew I had milked them dry to a certain extent but I was very aware of what Victoria was doing and I had my own plan. Before the NSW Government had time to reply I met with Steve Vizard and Peter Abrahams of the Major Events Company to pitch my 'crazy' idea: 'What about if we broke international precedent and presented the autumn/winter collections of MAFW in an alternative host city to Sydney? What say we establish the event in Melbourne where the historic manufacturing centre is based and play to the strength of that city's designers who are used to creating collections for a cooler environment?'

Vizard liked my vision and I liked Vizard. He was the perfect man to chair Major Events. He was equal parts businessman and showman. I had always been a fan of his television work and a great admirer of his business acumen. Unbeknown to me at the time, Steve was also on the board of the National Gallery of Victoria, which had nearly completed its new gallery, the Ian Potter Gallery at Federation Square. He proposed that this venue was perfect for the MAFW autumn/winter collections. We had the support of Major Events and potentially a beautiful new home; now all we needed was to strike a deal that new premier of Victoria Steve Bracks would approve. We then went into an intense period of due diligence and aggressive negotiations.

I was adamant that to make it work the industry needed huge support for the next five years until it could make the autumn/winter collections commercially viable. I needed extra support to get the Sydney-based designers to come and participate. I needed to fly most of the national fashion media to Melbourne. I needed a huge international marketing budget. I needed, I needed, I needed … and on behalf of the industry I got it. Our little company, Australian Fashion

Innovators, signed the biggest fashion sponsorship deal that had ever happened on our side of the planet, in excess of $5 million! Then on top of that, because I had originally asked for a whole lot more, we were separately given support for four international showcases to promote the event in New York, London, Shanghai and Tokyo.

Only three weeks after 2002 MAFW, on 28 May, Steve Bracks, Steve Vizard and I stood on a podium in the middle of Federation Square surrounded by the fashion community in Melbourne and announced that from October that year, in six short months' time, their city would be joining the international fashion week circuit. Melbourne not only had the country's leading public fashion event in the L'Oréal Melbourne Fashion Festival (LMFF), held in March, it now also had an industry-focused international fashion week.

During this period another instrumental change had happened internally at Australian Fashion Innovators. The three-person executive team of Jodi Pritchard, Jarrad Clark and me realised we were missing a wheel that we attached in Melbourne in the form of Graeme Lewsey. Graeme had won the Woolmark Prize, took himself off to London to learn fashion PR at the feet of Sir Paul Smith and, on his return, was immediately snapped up by me to join Spin in Melbourne. For years he ran the agency alongside Brett Chittenden and oversaw our contract for the Melbourne City Spring Fashion Week, an event for city retailers run each September. Graeme is a communications strategy genius. I was able to convince him to leave his role with us at Spin and join AFI full-time as our communications director. This could not have happened at a better time for us. To a certain extent we were getting further and further out of our depth in dealing with government agencies, sponsors, designers and PR people, not to mention the national and international media. I continued to shoot from the hip with the media and climb up onto my soapbox at a moment's notice, but MAFW was big now and we needed to act and behave more maturely when it came to our communications. Graeme was a godsend and was to become a very close friend and is still a personal advisor to me to this day.

The fabulous four were together: me, the ringmaster; Jodi, the orchestrator; Jarrad, the production and creative guru; and Graeme, the communications genius. We hit the ground running and took off for New York to produce our first-ever international showcase for MAFW to tell the world to come to Sydney *and* Melbourne. We also said, if you won't come to us we will come to you and show you what you are missing. The travelling showcase combined a cool collection by all the leading designers from MAFW and a two-day showroom where buyers and media could come and review and buy the collections. For this and each subsequent international showcase we selected about eight designers to join us, the ones we felt were best suited to that market. Over the next six months the circus was on the road and while it was beyond hard work it was such fun.

We worked alongside the Victorian Government, which footed the bill for everything, the Australian Tourism Commission, Austrade and the Department of Foreign Affairs. Again, this was Team Australia at its very best. Each event saw hundreds of influential buyers, media and industry influencers being exposed to Australian fashion, many for the first time. The strategy worked brilliantly. Attendance at both seasons of MAFW was increased, designers generated new orders and it definitely showed a new side to Australian culture. We hit milestones, not only for our industry but also for my long-held ambition to promote Australia as a sophisticated, innovative and creative nation.

In New York our venue was an incredible warehouse space in the Meatpacking District. Steve Bracks attended and spent quite a lot of time with us—great premier and really nice guy. The high commissioner to New York also hosted a cocktail party for us at his mansion near the World Trade Center site. Boy, did we feel grown up. It impressed the New York buyers to get an invitation with the country's crest on it, inviting them at the pleasure of the high commissioner. In London we scored a rehearsal room at the Royal Opera House at Covent Garden as our venue and our showroom was at Australia House on the Strand. In Shanghai we took over the Grand Hyatt Ballroom and the then Lord Mayor of Melbourne, John So, accompanied us to represent that city. Then we went on to Tokyo, where we hired one of the best film studios and produced a beautiful show. Australia's ambassador to Japan also hosted a cocktail party for us at our most beautiful consulate in Tokyo.

In all, over thirty Australian designers travelled with us on these showcases. For many it was their first international fashion experience. For others it reinforced their presence in key markets. A few special moments from the trip stand out above others for me. Welcoming guests on the spiral staircase at our consulate in New York made me feel, for the first time, like I really was the 'Fashion Ambassador for Australia', even if self-appointed! Accepting an invitation in Shanghai to a private dinner of seventeen courses as special guest at the Dalai Lama's ex-palace and holding artefacts that were five thousand years old. Clubbing with Dan and George from Tsubi and Wayne Cooper on a wild night in Roppongi in Tokyo and being chased down the street by guard dogs. However, the memory that shines brightest happened at our consulate in Tokyo. Our ambassador at the time was quite a good-looking man and very elegant. The very creative and interesting Alannah Hill, who was with us in Tokyo, was known for her outspoken, funny and irreverent comments. Alannah walked straight up to the ambassador and introduced herself in a very humble way. She bowed her head, regally shook his hand, and I actually heard her talking to him in Japanese! The ambassador stared at her wild hair and geisha make-up; he didn't quite know what to make of our fashion star.

And then came Alannah's little bombshell! 'Do you know, Mr Ambassador, that I feel we should marry right here, right now in your garden of paradise. I would love to be married and I don't feel that you are married? Why are you not married, Mr Ambassador, as I would be the perfect wife, don't you think? Let's get married, love! I am almost a Western geisha girl, don't you think?' The ambassador calmly shook Alannah's hand and moved on!

With a number of the showcases under our belts we headed back to Melbourne for our first-ever MAFW autumn/winter collections in November that year. Jarrad had worked his magic and together we designed a series of collection showrooms and exhibition areas at Federation Square. We had one collection showroom in a brand new gallery space at the Ian Potter Gallery. We created a majestic and impressively long catwalk in the Federation Square Atrium, turned the Edge venue into a fashion theatre and spread our exhibition, VIP rooms and registration throughout the entire precinct. Crown Casino came on board as our official hotel and Jarrad and I produced a great Opening Ceremony around the grand staircase at the entrance of the casino. I must say it was nice having a villa at Crown for the week—thank you, Mr Packer.

It was going to take a while for the industry to believe enough in themselves to gather momentum behind the MAFW autumn/winter collections and I take my hat off to those designers who supported us the first year and really showed what was possible. Big kudos needs to go particularly to the designers who mounted individual collection shows at the inaugural event in Melbourne: Alannah Hill, Melbourne showgirl; Gwendolynne, Australia's answer to Queen Elizabeth I of England; gutsy newbie HUONG; Lisa Ho, the fuss-free stylemeister; Nicola Finetti, the Italian fabric magician; S!X, the teachers leading the way; Tina Kalivas, Mondrian reinvented; Toni Maticevski, 'I still call Footscray home and I'm as good as anyone from Paris'; Vicious Threads, where music meets fashion; Vixen, the silk georgette goddesses; and 'Look I can be grown-up too!' Wayne Cooper. The group show also delivered a number of standout collections, including Claude Maus, Glen Rollason, Lorinda Grant, TL Wood, Ty & Melita, Dorian Ho and Joe the Taxi Driver.

While we were focusing on Melbourne we were at the same time renegotiating our contract with the Centennial Park and Moore Park Trust, which controlled our venues at Fox Studios. The entertainment quarter at Fox Studios was now totally complete, with restaurants, bars and two picture theatres. Every May MAFW brought tens of thousands of people to the precinct, and they paid for car parking, dined out and went shopping. However, all the trust wanted to do was put the rent up yet again. We had been at Fox for seven straight years and the new venues in Melbourne had added real excitement and driven innovation and creativity. We decided to pursue an alternative venue, which would be a fraught process. First we needed to position the event somewhere out of the ordinary. We couldn't go to the exhibition centre in Darling Harbour, for example. It needed to have immense flexibility in venue configurations. We couldn't go to the Sydney Dance Company, as it was just not big enough. The space also needed to reflect the nature of its host city and be inspiring internationally.

Back in 1996 it was Jarrad who had brought to my attention the sprung structures at Fox and again in 2002 he came up with another totally brilliant idea: the Overseas Passenger Terminal at Circular Quay, opposite the Sydney Opera House. Absolutely perfect. Totally unexpected by the industry, we were going to move the event before anyone got bored with Fox Studios. It sounded easy but the process was arduous. We had to deal with an independent events company, David Grant, which had been given the rights to operate the venue, along with a whole range of government departments from the Maritime Board to the Sydney Cove Authority. Finally we got a deal that gave us a new home for the next ten years. As usual I got back up on my soapbox and told the industry that if they thought Fox and Federation Square were great, wait until they saw what we had in store for them at the OPT. I hired a tall ship and sailed into Circular Quay with a group of models to announce the new venue—maybe a little over the top! But it turns out not everybody was ecstatic about our new direction.

Victoria and Robert Fisher and partner Tony Assness had been at odds with what we were doing creatively. For the designers they were working with, including Tigerlily and Terry Biviano, they had grand visions in regards to the creativity of their shows. These visions required very long bump-in schedules and for that reason they had always opted for doing collection shows in off-site venues so they could have the production lead time they required. Our central venue bump-in times were limited to twelve hours overnight if you were the first show the next day, or three to four hours during the day, as the venues needed to be rotated. When we announced the new venue and a schedule that again only allowed one show in the evening to be off-site, Mrs Fish hatched a plan that she thought best serviced the needs of her clients. She approached us through Jarrad and requested that on behalf of Wayne Cooper, Terry Biviano, Kerry Grima, Leona Edmiston, MARCS and Gabriel Scarvelli she would like to secure the off-site time slots each evening after we finished at OPT. The shows were going to be scheduled at 9 p.m.

From the beginning this was shaping up as dangerous territory because Mrs Fish was going to be using a single venue called Wharf 3, just around the corner from the OPT. She was going to spread the cost of the venue and production across her designer clients. This is exactly what we were already doing, in addition to being partly underwritten by sponsors and the government. We formed a very uneasy agreement that gave them the confirmed time slots on the schedule—biggest mistake I ever made!—and agreed to cooperate, providing volunteers and coordination with international delegates in the best interests of the designers. We were already disappointed that two big designers, Wayne Cooper and Leona Edmiston, had turned their backs on us and gone with Mrs Fish. What we didn't realise until it was too late was that Mrs Fish had secured sponsors for her venue that were in direct conflict with our designer agreements.

For any designer to be on the official schedule they needed to agree not to have individual sponsors that were in conflict with MAFW's event sponsors. We had also banned retailers and media organisations from sponsoring individual designer shows. I felt that a show sponsored by Myer would not be attended by DJs and a show sponsored by *Vogue* would not be attended by *Harper's Bazaar*. Pretty reasonable rules, I thought, and in the best interests of the industry. Ten days out from the event we discovered Westfield had

signed on as Mrs Fish's naming-rights sponsor. It was to be known
as Westfield Wharf 3. Not quite a retailer but about as close as you
could get. My nervousness built as we edged closer and closer to
the kick-off of the official schedule in 2003 and the first show at
Westfield Wharf 3. It was to be my worst nightmare.

We had just finished the sass & bide show at the new Harbour
Pavilion venue built in the forecourt of the OPT and I had just
arrived at the Paablo Nevada show when I got the call from Jarrad.
We had been up to our eyeballs bumping in the new venue and
hadn't had a minute to go down and check out what Mrs Fish was
up to—biggest mistake number 2! Jarrad was beyond exasperated
and told me to get down there straightaway as we had huge issues.
At the time I had a bright yellow SLK Mercedes and it didn't take
me long to hightail it down to Wharf 3. As I arrived at the huge car
park outside, where containers would formerly have been stacked, I
was greeted by a row of brand new cars under spotlight—I am not
going to reveal the brand of the car because all these years later I
am still not interested in giving them the slightest bit of exposure or
association with the fashion industry! To say I flew into a rage would
be the understatement of the century. Mercedes-Benz had supported
me and my industry from day one. If it weren't for them none of
MAFW would have been possible. I was prepared to fight to the
death to protect them and our sponsorship partnership.

As is often the case when I'm under huge pressure at an event,
I became very calm. I surveyed the situation and figured out my
next move. I then proceeded to drive my Mercedes directly into the
doorway of the venue. As great fortune would have it, it fitted like
a cork in a bottle. I climbed out over the bonnet of the car into the
venue to be greeted by Jarrad, who was in a heated discussion with
Wayne Cooper, the designer opening Westfield Wharf 3. To me at
that moment Wayne was Judas, after all I had done for him!

I then discovered another car sitting in the foyer inside the venue.
There was also signage and brochures everywhere for these cars.
I marched straight backstage, where about a hundred volunteers

provided by our MAFW organisation through our schools program were busy preparing Wayne Cooper's collection and starting to get models into first outfits. It was now 8.30 p.m. and the show was to start at nine. I really did get up on my soapbox this time and asked all the MAFW volunteers to gather around. I told them precisely who I was and if they didn't do exactly what I told them to do I would make it my personal mission to make sure they never worked in the fashion industry again. I very quickly explained the situation and then to their surprise I told them all to go to the far end of backstage and not to touch another piece of clothing. I could tell that every kid in the room knew I was not joking. Without further discussion they dropped everything they were doing.

Next I picked up my phone and called my trusty lieutenant, Jodi Pritchard, who was about to board a bus and lead a convoy of international delegates down to Wharf 3. I told her to get everyone she possibly could onto those buses and then drive them around in circles through the city until she heard from me again. No one could get off, no one could know what was going on and they couldn't come to Wharf 3. I'm the only person, I believe, in fashion history who has taken over one hundred of the most important people in the fashion industry hostage.

Vic, Fish and Wayne had gathered in the Wharf 3 foyer. I now calmly went up to them and told them I had completely closed them down. No one could get in thanks to my car and there was a huge line outside. No fashion show was going to take place because there were no dressers, and no international buyers or media were coming. Furious, confused and concerned, Cooper just stood there with his mischievous grin saying, 'Come on, Lockie, I want to do my show.'

As you can imagine there was a plea-bargaining exchange from Vic and Fish, who I believe genuinely faced bankruptcy if the show didn't at least partially go on. There were also the designers to be considered who, although ill advised to support this renegade venture, still needed to do business. But there was no compromise. There was my way or the highway. The branded cars outside were driven away and the lights switched off. The car in the foyer was wrapped in black plastic so many times it resembled a swollen marshmallow. The one hundred volunteers were set to work removing every last piece of car-branded signage and promotional brochures from the venue, including from within all the show bags. Only after all this had been done and I had personally checked every part of the venue did I back up my yellow Mercedes-Benz SLK just slightly, enough to let people pass in single file. This was now a Mercedes-Benz event and no one could miss it! The last thing I did was call Jodi and tell her to bring the hostages back. I really admired her because that night she had the worst job of all, trying to keep the fashion pack calm as they drove around and around Sydney, with her pretending to be lost while the collective tempers of some of the biggest buyers in the world were rising.

At nearly 11 p.m. the Wayne Cooper show started. It was classic Wayne and the production was spectacular. I sat front row next to Wayne's partner, Sarah, as I always did at his shows, pretending nothing had happened. Wayne, though, just couldn't resist. He knew exactly the trouble he was going to cause on this night and he was fully prepared. He strode to the very end of the catwalk right in front of me and the gathered photographers and turned around to reveal a printed T-shirt that said, 'THEY MADE ME DO IT'.

If only that was the end of it there. The shows kept happening each evening at Wharf 3, serving champagne that wasn't our sponsor's, water that wasn't our sponsor's, using make-up that wasn't our sponsor's, etc., etc. Battles were fought, compromises made. The media had a field day and Graeme was doing his best to control the fallout. Everyone in the industry was chiming in with an opinion and fuel was being added on a daily basis because the shows that Vic, Fish and Tony were producing were some of the best the industry had ever seen. Following Wayne with his huge screen backdrop, the next day Leona presented a collection set in a beautifully prepared English garden—the perfect backdrop. Vic and Fish pulled out the wall-of-water trick for Kerry Grima and then the biggest front page

of the week was Terry Biviano, when she arrived like Lady Godiva
on a horse. All these amazing productions were only possible in
a venue that allowed long bump-in times. Mrs Fish had proved a
point. She may not have gone about it the right way but what she,
Fish and Tony did in 2003 has left a legacy that is felt to this day.

The issues that had been raised by the Wharf 3 debacle had
to be dealt with immediately. If the Mrs Fish concept had been
left to gather momentum Fashion Week as we knew it would have
fallen apart. A third of fashion week's revenue comes from sponsors. Sponsors only see value in exclusive partnerships—they don't
want to be competing on a daily basis against conflicting brands.
Expenditure would soon be undervalued and sponsors would drop
out. At the same time we couldn't be the organisation bringing in all
the internationals and providing the services for another organisation to come along beside us and steal our thunder. The Australian
fashion industry is a small one and its key asset is unity. We have to
work together on the same team. Initiatives like this might work in
New York or Paris but our market is too small.

Immediately following the MAFW spring/summer collections
of 2003 I called a town hall meeting of everyone in the industry.
I needed to create rules that would prevent designers being on
the official schedule if they intended to support initiatives such as
Mrs Fish's. Again, there was only one way forward as far as I was
concerned: with me. These, however, are only shallow words without the support of the industry and I wasn't convinced that I had it. It
was the ultimate litmus test for the future of MAFW. Every designer,
PR guru, fashion media and retailer turned up and I put forward
my case with passion based on what I had done for the industry
and the fact that we had a solid strategy in place for the future—but
we needed the support of everyone in the industry. Fish spoke at
length on behalf of his team, with Victoria contributing at relevant
points. In the end it was put to a vote and a show of hands. It was
with huge relief that the industry saw the sense in what I was saying
and voted for unity. They upheld the three basic rules: no individual

sponsors that conflicted with the event sponsors, no retailers or media organisations as sponsors and, the nail in the coffin for Mrs Fish, no utilising shared venues unless they were operated by AFI.

It seems harsh now but we were still an industry coming of age and needed to stick together. If I had to be a bully, I'm sorry, but the alternative was unthinkable. The sad thing is that Victoria, Fish and Tony have produced very few shows at MAFW since and that is a huge shame. However, as a result of the marvellous shows that Mrs Fish and her team were able to create, the official schedule was opened up to allow off-site shows in the early morning as well as the evening, giving the industry the production times they needed and the chance to use some amazing venues, including Government House, the Opera House, mansions around the harbour and myriad other wonderful venues. Thanks, Mrs Fish, for helping to make this happen.

There is a twist to this tale. During a lot of this time an ex-staffer from *Harper's Bazaar*, Kirsten Doak, had joined the events team at Mrs Fish. Over the next few years we would be in the same room many times but never actually meet. Twelve years later I finally met her in Dubai, fell in love and married her. Victoria Fisher just about toppled off her chair, I believe, when she found out. Kirsten and Vic were close friends for years and we invited Victoria and Fish to our wedding in the hope of finally burying the hatchet. They didn't come, but I would still love to sit down with Mr and Mrs Fish and have a glass of champagne—as long as it is from our current sponsor!

*

In 2003 MAFW's spring/summer show was a bumper season even though the Wharf 3 sideshow was taking up a lot of our energy. The main event at Circular Quay was kicking major goals all around. Jarrad and his team had built a spectacular set of venues, including an enormous tent on the OPT forecourt called the Harbour Pavilion, which could accommodate eight hundred people. We also had an edgy warehouse space called the Cargo Room, a great gallery space called Rocks Warehouse and, through a deal with the Museum of Contemporary Art, we had taken over the Foundation Gallery and turned it into a stylish collection showroom. The upstairs and down-stairs in the OPT had become our new exhibition, The Source, aptly named by our designer liaison manager at the time, Lucia Labbate. All around The Rocks precinct were sponsors' lounges, VIP bars and, sitting high above it all, was Posh Bar, the ultimate MAFW VIP bar and lounge overlooking the Opera House and our glorious harbour. Move over Bar Bazaar … well, actually, move out, as Vic's bestie editor, Alison Veness, and Bar Bazaar ended up at Wharf 3.

There were some amazingly memorable moments from our first year at the OPT. A young niece of ex-royal Sarah Ferguson, Ayesha Makim, made her modelling debut in the debut show of creative chameleon Alex Zabotto-Bentley in his first Fashion Assassin show. It made the front page in the United Kingdom when Ayesha flashed her knickers to expose a Fashion Assassin logo in just the right place. We were also first introduced to Abbey Lee Kershaw, who was to go on to international modelling fame. Radio and television personality Jackie O made a star appearance on the catwalk for the Hong Kong designers. Director Baz Luhrmann had now become a regular at certain shows with his wonderful partner, Catherine Martin. But the huge news for us was the debut of both Gemma Ward and Nicole Trunfio. Our television production company had been making the first series of *Search for a Supermodel* and Gemma was uncovered in Perth and eventually came second overall in the show. We were lucky she was still in Australia that year to star at MAFW.

The schedule for spring/summer 2003 was our biggest yet, with thirty-one individual designer shows. As well as all the regulars there was a new breed of Australian designers really making their mark felt, including Gabriel Scarvelli, Kitten, Marnie Skillings, Rebecca Dawson, Tina Kalivas, Willow, Trelise Cooper, Kirrily Johnston, Azzollini and Gary Bigeni. Also, another new star was born at the New Gen show; well, two actually: sister and brother designing duo Camilla and Marc Freeman.

10
Ten Years Young

TODAY WE ARE back in New York and it has been a very good day. One of the country's most respected designers, Jason Wu, has just become part of the ORDRE Designer Portfolio. The CEO commented to us that what he likes about what we are doing is the fact that it is global and has been internationally inspired from its inception. I truly believe that having a global view and being internationally aware and inspired formed the foundations of our success at MAFW. We never set out to be the best fashion event in Australia or the event that showcased the best Australian designers. From day one our vision was global. Our ambition was to become a respected and permanent fixture on the international fashion week circuit, presenting designers that were world class. The fact that they were from Australia was just an advantage.

*

The twelve months prior to the 2004 event had been hugely productive for MAFW. We had established the autumn/winter collections in Melbourne, embarked on our first international showcases, had moved our home to Circular Quay and, together with the industry, had confronted an issue of unity. Enough for anyone to cope with, but on a personal level it had also been a milestone period for me.

Since Hannah and Jules were born, Lorraine and I had taken the unprecedented step of moving each year for the ski season from Sydney to Mt Buller, the resort in Victoria where my father had been an early pioneer and I had grown up. There were a number of reasons for this. Hannah and Jules' brother David lived in Melbourne with his mother and he also came out of his school to live with us each year during this time. It was important to me that all my children grew up together. It was also an opportunity to live together as a family in a small village community away from the pressures of the fashion industry and Sydney. This was all under-pinned, however, by my enduring love affair with the mountains and my complete passion/obsession for skiing.

Following the first business I established in my early twenties, the ski shop and touring company called Pro Ski, I continued to have a career in this industry as well as fashion. Alongside the development of The Lock Group and its various companies, including MAFW, I had kept up my professional skiing career. For ten years I was a member of the Mt Buller Ski Patrol, qualifying to National Patroller Level and then eventually becoming an examiner for the Australian Ski Patrol Association. I even worked profession-ally for one year on the Aspen Highlands Ski Patrol. I then joined the Mt Buller Snowsports School and started my training as a ski instructor and race coach. Following my initiation into ski school I embarked on a personal ambition to be the only part-time instructor to gain his Level 1 qualifications through to Level 4 in consecutive years. I was really proud when I got Levels 1, 2 and 3 on the trot but, unfortunately, it took me three attempts to get my fully certi-fied qualification. I got this in the ski season immediately following the Wharf 3 incident. For me this achievement is on par with the Australian Fashion Laureate I was to receive in later years. Both help define who I am as a person.

I have continued with my ski career in tandem with my career in fashion. At Mt Buller we eventually built our own ski lodge, aptly called Pro Ski after my ski shop. During this time I went to Canada and trained with the Ski Coaches Federation and got my Level 2 Race Coaches qualifications, and then continued with my training and qualification in Australia. For a number of years I was a trainer and examiner for the Australian Professional Snowsport Instructors and head coach for the Master Program at Mt Buller, a position I just loved and adored. When my work in fashion became a bit more international I became a member of the NISS Ski School in Niseko, Japan.

Most winters saw me travel from Sydney or wherever I had been on a Wednesday night to be with the family and instruct for four days before returning from the mountains on the Sunday night or Monday morning. It was a huge effort to make but it was absolutely worth it. All our children went through Mt Buller Primary School and the secondary college there until year 10, when it finished. Pro Ski Lodge for many years was also used as a company retreat, hosting the crew from Spin and Australian Fashion Innovators over many hilarious weekends. Skiing has always been the glue that keeps our family together. It's a common bond that I share very closely with them, particularly with my three children, and it has helped keep me sane throughout the many years of fashion chaos.

*

Following our showcases in the United States, Europe and Asia in 2002–3, AFI and MAFW were starting to attract a lot more international attention. This time it wasn't all about the Australian designers but also what services Australian Fashion Innovators could provide. We were about to become an exporter in our own right. This wasn't going to be the first time our Group had experience overseas. Simon B and I had opened the Spin showroom in New York in 1998 and ran it for three years, presenting ranges of Australian designers.

As has often been the case in my career I have been too early to market with an idea and, while we gave it a really good shot, the Australian designers just weren't well known enough at that time to be commercially viable. I know things would be completely different now. We made some great inroads for designers like Karen Walker, actually getting her pants on Madonna, Wayne Cooper, Saba, Zimmermann and others. Other highlights included opening the first-ever boutique for an Australian designer in New York—Saba on West Broadway—and the first show from an Australian designer at New York Fashion Week with Wayne Cooper.

During one trip to New York with Wayne to show his collection we had a huge night out and Wayne for the first time introduced me to his friend Jack. Well, Mr Daniels and I had a bit too much of a good time and we fell asleep in the early hours of the morning. With only about an hour's sleep and clearly still fully under the influence of Mr Daniels, I was woken by an exasperated Lucia Labbate in the lobby desperately calling for me to come down. After months of planning and scheduling I was due to appear live on CNN to talk about MAFW and the progress we were making internationally. This was going to be broadcast to a global audience of millions. I had completely forgotten about it. I put down the phone and gathered my thoughts. Smiling to myself, I thought, I can do this, and away I went.

I was in the green room at the CNN centre fifteen minutes later, getting my make-up done and joking with the girls. 'Wow, you are very lively in the morning, and what's that fragrance you are wearing? It smells like Tennessee!' I'm ashamed to say that Mr Daniels and I went on CNN live and he had a great time, joking with the presenters and gushing forth about Australian designers. Apparently they thought I was great and wanted me back. I don't think so. Got away with that one, just!

Internationally there were now a number of opportunities presenting themselves and it was only because of the talent and strength of the AFI staff and extended crew that we could even possibly consider any of them. Over these years the A Team at AFI had really come together. Some crew had been with us from the beginning and others were now an integral part of the team. One staff member, though, particularly stands out for the help he gave me as a friend and for the enduring role he played within the industry at MAFW each year.

I first met John Flower when he was the owner and manager of the Last Aussie Fish Café in South Melbourne many years ago. When he left the restaurant world, he joined our PR team at MJ's suggestion. A number of years later when I separated from Mary, my first wife, his home in Sydney was to become my halfway house. John, because of his hospitality days, always knew the who's who in the zoo socially in Sydney and it just made sense to involve him when in the first year of MAFW we needed someone to help organise the VIP seating. He made the role of seating director at MAFW his own for many years, right through to our move to Circular Quay. Behind the scenes he helped develop our delegate registration program and unique seating allocation system right up to when it was automated. For years and years prior to this John, often with Lucia, had worked burning the midnight oil, manually preparing the seating plans for each designer show, placing every buyer, media representative, designer VIP, industry rep and celebrity exactly in the right seat, given their pecking order in the industry. John and I used these seating plans and the kudos they provided to great effect. We positioned buyers opposite each other to spark competition, we positioned magazine editors just so to create rivalry and, in conjunction with designers, we rewarded big orders and favourable coverage with front-row seats. We banished enemies to the back row, we used the seating arrangements to ingratiate ourselves with sponsors and government ministers and we made sure our good friends and family were sorted.

Unlike many other venues such as theatres or auditoriums, everyone at a fashion show can see the front row. When you are in a picture theatre you can't see who is up front if you are in the middle or at the back, but you certainly can in a collection showroom. The way the seating is tiered in a collection showroom ensures everyone can see the catwalk and, just as importantly, that front row. For a period of time before the lights go down you are seen as a fashion god if you are sitting in the front row, particularly towards the end of the runway. It is the most public acknowledgement of how that organisation or designer sees you. If you are in the front row you are liked; the further towards the back row you are the less relevant you are. Everybody wants to be liked and seen as relevant. So based on that I permanently located my seat in the front row at the very end of the catwalk. I was going to make myself the most important person in the industry, self-appointed of course!

Combining the physical reality of the space with a gathering of people with healthy egos, who each think they are the most important person in the room, arranging them from highest to lowest in a pecking order and seating them accordingly can be a recipe for success and disaster. John was a success. His real skill, though, was not just behind the scenes, working with designers on their master seating plans, but was actually in the theatre performance he gave when it came to seating time. His ability to warmly greet people with an air kiss and escort them personally to their front-row seat was rivalled only by his ability to see right through them, even if they had been standing in front of him for ten minutes to discuss why they had a row B ticket. He was always polite and charming when he needed to be, even more so when he wanted you to move, had an incredible sense of humour and timing, and for years kept us all amused with his antics in the front row. But at the end of the day he had an important job to do and was not about to suffer fools. My fondest memory of John is always when he would run up and down the front row telling the fashion pack to uncross their legs and tuck their feet under their seats so as to not spoil the catwalk photography. When he eventually retired and handed the baton to Miro Kubicek he set up his own Hothouse Media agency, based around managing front of house at major events, including the Logies. Miro also did the same thing eventually, setting up Miro House.

Given the amazing breadth of talent we had in our staff the thought of international expansion was now possible with AFI. Internally, Jodi Pritchard had taken on the role of International Marketing Director, relieving me of some of MAFW's market visits so I could capitalise on a number of the opportunities that were coming our way. One of AFI's first endeavours internationally was very much a mouse-that-roared moment.

In 2001 on one of my many trips to New York I had met with Fern Mallis, the executive director of the Council of Fashion Designers of America and founder of 7th on Sixth, later to be known, as it is today, as New York Fashion Week. Fern was heavily in negotiation with IMG at the time, which was trying to make its first acquisition of a fashion week. I was keen to throw my hat into the ring as a bidder. At the time I had appointed Greg Daniel, ex-chairman of Clemenger and a board member of the Sydney Olympic bid, as the chairman of The Lock Group and immediately phoned him to find out whether, if I was successful, he thought he could raise the money. He was enthusiastic so AFI put in a bid of US$7 million to buy New York Fashion Week. The bid was rejected out of hand, not because of its value but because of the lack of added value we could provide New York Fashion Week by comparison to the goliath IMG. I found out years later we actually just topped IMG's bid.

AFI was slowly being recognised for the job it had done in establishing a new stop on the international fashion week circuit, and other industries were interested in tapping into our expertise and experience. At the time no one really had much experience in doing what we had done. Fashion weeks had been established only in Paris, Milan, New York, London and Tokyo before 1996, so MAFW can lay claim to being the sixth in the world. Currently there are about two hundred and ninety fashion weeks around the world, although many of them are hybrid events combining both industry and consumer components and not purely industry-only events based on wholesale collections. I do believe, however, AFI and MAFW provided a great deal of inspiration to many other entities that felt they had legitimate reason to establish a fashion week in their country or city. Certainly, if one of the most remote major cities in the world with an industry that basically was unheard of can successfully launch an international fashion week, then perhaps they can as well ... so who you gonna call to help? Our first big job overseas came when we were approached by the Singapore Tourism Board to take over the management of the Singapore Fashion Festival.

It was a great event to cut our teeth on internationally and was going to help AFI build even stronger relationships with the Singapore-based media and buyers for MAFW. As the law required, we formed a local joint venture with event infrastructure experts Pico to produce the event, and AFI-Pico was born. As is usually the case with all new ventures, Jodi was sent off to Singapore to manage the initiative and we ended up opening an office in Singapore. The major players all got involved in producing the event, including Jarrad Clark and Graeme Lewsey, Iain Reed, Troy Daniels, Jack Bedwani, Sophie Miller and Vanessa Van Zyl.

The great thing about Singapore was that we started to produce shows for international designers like Chanel, Diane von Furstenberg, Salvatore Ferragamo and many others. We also brought a lot of top supermodels and superstars to Singapore, including Lily Cole and Jimmy Choo, and worked with a lot of great local talent such as model/presenter Denise Keller, who I still work with today. One of the highlights of working on the Singapore Fashion Festival was bringing the concept MTV Fashionable Loud to the event. MTV Fashionable Loud was born in New York, and involved bands like Hole and Foo Fighters playing live at a fashion show of the country's best designers. In 1998 we produced a version at MAFW, starring Sarah O'Hare and Skunkhour. At Singapore Fashion Festival we stepped things up a bit and worked with international band Placebo.

Somehow the Indian Government got wind of what we were doing in Sydney, Melbourne and now Singapore and they asked us to tender for a huge fashion industry event called DSYN 04. We won this international tender and Jodi and I went over there to set everything up. It was to be a very big learning curve in more ways than one. I could actually write a whole other book about our Indian daze but there are a number of things I learnt from the experience that I should note. Never fall for the trick of staying in a 'Government Guest House'; it is not a glamorous colonial mansion but a rat-infested cell block on the outskirts of town with Quasimodo as a house boy who can't cook. Never go there in summer when the cricket is on because when the Test starts and everyone turns on their televisions power blackouts kill the air conditioning. Never take on your host at yoga poses after an evening of scotch and curry. Always make sure you have pizza for the models backstage: in India it's a 'No Eat, No Walk' policy … go figure! Never try to introduce on stage one of India's most renowned musicians without practising his name. The most important lesson I learnt, though, is to always check the fine print of the venue contract to make sure it includes air conditioning during bump-in, otherwise it will be you and a billion mosquitoes trying to build a catwalk. The entire team came over to New Delhi to work on the event and John Flower was based there for six months, heading up our office.

Back in Australia during this period, from 2003 to 2005, we had decided to set up a new feeder event for MAFW that was to also take flight around Asia Pacific and add to our international expansion. We had always been passionate about helping and supporting emerging talent in Australia. This had been the driving force behind the establishment of the New Generation Collections show at MAFW. The selection process of New Gen had been on a submission basis and we thought it was time to establish an emerging talent program to both find and invite designers to be part of New Gen and to mentor them in their growth and development. Mercedes was also interested in working with us to try to create more of an impact for their sponsorship in dealership states, as well as in

Sydney and Melbourne, where MAFW was based. The end result was the launch of the Mercedes Start-Up Program. Named by Brett Chittenden in our Melbourne office, it was to become Graeme's baby over the coming years. The program ran for three years until funding ran out and it covered all the states. Each year there was a very thorough search program to identify new local talent. Finalists would be selected, and then a judging day and fashion show would be held using our A Team to produce it.

It was for many designers their first experience of being involved in a fashion show and right from the beginning they were trained by the best. We had all the leading buyers and media involved on the judging panel, who in turn were being exposed at a grassroots level to Australia's best new talent. Start-Up also involved an extensive mentoring program that really helped a lot of designers get a foothold in the industry. It unearthed some amazing new talent who then went on to make their debuts at MAFW in the New Gen show, including Camilla and Marc, Gail Sorronda and Flamingo Sands. The concept was later taken to Canada by Mercedes-Benz and was also the catalyst for a program in the Asia Pacific. One of my great memories of our Start-Up was when we booked a random model to be the change/fit model for the day and a new young girl turned up: Miranda Kerr. She proved to be quite good!

With Jodi now set up in Singapore we went about creating another feeder event for MAFW to discover new talent in the Asia Pacific and to introduce them to MAFW. Together with Mercedes-Benz in the Asia Pacific we created the Mercedes-Benz Asia Fashion Award. It was basically the Mercedes Start-Up Program under another name but now included Asian countries like Singapore, Malaysia, Hong Kong, Vietnam, Thailand and Taiwan. AFI and MAFW's influence was seriously spreading around the region. Each year the regional final for the Asia Fashion Award was held at the Singapore Fashion Festival, which we were producing, and the winner would receive an individual collection show at MAFW.

It was a very big deal. Sven Tan, one of the winners of the award, went on to have a stellar design career in the industry as principal designer for many years of women's label alldressedup.

Given AFI's extensive work in Australia and now in Singapore, India, Malaysia, Thailand, Hong Kong, Vietnam and Taiwan and through the international MAFW showcases in Shanghai and Tokyo, we had become Asia Pacific's leading fashion event company. Never planned on this, it just sort of happened. All I wanted to do was set up a fashion week for my industry and one thing led to another. Who am I kidding, I always had world-domination plans—ha! While our international expansion was in full flight, our priority always remained our flagship event, Mercedes Australian Fashion Week. With the exception of India, basically everything we were doing had a positive impact on the growth of MAFW either by introducing new designers and building its position as *the* Asia Pacific fashion week or by continually promoting the event to media and buyers in the cities we were working in. All our work was really helping MAFW and it was showing on the schedule.

*

In November 2003 we were back at Federation Square for our second year of showing autumn/winter collections. Momentum was slowly starting to build and the schedule was looking stronger. Melbourne was also about to experience its first major fashion celebrity moment when both Paris and Nicky Hilton attended the event. Getting the sisters to attend was one of the hardest deals I have ever negotiated but it was definitely worth it in the end. Even in our second year Melbourne was still suffering from being seen as the poor cousin, media-wise, in comparison to the monolithic spring/summer collections in Sydney, and so a media star like Paris was going to work well—and she did. She took a star turn in the Wayne Cooper show and her outrageous party antics at night kept us all highly amused and the media constantly engaged. I will always remember the effect Paris had on two very different boys. The first was Grant Pearce, the stylish editor of *GQ* and publisher at *Vogue*, who lost all control on the dance floor and fell to his knees to shimmy in front of Paris as she stood over him gyrating. The other was to see my own son David, who was fifteen at the time and had come backstage to meet Paris with his mates, all full of bravado, left speechless with mouth agape as Paris worked her charm and gave them all kisses.

Two other beautiful stars also joined us in Melbourne and so did one very ugly one. Erica Baxter and Alyssa Sutherland were the standout girls on the catwalk and between them they appeared in just about all of the twenty-five individual and group shows on the schedule, double the amount from the inaugural year. The other was Chopper Read, the convicted hit man who was notoriously known for having cut off his ear lobes. Not really the sort of plastic surgery the fashion industry was used to. The designer from Vicious Threads, Ivan Gomez, had come up with the crazy idea to present his collection with spoken word poetry read live by Chop Chop himself. While perfectly well behaved, Chopper just had a sense of menacing violence around him. I must say I was nervous meeting him. Ivan certainly got the tension he wanted to express in his collection and had really put forward a point of theatrical difference in presenting his show. It was brave in more ways than one.

It was great to see the Melbourne designers coming out in force at the MAFW now hosted in their home city. Vicious Threads, Alannah Hill, Bettina Liano, Claude Maus, Gwendolynne, Scanlan Theodore and Ty & Melita all presented standout collections. Both the ready-to-wear collections and the New Generation group show had now been established in Melbourne and were presenting the debut collections of a number of designers who would go on to great things, including Arthur Galan at AG and a little-known brand at the time called Platform by designer Josh Goot. It was really pleasing to see in the second year that all the regular crew from Sydney had made the effort to show autumn/winter in Melbourne as well.

There was real thought given at this stage about whether we could make MAFW autumn/winter work long-term once the Victorian Government support stopped. The international showcases we had completed in the previous twelve months were having an impact and we were getting a good roll-up of international buyers to complement the Australian buyers coming regularly. The predominantly Sydney-based national media were also being really supportive. Graeme, being a Melbourne boy, had made a real difference in not only getting our media strategy right but also in making sure the Melbourne industry embraced us. The Major Events Company and the Victorian Government seemed happy and we had arrived at an uneasy truce of sorts with the L'Oréal Melbourne Fashion Festival, having now invaded their city.

After a strong autumn/winter season in Melbourne it was soon back to Circular Quay in May 2004 for spring/summer. Thank heavens there was no Wharf 3 on the horizon and the lead-in was pretty smooth sailing, except for the start of a media phenomenon that was going to be with us forever and a day. It shaped up to be the biggest season to date with thirty-nine individual shows and ten group shows. A mammoth year! However, the media, or should I say News Limited, decided that the story wouldn't be how this year was a bumper season but instead how many designers who had showed in the past wouldn't be in the schedule this year. It was a classic case of not saying we are half-empty or half-full but worse: we were 95 per cent full. So why the focus on the 5 per cent empty? Really, why was that the story? The industry was busting to drive itself forward and all of a sudden the media decided to take a negative stance on things. The reality will always be that not every designer will show each year. The reality at this time was that designers were starting to spread their wings, showing at other fashion weeks around the world. For us this was joyful because designers were growing through MAFW and then moving on to bigger and better things. That is what I built the event for. But, oh no, the story was 'Designers desert MAFW to show overseas', 'Designer no-shows

at MAFW', 'Collette snubs MAFW for Paris'. This attitude started
to creep in during 2004 and stay, and News Limited has recycled it
every year since.

It is interesting to think about this. We know for a fact through
journalist friends that directions have come from editors and chiefs
of staff to take potshots at MAFW and do negative stories. Editors
always think they are reflecting the attitudes and wants of their
readers but I disagree wholeheartedly with this often-negative take
on a number of popular culture subjects. I *get* sensational journalism. I understand that the supposed private lives of public people
are intriguing and sell newspapers. But I don't get the tall-poppy
syndrome. Why, when something or somebody has been built up
in a positive way in the public eye and is doing good things for the
community, is it of interest to find the negative slant to try to create
that sensational angle and drag them down? Do editors actually help
create a profile for events, companies and people with the thought of
drawing an audience to the story and then keeping the story going
to sell more newspapers by turning it negative? If so, I think they are
completely underestimating their audience and don't understand the
true spirit of being an Australian in the lucky country.

As a nation we have never thrived on negativity. We have
blossomed and grown through being positive and being inspired.
Don't get me wrong, when it comes to MAFW we have always
held ourselves open to media criticism and have often reacted and
changed things as a result, but why lead into a nationally important event with a story that has such a negative slant? Wouldn't a
better angle be 'MAFW celebrates the success of Australian designers showing in Paris as they make way for a new pool of talent
in Sydney'? I have enough confidence in the Australian public's
attitude about pride in country and sense of self to believe that this
will sell as many papers.

Another favourite headline of some media is the 'skinny model'.
Everyone has read/seen the skinny-model stories that have come
out of MAFW over the years. They could have all so easily been

replaced with stories about how in fact our modelling industry is
one of the best in the world and delivers way above our punching
weight on the international stage. What do they think—that we
never feed our models and when we do it is lettuce leaves? That we
also encourage them to swallow cotton wool so they will feel full and
won't eat anyway? That we tell them to go on starvation diets in the
lead-up to the event and do active cellulite on-the-spot testing? Or if
you get caught with even one dimple you are immediately sacked.

I have lived around models for twenty-five years. I have worked
with them all my professional career. I have spotted models and I
have helped models become famous. I have cast models and spent
years backstage with them. I've directed models at fashion shows,
I've lived with models, I have model friends, I have travelled with
models, I have partied with models, I even went out with a model
for a while and, yes, I have been both Claudia Schiffer's and Gisele
Bündchen's date. So I know what I'm talking about. The skinny-
model story is a beat-up, just about every single time. Let me tell
you the real story.

Young Australian girls who become models generally come from
two schools: those who aspire to the life and those who have no idea
about it but because of their physical attributes someone has tapped
them on the shoulder. Models are born with that X-factor gene that
makes them slender and well proportioned and generally about
175 to 180 centimetres tall. Designers like this size because clothes
hang on these women the right way, particularly as a lot of the time
they have to be walking clothes hangers. We have fashion shows
so buyers can see how a particular outfit moves and drapes when
someone walks in it. So over the years the industry has standardised
the garment size to 'fit model' or 'sample size' and the industry looks
for models who fit this size. It makes sense, logistically.

Models are introduced to the industry through agents when they
are sometimes as young as fourteen or fifteen but generally when
they have finished growing. Our agencies are some of the best in the
world and straight away they advise girls coming into the business

on diet and fitness. One of the best things about Australian models is their skin and complexion and this is generally a direct result of our great food, unpolluted environment and sporting lifestyle in which healthy activities are encouraged. Young models usually work only during holidays until they have finished year 12, taking selective 'training' jobs identified by their agencies. Some choose to keep doing this through university or take leave from university or work to take up the profession full-time. Usually a good model can work until they are in their mid twenties, and some go well beyond.

When you start a full-time modelling career you basically have a coach/booker who runs your diary and looks after you. It can be a really hectic life with long hours, lots of travel, hours standing around doing nothing and constant rejection at casting calls. To do all this you need to be both mentally and physically fit. Often models at this stage will be living in a share house with other models that is nothing like the fantasy of the *Next Top Model* shows. The routine in the house is often focused on diet, yoga, fitness and work. Sure, they are young girls and everyone parties and, sure, some go too hard but the majority know what is at stake here: money ... and lots of it.

If a model is good enough and ambitious they can really make good money over a five- or six-year career and then go back to university or whatever. To get work they need to be 'fit model' size and have the endurance for a long day's work, have a great complexion and a great attitude. You cannot do this without good nutrition and every model at this level has been coached into a position of understanding that if you get sick you won't work. They are professionals. They get well looked after and are greatly loved by the industry. They get treated specially because of the job only they can do.

There are those who get the balance of the model life wrong for whatever reason. They work too hard, skip meals, have low energy levels, party too hard, fall in with the leeches who often hang around or end up depressed and very underweight. These girls 99.99999999 per cent of the time never get near a catwalk.

The problem is identified by their family, friends or their agent and something is done to change this and help. In all my years of running fashion events all over the world there has only ever been one girl who slipped through the net and made it onto one of my catwalks who shouldn't have. She was in my opinion the only skinny model that anyone should have been talking about and nobody did because the industry identified the girl and sent her home before she was made to feel bad in any way by some picture editor at a newspaper.

I stand proud to say that all the models at MAFW have been and continue to be working fit. It's easy to take one of these working-fit models, any one of them, get them to stand at the end of the runway in an ill-fitting bikini, which is not their fault, and blast them with white light from the front, which completely washes the colour out of their complexion. If you then spotlight them with super-strong Vari-Lite lights from above and get them to twist their upper body around and lean back in a pose, what happens? Their four bottom ribs show and the shadow cast over them from the downlight empha-sises the way the ribs protrude. There you have it: the classic 'skinny model' shot. It is possible to get this shot every day of fashion week and the picture editor can just decide whether to run the picture or not. It is usually about day three or four when the editor is sick of all the good news stories and starts looking for the negative slant. So rather than being inspiring or creative about covering a new angle on MAFW, let's just roll out the skinny-model story again. We are all over it!

I also find it insulting because it goes to the heart of our duty of care and that is something I take very seriously. What you don't read about in the media is that we were the first fashion week in the world to impose a working age on models and adopt a chaperone policy for underage girls while they are working in an adult work-place. What you won't hear about is the great lengths we take to have 'Model Mammas' tour with our girls to new events to look after and chaperone them. What you don't see is normal young girls going crazy on takeaway or stuffing their faces with Mars Bars because many have those unbelievable metabolisms that allow them to eat anything. What you would not have heard about is my work on government boards to promote positive images of women in the media. What you won't hear about is our condemnation of night-clubs that lure young girls through model nights with free drinks and illicit substances. What you won't hear about is how we escort home young girls who have found themselves in compromising situations at one of our fashion parties. And you will never hear about the catered model lounges backstage at a lot of our events, which are stacked with sandwiches and salads. No story there.

I can't talk for my colleagues around the world who run other fashion weeks or big fashion events but I can tell you the models on my watch get looked after like they are my daughter Hannah. The fact that someone might put Hannah on the front page of *The Daily Telegraph* and tell the world that she is too skinny for her job and assume by default she is being abused by our industry or has an eating disorder, just for doing the job she is paid to do, really makes me mad, in case you haven't noticed.

*

MAFW spring/summer 2004 was shaping up to be a bumper season. Jarrad had already made some modifications to our new home at Circular Quay, Jodi had been hard at it rounding up inter-national buyers and media from around the world and Graeme was superbly expanding our communications in every direction possible. The big news that year was that another one of the supermodels, Helena Christensen, had been enticed to be the guest editor of *Harper's Bazaar*. She is a lovely lady and it was great to hear her reminisce with Peter Morrissey about her previous time in Sydney with Michael Hutchence.

We kicked off the event with *marie claire*'s huge opening at the Opera House and asked designers to present a red dress to support the Heart Foundation as part of an international initiative. For the first time we had installed huge live screens in Martin Place and in front of the MCA so the public could get a glimpse inside our industry shows. It was very forward-thinking at the time and a sign of things to come.

There were some absolutely spectacular shows in May 2004. Nine years in and our industry was really stepping up. I can't tell you how proud of everybody I was that year. One of my all-time favourites, the ridiculously talented Jayson Brunsdon, made his long-awaited solo debut at MAFW. After years of being a creative director, first at Morrissey Edmiston and then at Morrissey, it was a wonderful moment to see him step out on the catwalk after his own show. Jayson had turned to me when he was trying to give a brand to his new company, not confident about using his own name. I immediately flew into a spiel about why he absolutely had to use his own name and in the process must use his beautiful signature as the logo. He listened. Willow also presented her follow-up collection to huge applause. The image of a nearly naked Tanya G in the beautifully executed Sarina Suriano jewellery show will stay with us forever. Andysoma put on a great show—this label should have gone on to bigger and better things in menswear. Finally, Lover decided to grace us with their presence and it was worth waiting for. One Teaspoon's collection exploded onto the scene. The cultish Platform made the move to a solo show in a car park underneath the Domain—watch this space, as a real designer was to soon emerge! Alice McCall made her debut and left her calling card for the future. And Tsubi! Bloody Tsubi …

The Tsubi team locked the doors to the venue until an hour after the show was supposed to begin. In the meantime they completely wrapped the first two rows of seats in cling wrap so no one could sit down on them, and dressed up all their mates as fashion celebrities, like Karl Lagerfeld and Anna Wintour, placing them in the front row. They had allocated all the important media and buyers seats in row Z, and then proceeded to get drunk backstage. The crowd outside at Circular Quay was beyond heaving with Tsubi kids and fans going berserk. John completely lost the plot with his seating plans. I was fighting battles with international delegates who were asking why they had been assigned seats in the nosebleed section, and then all hell broke loose. Someone finally opened the doors to the Harbour Pavilion and it was on for young and old as legitimate delegates headed for the front row only to be confronted by the cling wrap, which John took to with a pocketknife. Meanwhile 'Karl' and 'Anna' looked on, swigging from a champagne bottle. I believe about a thousand people jammed into the venue that night—we were so overloaded. I can still remember Pip Edwards (Dan Single's ex), who for some bizarre reason was in charge of the backstage door that night, letting about a hundred buddies slip in. I used to think the Morrissey night at MAFW was the big one. Tsubi had taken big to a new level!

The group shows that season were equally impressive, with collections from designers from Hong Kong, Singapore and Kuala Lumpur. Our push as *the* Asia Pacific fashion week had really taken hold. The New Gen Collections were also off the wall, introducing Rachel Gilbert, Brent Wilson and Bec & Bridge, all of whom have gone on to greatness. It was also the first year that we introduced Nicholas Huxley's show—well, his top students from East Sydney Design Studio, as it was known back then.

It was a very busy year in between the spring/summer and autumn/winter shows in 2004. We produced events in New Delhi, Singapore, Hong Kong, Malaysia, Vietnam and Taiwan. When we returned to Melbourne it was to be a season of firsts. Delegates and guests attending the Wayne Cooper show at an off-site venue, Rosati, normally a warehouse dining venue in Flinders Lane, got locked in at the show. The anti-fur movement, always very active around international fashion weeks, went nuts when Wayne introduced possum fur into his collection. The protestors kicked up a huge fuss on the street during the show and then blockaded the exit, not letting anybody out. Other firsts in Melbourne included appearances from Alice McCall; Camilla and Marc, who were now really building momentum behind their label, stepping out of group shows and doing their own thing; Jayson Brunsdon; and Mimco. It was our third season in Melbourne and we now held up to twenty individual shows, four group shows and a very healthy exhibition.

Spring/summer 2005 was always going to be a milestone event in our history as it was our 10th Fashion Week. I certainly felt a sense of achievement as we prepared to launch our record-breaking season, with more designers showing that year than any other to date. After ten years on the international fashion week circuit I think we had rightfully earned our place and status internationally. We were a regular and high-profile stop on the circuit, no longer treated as some novelty as we had been in the early years. What we were celebrating this year was not so much what MAFW had achieved but the development our industry had undergone in just ten years. Together we had grown the domestic market for Australian designers enormously. I couldn't even put a figure on it, other than to know that if you walked onto the designer floors at DJs and Myer you were now surrounded by my friends.

When we started people maybe knew of Carla Zampatti, Trent Nathan, Stuart Membery and Harry Who, but now they knew Akira Isogawa, Alex Perry, Alice McCall, Aurelio Costarella, Bare, Bettina Liano, Camilla and Marc, Charlie Brown, Jayson Brunsdon, Leona Edmiston, Lisa Ho, Lover, Mimco, Nicola Fenetti, Scanlan Theodore, sass & bide, Toni Maticevski, Tsubi, Wayne Cooper, Willow and Zimmermann, among a host of many others. All these designers had been brought to prominence and had developed their businesses through MAFW. For many of them, MAFW had been their launching pad globally and by our tenth year there were about thirty designers exporting as a direct result.

Annually MAFW was generating tens of millions of dollars in both domestic and wholesale orders for the industry; seasonally we were the catalyst for a national and international publicity blitz that raised the profile of our designers. Along the way the industry had achieved a lot together. We had learnt how to produce international standard fashion shows and developed a new group of home-grown producers and events people to work with the Australian designers. We had created experts in hair and make-up and styling, nurtured a whole industry of fashion PRs who weren't even around in 1996, shone a very bright spotlight on our local modelling industry and created stars. We had shown inexperienced buyers how to do business like the rest of the international fashion industry, encouraged the fashion media to realise the value they had within their own industry, generated new jobs in the industry for designers, pattern makers, sample makers, fabric wholesalers and salespeople and provided industry work experience to thousands of students. Yep, in 2005, after ten of the hardest years of my life, we had a lot to celebrate and we were going to do it in style.

I wanted to do something really special and memorable to celebrate. For me it was really important to recognise those people in the industry who had been there from the beginning, believing in my vision and helping me carry the industry forward. These weren't just the designers but also our staff, the retailers, the media, the production and creative people, the models, the sponsors, the government and my family. I decided to host a dinner to recognise about a hundred people without whose support MAFW would not have been possible. Working with Christine Bookallil, now employed by Autore; Mariela Demetriou, who was now our general manager in Australia; and my good friend Maurice Terzini from Icebergs restaurant at Bondi, I hosted the ultimate thank-you dinner on the eve of MAFW. It was an absolutely glorious night at Icebergs, which Maurice had looking magical. The stars sparkled over Bondi Beach and our invited guests had gone to a great deal of trouble to look fabulous. The evening engendered an amazing spirit as it started to dawn on everyone what we had been able to achieve together.

Through our unity, camaraderie and hard work we had all done something that we could not have done as individuals. We had put

Australian fashion on the global map. In my speech that night I likened our industry to beautiful individual glowing pearls, stunning in isolation but spectacular when brought together in a complete strand. As I finished these words the doors of the restaurant swung open and in walked a procession of volunteers dressed head to toe in white, wearing white gloves. Each of them was carrying an individual pearl-shaped jewellery box made of shining copper that had the name of a guest engraved on it. Inside each box was a single magnificent Autore South Sea Pearls necklace to commemorate our tenth year. I took each box from the volunteers and handed them to each of our special guests, thanking every one of them personally. It was a night I will always remember.

There was one person missing that night and it broke my heart. After standing beside me for ten years at MAFW Jarrad Clark had inexplicably resigned six months before our 10th Anniversary year. For some reason he had decided to spread his wings in the lead-up to our biggest year, when I really needed him. To this day I still don't understand it. I was actually devastated for the next few years because of it. Perhaps my reaction was more about my inability to cope with rejection than anything else. The good news was I actually got over myself and pleaded with Jarrad to come back. He did after about twenty-four months and I think it turned out to be the best decision he ever made.

Eighty-four designers presented collections on the catwalk that year at MAFW and another one hundred and fifty showed in the exhibitions and showrooms. All the major stars came out to play and there were standout collections one after the other. Josh Goot finally came out from underneath Platform to make his solo debut. Scanlan Theodore presented a collection acclaimed by many to be their best. Akira presented his show at the Sydney Dance Company, which he was now in collaboration with. Tsubi changed their name to Ksubi and went fluoro. And other highlights included the Canvas Project, where we supplied leading designers with pieces of canvas, each the same size, and asked them for their interpretation of

Australian fashion. We raised a huge amount for charity by auctioning them off and by staging a retrospective photographic exhibition of MAFW by Robert Rosen. Robert for years had documented MAFW for *Vogue* and his exhibition was a standout of our 10th Anniversary celebrations.

11

There is No 'I' in IMG

KIRSTEN AND I are back in Sydney. We were in Paris when a call from my mother made us cut short our European trip, drumming up designers for ORDRE, to fly home and be with my father. The inspiration for my life and career is close to his last days. I've written a number of these chapters as I care for him, while he sleeps. It has been such an honour to be able to look after him. As I think about the dramatic changes about to happen in my career at this point in my story, I'm reminded that, as in most things in life, my father showed me by example how to take them on. For years around the dinner table I had listened to the daily trials and tribulations of his struggles and his innovative and aggressive approach to problem solving within the framework of corporate bureaucracy. Little did I realise after MAFW 2005 that everything I had learnt from my father I was going to need over the next five years.

*

I was in a closet under the stairs in a typical Bavarian farmhouse high in the Austrian Alps in a little ski town called Maria Alm.

This is where we were staying on a family ski trip. Outside the snow was packed up around the windows and you could hear the faint mooing of the cows housed for the winter in the barn next door. The only internet connection available was a landline that made its way into the makeshift office under the stairs. The service provider, the Austrian Dairy Farmers Association, had taken it upon themselves to provide internet to their member farmers. While I'm sure the association excelled at dispensing advice about how to deal with clogged milking machines, when it came to reliable internet connections that was another thing. The German keyboard also didn't help matters.

I had been up all night trying to get an email through to New York and a deadline was rapidly approaching. I sat there in the dark cupboard watching the spinning wheel on my laptop's screen, trying to send the one email in my outbox yet again. I looked down at the screen one more time and finally it had gone. I had just agreed to sell Mercedes Australian Fashion Week to IMG. Had I done the right thing for the industry? Only time would tell.

It seemed like a huge jump after spending fourteen years building and developing MAFW to be now contemplating selling it after we had just celebrated our very successful 10th Anniversary. The money that had been offered was not a major component of the deal as it wasn't enough to change my life. The deciding factor was that at the time I thought it was absolutely in the best interests long-term for the Australian industry so that MAFW could be a part of the global IMG Fashion network.

IMG is an international organisation that at its peak employed over five thousand people. The company was established by Mark McCormack based on a handshake with Arnold Palmer, the famous golfer and the first sportsman Mark would represent. Through Mark's entrepreneurial style IMG grew into a world leader in sports management and representation, managing the careers of some of the world's most famous sporting stars. The company went on to develop diverse interests in many sports, events and media.

It operated in thirty-three countries around the world and was head-quartered in New York. After Mark McCormack passed away his estate sold the business to Forstmann Little, which at the height of its success was one of the largest private equity firms in the world with an impeccable reputation for buying struggling companies and reselling them at amazing multiples. Chairman Ted Forstmann was a charismatic player who liked to surround himself with the trappings of a fabulous life, including famous people. IMG was a natural acquisition target for him and in 2004 he bought it for US$750 million.

One of McCormack's leading lieutenants was Chuck Bennett, who many credit with the foundation of the women's professional tennis circuit. He is a gregarious larger-than-life character who counts Lou Reed and Anna Wintour among his best friends. The stories of his professional and romantic pursuits are the stuff of legend, but legend and hearsay they will stay. Chuck is an expert at staying under the radar and pulling all the strings from a well-camouflaged position. His memoirs, which will never be written, would be a global bestseller. In the late 1990s McCormack had tapped Chuck on the shoulder to head up the newly formed IMG Fashion division. The division was a ploy to do to the fashion industry what IMG had done to the sports industry for years: own the performers, own the events they performed in and own the media rights to those events. Chuck rose to the challenge and launched IMG Models, signing Kate Moss and Naomi Campbell, both of whom had fallen in love with him and his ability to make them money.

All the top models in the industry beat a path to Chuck's door and along with Ivan Bart he established the powerhouse that is IMG Models today. Chuck then turned his attention to what fashion events IMG could own. The star in any crown was always going to be New York Fashion Week. In July 2001 it was announced IMG had acquired New York Fashion Week from the Council of Fashion Designers of America—I estimate at a cost of US$6.5 million—and Fern Mallis, the executive director of the CFDA, went on board at

IMG as a senior vice president of IMG Fashion in North America. Chuck had also appointed Massimo Redaelli as the senior vice president in Europe, running both IMG Fashion and IMG Models there. The plan was global domination of the fashion world, bringing together a unique portfolio of fashion weeks and events and the world's best model talent and, through sponsorship and other commercial initiatives, generating profits.

In 2004 when the McCormark family sold IMG, Chuck in his usual stealth move found himself at the right hand of Teddy, riding in the Gulf Stream and with new acquisition funds to expand the IMG Fashion and IMG Models empires. It was at this time that a conversation started between IMG and Australian Fashion Innovators about the acquisition of MAFW. Martin Jolly, who was Asia Pacific senior vice president, took the lead on the acquisition discussions. Martin was always a fan of adding a fashion and models division to the Asia Pacific region and was well aware of the impact that MAFW had made in the region. Along with regional Finance Director Max Davis and Chuck pulling the strings from New York a deal came together that would ultimately result in me sending that email from a little ski town in Austria.

There were two parts to the IMG deal: we got cash and they got me. Part of the deal was that I would be appointed senior vice president and managing director of IMG Fashion & Models Asia Pacific. The position was eventually to be based in Hong Kong. My thought process on selling MAFW was this. What was going to happen to the event if something happened to me or The Lock Group? If I got hit by a truck we had no contingency plan. If The Lock Group got wiped out in a financial crisis MAFW would go down with it. The industry rightly or wrongly had no industry association to take over and run the non-profit management of the event like the Council for Designers in New York or the British Fashion Council did for their regions' fashion weeks. International precedent had already been established when the Council sold New York Fashion Week to IMG. How much longer could I keep going—ten, twenty, thirty years?

What would happen then? I felt I owed it to the industry as part of establishing and building our fashion week to ensure that its future was rock solid forever. Part of my job was to ensure MAFW could continue always, not just while I owned it.

The proposal that IMG presented was very attractive. Firstly the money on offer, slightly less than what they paid for New York Fashion Week, was a bit over US$5 million. This allowed us to finally pay off the accumulated debt that MAFW had rolled over year after year. We gave key staff bonuses and, as AFI had a number of shareholders involved in The Lock Group, there was quite a number of allocations. While I was the largest single share-holder, after tax was paid it was a nice lump sum but wasn't enough to change my lifestyle or permit me to stop working. Anyway, I couldn't—I was sold to IMG as part of the deal. MAFW for me had never been about the money and it wasn't when I sold it. The fact of the matter is that what I got out at the end was nowhere near the cash I had put into the event in the first five years. I will always have an investment in MAFW.

The opportunity for the event to be part of the IMG network was very promising. It was hoped that as part of the alliance other IMG fashion weeks would be used to promote MAFW, as we would promote other IMG events. Access would be provided to various global databases of buyers and media. Australian designers would get the inside running and support to get on the schedule at New York Fashion Week and potentially other fashion weeks. Introductions would be made to international designers interested in presenting collections at MAFW to access the Asia Pacific market. Priority access to IMG models in regards to attracting top girls to Australia would be on offer. One of the most promising benefits was access to the IMG sales team, particularly in Australia, to help grow commercial sponsorship for MAFW.

For me, the career opportunity was interesting. Along with Fern and Massimo I would report directly to the infamous Chuck Bennett, who I had met in Hong Kong during our early discussions, and I would also work alongside Martin Jolly in the region. I would remain the head of MAFW and was given a brief to also expand the business, growing and securing other fashion weeks and events around the region into the IMG portfolio. As the head of the model division for the region my brief was to sign new models and identify opportunities for the existing talent pool. My territory stretched from Australia and New Zealand to Japan in the north and from the Philippines through to India and the Middle East—a very exciting playground. I was also to be appointed a board member of Lakme Fashion Week in India, an event that was already in the IMG portfolio. One of the other conditions of the deal was that I would be able to retain my role as CEO of The Lock Group and be available to the Group's companies as required, but on a day-to-day basis my focus was to be IMG business.

Another part of the agreement was that all AFI staff would become part of IMG Fashion & Models Asia Pacific. This could have been a deal breaker, as it was a priority from my perspective. One of the experienced sales executives, Dan Hill, from IMG was going to join the fashion division and help us assimilate into corporate culture. Good luck with that, Dan! We started life at IMG in The Lock Group's office in Riley Street, Darlinghurst, but it wasn't long before we moved into IMG's headquarters in the Sydney CBD. Our first Asian office was in Singapore and we soon moved that to Hong Kong. Both Jodi and Graeme were excited about what lay ahead but there was one cog missing: Jarrad. After a time in the wilderness I convinced him to come back and join us as regional production director for IMG Fashion & Models Asia Pacific. He accepted. The gang was back together again and we hit the ground running.

A new chapter began and it took off in the most unexpected and pleasant way. The call went something like this: 'Hi, Simon. Look, Gisele is going to Hong Kong with Marc Jacobs for the opening of the new flagship Louis Vuitton store in Central and we need someone to be her date for the night. Pick her up at the hotel, accompany her on the red carpet and make sure everything goes smoothly for her at the private dinner and party.' Hmmmm, yes, I think I can do that. I was in Singapore at the time and so I hotfooted it to Hong Kong. The story got better as now I was flying business class for the first time in my life, and on top of that I got upgraded to first!

I arrived at the Four Seasons Hotel to be invited into Gisele's room, where we hung out and discussed commercial opportunities for her in Asia before heading off to the event, negotiating the red carpet, the private dinner with Marc and Peter Marino, etc., etc. Then we attended the after-party. The Hong Kong paparazzi had been let into the party and while not quite like their peers in London or Los Angeles they were still pretty annoying. Clearly my 'date' had had it, and fortunately I knew a lot of the guys who were going flash crazy. I walked into the middle of the pack and asked them as a favour to me if they could turn on their heels and go, enough was enough. To my surprise they all immediately packed up and left. I slipped quietly back under the velvet rope of the VIP area and next to Gisele. She just turned to me and said, 'I've never seen that done before. That was incredible. Thank you so much.' Oh yeah, baby, I'm the regional head of IMG Fashion, I talk and people walk—well, that's what I said to her in my deluded mind!

It wasn't long before our team bonded with key members of the IMG team around the region thanks to Martin, who was always our division's biggest fan. Dan was our go-to guy in Australia and I had created good relationships with the key managers around the region. With the additional resources our team had we were really able to expand our presence. Our first big home run with IMG was signing MasterCard to a three-year contract as the naming-rights sponsor of a new event I had created in Hong Kong called MasterCard Luxury Week. It was basically an upmarket fashion festival that presented collection shows of international designers to VIP clientele across the Asia Pacific. We also tied MasterCard into deals at the Singapore Fashion Festival as well as MAFW, and signed a big model endorsement with Denise Keller, who I had signed to IMG.

We headed to China and negotiated with the government on a number of potential fashion events that helped pave the way for a Chinese–IMG joint venture that is now in place. We established a new event in Australia at Sanctuary Cove in Queensland called Swim Fashion Week, where we presented swimwear collections based around the IMG event that had been so successful in Miami. We secured the commercial rights for Japan Fashion Week and did a string of model deals with a range of IMG stars, including Anne Watanabe, Du Juan, Erin Wasson, Ai Tominaga, Lily Cole, Jessica Gomes and Mischa Barton. We were also heavily involved in Lakme Fashion Week in Mumbai, alongside Fern.

My favourite project during this period, working very closely with Jodi Pritchard, was an initiative we started at AFI and continued with IMG. The chairman of the major media conglomerate in Pakistan, which among many other things owned GEO TV, had approached us. He was passionate about portraying Pakistan as more than a never-ending series of bombings and civil unrest and asked for our assistance to establish Pakistan Fashion Week, which he was prepared to fund. To think of such an initiative today in light of the political environment would be very foolish. However, at the time it somehow struck a chord with me: a country wanting to use fashion to help tell the world who they are. I immediately got it and went in with my heart on my sleeve, clearly not thinking about the possible outcomes. Jodi and I initially made many trips to Pakistan in an attempt to bring the industry together to support this brave initiative. In the end Jodi stopped coming to Pakistan and I continued on, trying to establish a framework that would unify the fractured industry to present a view of Pakistan's culture and fashion that wouldn't be seen as offensive to any long-held traditions within the country and would also attract international interest. I learnt so much during these trips, met some incredibly talented and passionate people and, believe it or not, attended some of the best parties of my life, which were graciously held in my honour. One of the highlights was when Jodi and I became the subject of the Pakistan equivalent of *60 Minutes*, talking about our plans to establish Pakistan Fashion Week.

The reality of the project was very different to the idealism I had built up in my mind. IMG would not cover me for kidnapping insurance. When I was travelling in Pakistan at peak times of civil unrest I had armed security with me 24/7, travelling in a convoy of two cars with three guards. I stayed at the Sheraton Hotel just ten days before the infamous terrorist suicide bombing and, two months out from our event, the Golden Mosque in Lahore, just 5 kilometres down the road from the venue I had selected, was blown up. I was the spokesperson in the media in Pakistan for the promotion of a western ideology called a fashion week. I might have been trying to tell the world that not everyone in Pakistan was a terrorist and there is wonderful culture to be celebrated but I was a fool. I put myself and, more to the point, Jodi in harm's way. I made myself an easy target in a culture I really knew nothing about. Immediately following the bombing in Lahore I called the whole thing off, telling the crew to come back as they were literally on planes preparing to fly in. There was no way I could ever make this event safe for people to attend, no matter what extraordinary lengths I was prepared to go to. Did I really think I could save the world through fashion and create peace and harmony? I was a long way from home and I had no business being there.

Closer to home, however, things were in much safer hands and IMG had delivered on a big promise for MAFW. Our naming-rights sponsorship with Mercedes-Benz was up for renewal in 2006. In conjunction with the Australian sales team, we targeted Foster Brewing Group, specifically Rosemount wines, as a prime prospect. The price tag was now well over $1 million a year and this priced us out of the relationship with Mercedes-Benz. MAFW was about to become Rosemount Australian Fashion Week (RAFW). It was a bittersweet decision given the loyalty I had to Mercedes-Benz but the funding from Rosemount was going to be critical to ensure Australian Fashion Week continued to develop at the pace I was hoping it would and to take advantage of the opportunities presented by the partnership with IMG. We had one season left in Melbourne as MAFW in November 2005 and then a new five-year contract with Rosemount would take effect, seeing us through to the end of 2011.

There were two other events that I'm proud to say I created during this period with IMG. The first was launched in 2008: the Australian Fashion Laureate. Over the years I had been continually frustrated by my inability to extend the Australian Fashion Awards into an annual, nationally televised event following our attempt in 1998. The opportunity arose during renewed discussions with the NSW Government to establish a single annual honour to recognise outstanding achievement in the industry. The simple nomination and voting process involved the RAFW advisory board, which in years to come we would expand to include a broader cross section of the industry. Nominations were open to Australian citizens anywhere in the world who had made a major contribution to the development of the Australian fashion industry but staff of NSW Government or IMG were not eligible. While it might have been my concept, Dan Hill came up with the name.

The other event, which I think had the longest gestation period of any fashion event ever created in Australia, was the Sydney Fashion Festival. The concept was first pitched by me back in 2002 to the City of Sydney when Frank Sartor was the lord mayor. Graeme Lewsey worked on the original concept with me following our work together on Melbourne City Spring Fashion Week. This was to be the Sydney equivalent, also held in September to showcase spring/summer collections direct to the public consumers when these clothes were available in-store. They would be the same wholesale collections that the industry presented at RAFW in May. The event was eventually launched as the Rosemount Sydney Fashion Festival in 2009 and it became part of our five-year sponsorship program developed with Rosemount.

As IMG Fashion Asia Pacific we were about to embark on four editions of the RAFW autumn/winter collections, four editions of RAFW spring/summer collections and, at the end of 2009, the inaugural Rosemount Sydney Fashion Festival. The first-ever event in Australia by IMG Fashion Asia Pacific was RAFW Autumn/Winter 2004 in Melbourne. Chuck Bennett and Fern Mallis came over for it and they were suitably impressed, which was a relief all round. That season we had also added the Asia Pacific Fashion Forum, an expanded industry seminar that had attracted some regional heavy hitters as speakers, including the president of Lane Crawford, the Chinese retailer, and the CEOs of hugely successful Chinese brands Ports and Shanghai Tangs. Josh Goot also showed in Melbourne for the first time along with Marnie Skillings, Charlie Brown and a great new menswear designer, Mjölk. Another highlight was Caravana, who worked with a women's cooperative in Afghanistan to produce the most beautiful embroidery work. Bowie Wong made his debut at RAFW and we introduced a show for RMIT graduates, as we had done for those at the East Sydney Design Studio in Sydney. The concerning thing this season was the drop in the number of shows from the previous season, one of the indications that more needed to be done to establish the ongoing commercial viability of the autumn/winter event post the Victorian Government funding.

Back in Sydney the RAFW Spring/Summer 2006 collections were shaping up well under the Rosemount and IMG banners. We had come off the high of the 10th Anniversary, which had seen an all-time record of 115 designers participate on the official schedule, and this season it dropped to eighty-three. The major established players were there, as well as the growing groundswell of a new wave of Australian designers who had been launched at RAFW and were really starting to gather momentum. These included Alice McCall, Anna & Boy, Camilla and Marc, Fleur Wood, Lisa Gorman, Josh Goot, Kirrily Johnston, Lover, Marnie Skillings, One Teaspoon, Toni Maticevski and White Suede.

Our superstar model that year was Lily Cole, who had first starred with us at the Singapore Fashion Festival a few weeks before and then through another deal with Danny came to RAFW to walk in the Charlie Brown show as well as in Zimmermann's. As a young girl Lily was very impressive, as much for her keen intellect and interest in world affairs as for her pursuits on the catwalk. Anyone familiar with her career will understand what a special person she is. But like any supermodel she was not averse to a bit of glamour and boy was I able to deliver it that year.

In the lead-up to the event I had been approached by super yacht company Azimut and asked if I would like to borrow a 70-foot, brand-new, multimillion-dollar luxury motor cruiser, to be at my disposal for the week. Hmmm, yes, I think I can handle that. This amazing yacht was moored at Circular Quay in front of the Park Hyatt. It was like giving a kid the key to a chocolate shop. I hosted a party for Lily and Charlie out on the harbour, as well as a few special nights with Kirstie Clements from *Vogue* and, generally in between show and events, I acted like a cross between Don Johnson from *Miami Vice* and Aristotle Onassis. I loved being me.

This wasn't the first time I was to host or be part of a *Vogue* event. Kirstie, who was well into her fifteen-year editorship of the magazine, had really taken RAFW and the Australia designers into her heart. Not only had their presence increased in the magazine but when Kirstie famously likened Alex Perry to Valentino it made a lot of people sit up and take notice. Along with Grant Pearce, Kirstie had also been hosting a series of designer dinners around RAFW for a number of years. It was a great milestone in the career of a designer to be invited, and a real endorsement that they had made it. At the end of the day relationships are about people and Kirstie and I have always had a similar view on the reality of the industry and how best to support our local designers. At this time, though, there was definitely a rift between myself and the editor of *Harper's Bazaar*, Alison Veness, as a result of her involvement in the Wharf 3 shows.

The other big advancement that season was our first real foray online. Certainly there had been a few independent attempts at webcasts before but we formed a partnership with MSN to distribute

RAFW collection shows and this was the most significant online broadcast deal for fashion at the time, thanks to Dan Hill. Graeme was also taking a lead role in developing our internet presence. We were determined to be a global leader online in regards to international fashion weeks. Broadband was finally getting faster and more efficient, enough so that we could distribute video effectively, and this was going to be a game changer for our industry. We could slowly start to distribute our content around the world and not have to rely exclusively on buyers and media physically attending the event. Another partnership formed after many months of negotiation was with the New South Wales Minister for Tourism, Sport and Recreation, Sandra Nori. A $1.25 million, five-year funding package was announced and it was to be the catalyst that allowed us to establish the Australian Fashion Laureate program.

We returned to Melbourne for RAFW Autumn/Winter 2006 in October and it proved to be a difficult year for a number of reasons. The feedback coming in from the industry was that, given the size of designer companies and turnover, everyone was struggling with the investment required to produce fashion shows for both spring/summer and autumn/winter collections. The event in Melbourne was certainly growing their businesses but they questioned if it was fast enough to sustain the continuation of the event. Without Victorian Government funding the cost of participation was going to skyrocket and designers didn't have deep enough pockets. It was also starting to be made clear to me by IMG that I couldn't invest their money to prop up events until they could stand on their own two feet like I had done previously. We had already seen this in Swim Fashion Week at Sanctuary Cove, which was cut after only one season.

Regardless of what might have seemed inevitable, the team and I were still going to give Melbourne our best shot. Federation Square was now highly in demand and we were priced out of that space so we took the innovative and unusual step to relocate to the recently renovated St Kilda Sea Baths, the centre of hipster-ville. It was an would and to take advantage of the opportunities presented by the partnership with IMG. We had one season left in Melbourne as MAFW in November 2005 and then a new five-year contract with Rosemount would take effect, seeing us through to the end of 2011.

There were two other events that I'm proud to say I created during this period with IMG. The first was launched in 2008: the Australian Fashion Laureate. Over the years I had been continually frustrated by my inability to extend the Australian Fashion Awards into an annual, nationally televised event following our attempt in 1998. The opportunity arose during renewed discussions with the NSW Government to establish a single annual honour to recognise outstanding achievement in the industry. The simple nomination and voting process involved the RAFW advisory board, which in years to come we would expand to include a broader cross section of the industry. Nominations were open to Australian citizens anywhere in the world who had made a major contribution to the development of the Australian fashion industry but staff of NSW Government or IMG were not eligible. While it might have been my concept, Dan Hill came up with the name.

The other event, which I think had the longest gestation period of any fashion event ever created in Australia, was the Sydney Fashion Festival. The concept was first pitched by me back in 2002 to the City of Sydney when Frank Sartor was the lord mayor. Graeme Lewsey worked on the original concept with me following our work together on Melbourne City Spring Fashion Week. This was to be the Sydney equivalent, also held in September to showcase spring/summer collections direct to the public consumers when these clothes were available in-store. They would be the same wholesale collections that the industry presented at RAFW in May. The event was eventually launched as the Rosemount Sydney Fashion Festival in 2009 and it became part of our five-year sponsorship program developed with Rosemount.

As IMG Fashion Asia Pacific we were about to embark on four editions of the RAFW autumn/winter collections, four editions of RAFW spring/summer collections and, at the end of 2009, the inaugural Rosemount Sydney Fashion Festival. The first-ever event in Australia by IMG Fashion Asia Pacific was RAFW Autumn/ Winter 2004 in Melbourne. Chuck Bennett and Fern Mallis came over for it and they were suitably impressed, which was a relief all round. That season we had also added the Asia Pacific Fashion Forum, an expanded industry seminar that had attracted some regional heavy hitters as speakers, including the president of Lane Crawford, the Chinese retailer, and the CEOs of hugely successful Chinese brands Ports and Shanghai Tangs. Josh Goot also showed in Melbourne for the first time along with Marnie Skillings, Charlie Brown and a great new menswear designer, Mjölk. Another high-light was Caravana, who worked with a women's cooperative in Afghanistan to produce the most beautiful embroidery work. Bowie Wong made his debut at RAFW and we introduced a show for RMIT graduates, as we had done for those at the East Sydney Design Studio in Sydney. The concerning thing this season was the drop in the number of shows from the previous season, one of the indications that more needed to be done to establish the ongoing commercial viability of the autumn/winter event post the Victorian Government funding.

Back in Sydney the RAFW Spring/Summer 2006 collections were shaping up well under the Rosemount and IMG banners. We had come off the high of the 10th Anniversary, which had seen an all-time record of 115 designers participate on the official schedule, and this season it dropped to eighty-three. The major established players were there, as well as the growing groundswell of a new wave of Australian designers who had been launched at RAFW and were really starting to gather momentum. These included Alice McCall, Anna & Boy, Camilla and Marc, Fleur Wood, Lisa Gorman, Josh Goot, Kirrily Johnston, Lover, Marnie Skillings, One Teaspoon, Toni Maticevski and White Suede.

Our superstar model that year was Lily Cole, who had first starred with us at the Singapore Fashion Festival a few weeks before and then through another deal with Danny came to RAFW to walk in the Charlie Brown show as well as in Zimmermann's. As a young girl Lily was very impressive, as much for her keen intellect and interest in world affairs as for her pursuits on the catwalk. Anyone familiar with her career will understand what a special person she is. But like any supermodel she was not averse to a bit of glamour and boy was I able to deliver it that year.

In the lead-up to the event I had been approached by super yacht company Azimut and asked if I would like to borrow a 70-foot, brand-new, multimillion-dollar luxury motor cruiser, to be at my disposal for the week. Hmmm, yes, I think I can handle that. This amazing yacht was moored at Circular Quay in front of the Park Hyatt. It was like giving a kid the key to a chocolate shop. I hosted a party for Lily and Charlie out on the harbour, as well as a few special nights with Kirstie Clements from *Vogue* and, generally in between show and events, I acted like a cross between Don Johnson from *Miami Vice* and Aristotle Onassis. I loved being me.

This wasn't the first time I was to host or be part of a *Vogue* event. Kirstie, who was well into her fifteen-year editorship of the magazine, had really taken RAFW and the Australia designers into her heart. Not only had their presence increased in the magazine but when Kirstie famously likened Alex Perry to Valentino it made a lot of people sit up and take notice. Along with Grant Pearce, Kirstie had also been hosting a series of designer dinners around RAFW for a number of years. It was a great milestone in the career of a designer to be invited, and a real endorsement that they had made it. At the end of the day relationships are about people and Kirstie and I have always had a similar view on the reality of the industry and how best to support our local designers. At this time, though, there was definitely a rift between myself and the editor of *Harper's Bazaar*, Alison Veness, as a result of her involvement in the Wharf 3 shows.

The other big advancement that season was our first real foray online. Certainly there had been a few independent attempts at webcasts before but we formed a partnership with MSN to distribute

RAFW collection shows and this was the most significant online broadcast deal for fashion at the time, thanks to Dan Hill. Graeme was also taking a lead role in developing our internet presence. We were determined to be a global leader online in regards to international fashion weeks. Broadband was finally getting faster and more efficient, enough so that we could distribute video effectively, and this was going to be a game changer for our industry. We could slowly start to distribute our content around the world and not have to rely exclusively on buyers and media physically attending the event. Another partnership formed after many months of negotiation was with the New South Wales Minister for Tourism, Sport and Recreation, Sandra Nori. A $1.25 million, five-year funding package was announced and it was to be the catalyst that allowed us to establish the Australian Fashion Laureate program.

We returned to Melbourne for RAFW Autumn/Winter 2006 in October and it proved to be a difficult year for a number of reasons. The feedback coming in from the industry was that, given the size of designer companies and turnover, everyone was struggling with the investment required to produce fashion shows for both spring/summer and autumn/winter collections. The event in Melbourne was certainly growing their businesses but they questioned if it was fast enough to sustain the continuation of the event. Without Victorian Government funding the cost of participation was going to skyrocket and designers didn't have deep enough pockets. It was also starting to be made clear to me by IMG that I couldn't invest their money to prop up events until they could stand on their own two feet like I had done previously. We had already seen this in Swim Fashion Week at Sanctuary Cove, which was cut after only one season.

Regardless of what might have seemed inevitable, the team and I were still going to give Melbourne our best shot. Federation Square was now highly in demand and we were priced out of that space so we took the innovative and unusual step to relocate to the recently renovated St Kilda Sea Baths, the centre of hipster-ville. It was an inspired move, along with promoting the collections as trans-seasonal instead of autumn/winter to try to attract more buyers from Asia. What unfortunately was to be our last year in Melbourne was a really cool event. Alex Zabotto-Bentley came down and weaved his magic with Fashion Assassin, which was one of the hottest brands in the country at the time. Gail Sorronda presented a stunning collection and was becoming a fully-fledged star. Toni Maticevski again proved why he is one of the best designers to ever come out of Melbourne.

The event, though, will sadly be remembered by me as the 'cancer scare' season. For months and months I had been feeling unwell and had lost lots of weight. Tests were done, blood samples were taken and I was waiting for the results when the phone rang in the middle of the event in Melbourne. A doctor's receptionist told me that it was imperative that I came in to see the doctor immediately. She couldn't discuss the findings with me, only the doctor could, and he needed to see me now! I thought my worst fears were about to be confirmed … the Big C. I left St Kilda and went straight to their surgery. As soon as I arrived I was ushered into a room to wait for the doctor, who took only a few minutes to turn up. This was it! He then proceeded to tell me that it was nothing too much to worry about other than that I had giardia, possibly caught from ill-prepared food in Pakistan where I had just been. The urgency was that it had to be immediately reported to the infectious disease control authority and I needed to sign some form. I was furious. Did he not understand I had just spent the past forty minutes thinking I had cancer? Idiot!

*

RAFW Spring/Summer 2007 belonged to Miranda Kerr. Her career and profile had been building steadily from the first time we worked with her as a fit model at the Mercedes Start-Up judging a few years earlier. When she walked out in the most stunning floor-length evening dress in the Alex Perry show everyone knew a superstar had arrived. She stole the show and every one she walked in that year. The combination of her assuredness on the catwalk and her curves, as well as a smile complete with dimples, was just arresting. She is also a darling to work with. Nothing is too much trouble and she is very down to earth. I often find with the huge stars in the fashion industry that the bigger they are the nicer they seem to be, and that is certainly true of Miranda.

Miranda did have a bit of competition in the supermodel stakes that year, when the face of Maybelline Erin Wasson arrived as part of the Ksubi crew to open their show. One of my all-time favourite On the Couch with SPL interviews was with George, Dan and Erin. They were all trying to do their best Kurt Cobain impression, that of a laidback rock star, during the interview. It was hilarious. Another great moment this season was delivered by our brand-new shiny sponsor MAC. They used RAFW to launch their Viva Glam range, developed in conjunction with Dita Von Teese. Dita brought her entire burlesque show to RAFW, which we staged in the Museum of Contemporary Art, complete with a 2-metre-long lipstick that she rode like a bucking bronco. Dita was a sweetheart and attended a number of shows, always perfectly turned out.

The big news for us on the designer front was the arrival on the scene of a couple of duos who were going to become major players, growing their businesses through RAFW year on year. The first was Ginger & Smart. Sisters Alexandra and Genevieve Smart originally focused on luxury accessories but had now developed ready-to-wear. It was an instant success. Alex had been instrumental in publishing the first book on MAFW and was very familiar with the event, which gave her the inside running from a business perspective. The other pair's show, though, was not going as well and I was to blame.

Anna Plunkett and Luke Sales from Romance Was Born had chosen the Conservatorium of Music to launch their debut collection at RAFW. As designers of great expectation we tried to give them as much support as possible, including lending them one of our key producers, Nat Ratard. As is usually the case with Romance Was Born it was a hugely complex show—basically, a live-theatre performance rather than a catwalk show. The auditorium they had chosen suited the format. They were the last show on this particular night and due to start at around 9 p.m. I got to the venue straight after the last on-site show on my trusty (sometimes) 1950s Lambretta vintage scooter, which I used for quick escapes from Circular Quay. Backstage was beyond chaos—it was like the monkeys had taken over the zoo.

Virgin designers can occasionally bite off much more than they can chew. Romance Was Born had about fifty outfits in their collection and each was very elaborate. As a result no changes were possible and they needed fifty models. Having limited funds they got friends and some of the development models to do the show for free. On top of that they had limited hair and make-up resources and they hadn't even finished the collection by the night of the show. Models were half made-up, outfits were still being sewn, decisions were still being made on music and Nat was sitting in the middle of it, screaming for help. Meanwhile, our streamlined organisation had delivered about three hundred delegates to be ushered in on time. They were seated by 9 p.m., ready for action. They were still there at 9.15 p.m. ... 9.30 p.m. ... 9.45 p.m. ... 10 p.m. ... 10.15 p.m. ...

I was tearing my hair out. *What's happening?* Every magazine editor was on my case. The internationals wanted to go home to bed after such a huge day. Friends wanted to get stuck into the drinks. Basically, everyone's patience was running very thin. I went backstage again and the models were slowly starting to line up for the show and the producer was ready to call action. But a show never, never, never starts until the designers say they are ready, and Luke and Anna were still getting models into outfits. It looked like the show was going to be hours away. While they were concerned about the time they were adamant the show would not start until they were ready, as each outfit was just too important. I made one of those calls that was tough to make. Nat was on my payroll and I gave her a direct order to start the show. Shoot me now, guys. Yes, it was actually me—I did it!

By 10.45 p.m. the show began to the relief of the audience, most of whom had stayed because of my pleading, but to the complete surprise of Anna and Luke, who were still at the end of the model line sewing outfits on models. By the time the models at the end of the line had reached Nat their outfits were ready, at least I thought they were. The show was both startling in terms of some quite bizarre images of a bleeding Jesus and semi-naked girls, but the essence of their art-inspired fashion made Romance Was Born a hit. It was unmistakable. Anna and Luke were beyond upset, though, and no amount of apologising or trying to explain the situation would appease them. For a period of time we didn't speak. Their attitude was that people needed to wait sometimes for art. Mine was purely business, based on the fact that international buyers won't wait forever. I still feel that the balance between art and commerce was achieved that evening.

Next on our agenda was RAFW Autumn/Winter 2007. I was determined to make this work and had moved the schedule to Sydney in the hope that, as most designers were based there, we might be able to gather a new momentum. We put together a single venue event at OPT with seven individual shows and two group shows. Designers undertaking individual shows included loyalists Alex Perry, Wayne Cooper and sass & bide. Unfortunately the writing was on the wall. No amount of passion or enthusiasm from me was going to mask the fact that the Australian fashion industry just could not contribute the investment required to support international fashion weeks for both spring/summer and autumn/winter. The following autumn/winter season we produced a schedule to help a few designers who still wanted to present their collections on a catwalk to buyers, but that was the last time we officially had anything to do with an autumn/winter showing.

The reality was that by this period Australian designers were investing over $60,000 each spring/summer to present their collections on a catwalk. In regards to producing a show on-site at RAFW, the biggest cost is always the fabric and sampling costs of the collection, which on average can be $20,000. In addition to this, venue fees are approximately $20,000, models $6000, producers $3500, stylists $2500, catwalk photography and video $3500, accessories $4000 and PR fees $5000. These costs are basic and don't include any production extras, staff or travel costs, or any additional fees for big models or special guests. Many designers spend $100,000 on a show and others can spend a lot more than this. Designers see this as a valuable investment to support their showing. Most designers in Australian do two drops to retailers of their spring/summer collection, which basically represents about two-thirds of their annual turnover. Autumn/winter in Australia tends to be a small season, representing only a third of total production. To invest potentially another $60,000 plus to promote this collection on the catwalk to media and buyers in the end just couldn't be commercially justified. No one will ever be able to accuse me of not trying. I certainly gave autumn/winter my best shot.

*

RAFW Spring/Summer 2008 was another memorable year. By this time designers were really becoming very inventive about how to use our venues at OPT. While Jarrad and I were constantly updating the design of our on-site venues, designers were also exploring the immediate surrounds of the Circular Quay precinct. This included using various venues at the Opera House and on the water's edge with the harbour as a backdrop, which Bowie did to great effect. Team Easton Pearson, which now regularly included Jane Roarty and Kevin Harris as part of the stylist team, produced the most magical collection inspired by beautiful Indian fabrications. They hung a thousand lanterns from the roof of the Harbour Pavilion, which looked amazing. Akira also presented a collection based around an explosion of colour and it was very well received.

sass & bide, who were becoming international superstars, launched
their diffusion line S&B.

Of the forty-five individual shows on the schedule that season,
twenty were debuts, which really emphasised to me how strongly
the industry was growing. Our structure of presenting steps to grow
through RAFW, from group shows to individual shows, was really
working. There was never a better example of this than the group
shows, which presented for the first time collections from Dion Lee,
Christopher Esber—both in Nicholas Huxley's Design Studio group
show—and Michael Lo Sordo in the New Gen show, which again
was responsible for unearthing a new rising star.

Graeme and I saw a changing tide coming in and really started to
put a lot more emphasis on these new crazy people called 'bloggers'.
Graeme was passionate about the fact that RAFW should be a global
leader when it came to social media and what we were doing online.
As such we became the first international fashion week to support the attendance of a little-known blogger from the Philippines,
Bryanboy. Over the coming years RAFW was to break a lot of new
ground with bloggers as they embraced the rapidly growing social
media channels.

We had some great stars turn out as well. Mischa Barton, who
was represented by IMG at the time, made an appearance. My
daughter just about had a meltdown when she met her—I think
the photo is still in her bedroom. Dannii Minogue was a regular
along with two girls that Foxtel kept annoying us about, wanting
to bring them down to sit in the front row. We had never heard of
them. They were from some silly new reality program called *Keeping
Up with the Kardashians*. If Kim and Khloe were to come back today
I think we would make a slightly bigger fuss!

*

RAFW Spring/Summer 2009 was going to be a challenging season.
The global financial crisis had really bitten into the fashion industry

A thorn between roses Miranda Kerr and Megan Gale (*Getty Images*)

One of Wayne Cooper's
best shows, inspired by
his parents, presented
in the Cargo Hall at
Circular Quay
(*MAFW Archive* above;
Getty Images right)

After thirteen years
it was great to have
Marco Maccapani
back on board
(*Getty Images*)

The Lock children—Jules, David and Hannah—grew up backstage and in the front row at MAFW (*Getty Images*)

Dita Von Teese brought her Viva Glam burlesque show to MAFW and was an absolute delight (*Getty Images*)

One of the Australian fashion industry's biggest supporters and editor of Australian *Vogue* for fifteen years, Kirstie Clements at Swim Fashion Week (*Getty Images*)

Above: Bloggers move into the front row: Bryanboy joins Edwina McCann, editor of Australian *Vogue* (*Simon P Lock*)

Left: Rosario Autore making a presentation to MAFW's patron Annita Keating at the 10th Anniversary celebrations (*Simon P Lock*)

On my soapbox again, announcing a new partnership with the NSW Government and the establishment of the Australian Fashion Laureate (*Getty Images*)

Above: Alex Perry has made more appearances at Fashion Week than any other designer (*MAFW Archive*)

Right: Lydia Pearson and Pamela Easton, creative gems (*Simon P Lock*)

Easton Pearson, spring/summer 2013 (*Simon P Lock*)

Camilla reinvents theatrical presentations at MBFWA (*Simon P Lock*)

Above: With my fellow Australian Fashion Laureates (from left) Jenny Kee, Nicky and Simone Zimmermann, Carla Zampatti and Akira Isogawa (*Getty Images*)

Left: As creative director of Dubai Fashion Week I was to meet and later marry Kirsten Doak (*Getty Images*)

Co-hosting an episode of *Germany's Next Top Model* with Heidi Klum (*Kirsten Doak*)

On the road with ORDRE, establishing a level playing field for Australian designers (*Simon P Lock*)

all over the world and Australia wasn't immune. We had already seen collection show designers drop in 2008 and in 2009 it was going to fall to a low of sixty-three. It would fall again in 2010 to fifty-six. Our all-time high in our 10th Anniversary year in 2005 was 115. We were also feeling immense pressure from our masters at IMG to cut costs to shore up profits. The end result was that we reduced the venues to two: the OPT Gallery upstairs and the Cargo Hall downstairs. The Source exhibition had also been reduced and it shared the rest of the floor space with sponsorship activities. While the number of designers might have been down, with some major designers not wanting to make the investment, it allowed a number of emerging designers, who can often mount a collection with the support of friends and the industry more cost effectively, to shine through. As such we had a number of absolute standouts, one in particular.

Following his much-applauded debut in 2008, Dion Lee presented his first solo show in 2009. Godfrey Deeny from *Fashion Wire Daily* said it was the best debut collection of any designer on the planet in 2009. The season also saw both Christopher Esber and Michael Lo Sordo present individual collections to rave reviews. So did Ellery, Gary Bigeni, Manning Cartell and Romance Was Born, who presented the most amazing Neptune-inspired collection and installation at the Sydney Dance Company. It really did seem to be the future and it was looking very strong indeed.

A highlight this year was the attendance of Margherita Missoni, who starred on the catwalk, but it was her father who accompanied her who I was excited to see, Marco Maccapani. It had been eleven years since Marco last attended RAFW and it was a real thrill to have him back to show him what we had achieved since he left. I was the one who felt like a proud father. Another memorable moment, and maybe it was an aftershock of the GFC, was a power blackout in the middle of the Zimmermann show in the OPT. RAFW ground to a halt momentarily.

Our last event for 2009 was the inaugural Rosemount Sydney Fashion Festival. Finally Sydney had a major contender in the fashion festival stakes. By this time the L'Oréal Melbourne Fashion Festival was going from strength to strength and public fashion festivals had also been established in Perth, Adelaide and Brisbane. Thanks to the support of the City of Sydney we had secured Martin Place as our venue. Profile-wise it was fantastic, but from a production perspective it was a nightmare. As many know, Martin Place slopes down to George Street so the first thing we had to do was build a gigantic level platform out of scaffold. It was an ingenious design by Jarrad and the team and when completed the Martin Place venue boasted a reception area for our VIP bar, a catwalk and a collection showroom for seven hundred people. Downstairs among the scaffold was a backstage basement. For the first time the collections shown six months previously to buyers and media at RAFW Spring/Summer were now being shown to the adoring public, who could buy tickets to the shows, including the VIP front row. And then, whatever they liked on the catwalk, they could immediately go and buy in the shops.

We had done a cross-event deal with RAFW so most of the designers participating in our trade event in May were now involved in our consumer event in September. We opened the event with Sarah Murdoch and I hosting a great charity show for Fashion Targets Breast Cancer. It kicked off the week-long event to a great start and having actress Emma Roberts in the front row didn't hurt either. If only her aunty Julia had come with her.

*

This period as part of IMG had been exhausting in many ways. The team in Australia now under Dan Hill's general management had achieved a lot over the past five years. Without their focus on our flagship event, RAFW, we would have never been able to expand in Asia as we had. The team was now split, with Dan, Graeme and the Australian crew in Sydney and myself and Jodi based in Hong Kong with the rest of the gang. Jarrad was still overseeing the production of our events but was now starting to take on a global role within IMG Fashion.

In my pursuit of growing the business and my own personal ambitions the work/life balance I had been trying to maintain with my family over this period suffered. At IMG I was no longer able to spend all my winters with them at Mt Buller, being there only occasionally. Unfortunately I had to give up my role as head coach of the Masters Ski Program and could only give private lessons on the rare occasion I was at the ski fields. In the early years of IMG I was based in Singapore and then we set up the regional headquarters in Hong Kong. As Hannah and Jules were entrenched in their schools in Sydney and at Mt Buller it didn't seem to make sense for Lorraine to bring them to Singapore or Hong Kong. David had by then left school and was pursuing a degree in event management in Melbourne.

During this time Lorraine and I had a crisis in our marriage that just added to the difficult logistics of our life. It was something we were not able to recover from. We separated and eventually divorced, but in some ways nothing really changed for our family. Lorraine and I were determined to not let the demise of our relationship affect the stability of the family unit. The kids stayed put in our home at Billiard Avenue and we shared time at Pro Ski Lodge at Mt Buller. The kids would also often come and stay with me in Asia or when I was in Sydney. Lorraine and I remain close friends and for many years she continued to take her front-row seat next to mine at RAFW. The industry seemed to respond well to this as many had a great affection for Lorraine and were grateful for the support she had provided them over the years.

That year we suffered the power blackout at RAFW, but looking back perhaps that was more a reflection of the dark clouds I could feel hanging over me.

12
Life is What Happens

As I sit at the foot of my father's bed I am reminded about the origin of my passions and enthusiasm for life—he was my first role model. Strangely, I wasn't originally attracted to fashion, but it became one of my passions. Fashion is like art. To understand it, you have to be a fan first and foremost. Then you have to become educated so you can understand it and recognise outstanding creativity and genuine innovation. To live in the arena of a fashion week has always been a fascinating one for me. It is like a moving art gallery with an intriguing cast of characters. The special moments in fashion come when I see a designer present an amazing fabric or create a silhouette or pattern that I haven't seen before. It is like finding a rare gem. It is also hard to spot, as nowadays the success of reinterpretation makes it difficult to identify a clear single idea of uniqueness, something that has never been done before in that exact way.

As Kirsten and I travel the world looking for designers who have achieved these rare moments or have the potential to do this so that we can invite them to be part of the ORDRE family, it is very exciting: discovering the new shapes of ex-Dior artisan Nicole Zhang in Shanghai, the continual reinvention of Marni in Milan, the disregard for convention of Hood By Air in New York, the sublime fabrication of Coperni Femme in Paris and the new-age silhouettes of our own Kym Ellery. In similar ways that an art collector might be inspired by a single artist or painting to add to their collection, I love the opportunity that ORDRE provides us to build our own portfolio of designers. I have spent my working life collecting designers and scheduling them in various groupings at international fashion weeks. I never get tired of discovering and promoting them, as there is always something new to experience, something to make you think or feel differently, something to be inspired by. I like being a fan.

*

In a career such as mine, given the volatile highs and lows of the often-turbulent fashion industry, it's rare that you can pinpoint exactly, to the time and date, the absolutely worst moment. For me it was about 6 p.m. on Friday, 7 May 2010, at the conclusion of the New Gen show at the 15th Anniversary of RAFW. After being the head of MAFW and RAFW for fifteen years this was the last show in that role. After all I had done for the event and the industry I was being treated like a fashion leper! How could this have possibly happened?

It is difficult to explain fully how I ended up in this predicament. It is easy to say the ugly 'corporation' is entirely to blame but on reflection I don't believe that to be the case. In my opinion it has more to do with how individuals behave within the structure of a corporation, and this includes myself. I certainly responded in a way to the corporate structure at IMG that was ultimately going to lead to my demise with them. To a certain extent I only have myself to blame for the way I was treated. From day one I was a square peg in a round hole. I had never worked for a corporation before and never had ambitions to do so. I was as surprised as anyone else when my working for IMG was stipulated as part of their acquisition of Australian Fashion Innovators. I only did it because I had to as I thought at the time it was in the best interests of the industry.

When I became part of IMG I knew that the way I operated as an entrepreneur would have to change. It was made clear to me that the 'I' in IMG was not a pronoun. It was all about the promotion and the greater profitability of the company. I had always been the high-profile media spokesperson for the event and this way of marketing the event was to come to an end under their system. RAFW was to become faceless. As I understand it from a corporate perspective, having a media profile within a corporation makes others who are of similar seniority resentful because of the supposed status associated with a media profile. Employee rivalries are not encouraged. Having a media profile that has a positive influence on a particular event also provides an individual extra negotiating power when it comes time for salary review, especially if being a spokesperson for a particular event has a direct impact on revenues, be it ticket sales or sponsorship. Therefore the preferred corporate stance is generic promotion wherever possible or shared responsibilities, not wanting to give any individual leverage against the company or disadvantage any event if they leave. From a corporation's point of view I can see the sense in this. I always found it difficult because I had also felt that one of the key strengths of RAFW was the personal passion I had for the event and the industry, which was always evident in my media promotion of them. I truly believe the 'SPL' factor in the development of Fashion Week, especially for the first ten years, was a key advantage in our growth.

The other area I found challenging at IMG was the expected gestation period for an event to return a profit. Big events can take anywhere from three to five years to get established. I was under the impression when I started that our development program, especially in Asia, would have access to investment funds to support the new events we created. This didn't happen for two reasons. The first was the global financial crisis. Our development program perfectly coincided with the GFC. This meant that funds were extremely tight in every corporation, not just IMG. This was also coupled with the fact that from day one, when Forstmann Little bought IMG for US$750 million, they had publicly declared they didn't want to hang on to the company for long and had set a sale price target of US$1.5 billion. As a result there was incredible pressure to deliver profits. The easiest way to deliver profit is to cut expenses and not make investment funds available. Forstmann Little ultimately hung on to IMG much longer than they expected as a result of the GFC, as they were not able to find a buyer at their target price. This ultimately worked for them when they did sell the company in 2014 for US$2.3 billion to William Morris Endeavour. It was worth the wait. The GFC and the focus on profits had two other outcomes. The first was going to have a profound effect on RAFW and the other a devastating effect on me.

Since I first staged Mercedes Australian Fashion Week in 1996 a major part of our budget year after year was our international marketing. From day one I knew we had to punch above our weight in this area. We were on the other side of the planet from where all the major media and buyers lived and as an industry we were unknown. To combat this I channelled at least 20 per cent of the total budget, if not more, into marketing the event. This included our gruelling and never-ending road shows and visits to directly meet key buyers and media all over the world to invite them to the event, all our direct mail programs, video compilations, brochures, websites, social media and, importantly, support programs for media and buyers to attend. In addition we created very strategic and powerful relationships with a range of government departments to promote the Australian fashion industry globally. This involved the NSW Department of State and Regional Development, the Ministry of Arts and Tourism; the City of Sydney; the Australian Tourism Commission; the federal Department of Foreign Affairs, Austrade and AusIndustries; and a range of other players. As I spoke about previously, this was Team Australia at its very best. When pressure is put on an event to deliver bigger profits, as was the case when RAFW came under the ownership of IMG, the easiest and quickest way to do this is to slash the marketing budget. That is exactly what happened and the unfortunate thing was that it was never reinstated to the level it had been previously. When I owned the event all I had to do was try to pay down the debt we had accumulated and try to make enough money to send my kids to school. Not a very sound corporate-profit strategy.

The GFC and the chase for profits had another profound effect on IMG Fashion and that was the appointment of Maureen Reidy, initially by Ted Forstmann and then Chuck Bennett, to head up IMG Fashion globally. Maureen was given the responsibility of getting the company ready for sale and wringing every last ounce of profit out of IMG Fashion. Whether it was her idea, Ted's or Chuck's I will never know, but it was my understanding that a strategy had been created to completely wipe out the senior management level of IMG Fashion. This meant that Fern Mallis, who headed up the United States, Massimo Redaelli, who headed up Europe, and me in the Asia Pacific had to go. Rather than come to us with her/their corporate plan and come to an arrangement with each of us, a strategy had been created, as I was to discover after the fact, to put such pressure on us that we would ultimately resign of our own accord, saving the company huge amounts of money by not having to pay us out of our very tight employment contracts.

I cannot talk about the others but the twelve months that I reported directly to Maureen were the worst of my life. For the first time I was made to feel completely inadequate. I was criticised and chastised. I was required to have never-ending conference calls in the middle of the night week after week until I was exhausted. An Excel spreadsheet budget drove every hour of my waking day. The pressure I was put under was just plain unfair. In my opinion and in the opinion of others it was actually harassment. Inexplicably Maureen then just disappeared overnight, explained by an internal memo that said she had been reassigned to 'special projects'. We never heard from her again. However, my pain was not over. The baton was picked up by Peter Levy, who had been appointed to replace her.

By this time it was January 2010 and the lead-up to the 15th Anniversary of RAFW. I was in Niseko, Japan, with my three children skiing and contemplating life. I still had over twelve months to go on my IMG contract. Over a number of weeks of soul searching, magnified by being with David, Jules and Hannah, who I adore, I decided to return to Hong Kong and negotiate my way out of my contract. I had had enough. My loyalty to RAFW, the industry and the money I was due was just not worth it. I had started to second-guess myself in all my business dealings. My self-confidence was at an all-time low. I didn't know what the future held but it couldn't be any worse than this. I resolved to call Peter Levy on my return to Hong Kong.

Our holiday rental in Japan was literally buried under the annual 20 metres of snowfall when the familiar US number came up on my phone. Not again! Expecting another gut-wrenching conversation about whom I had to sack next week or what other extremity of RAFW I had to remove, I rightly expected it to be Peter Levy. In a conversation that lasted less than sixty seconds he told me that IMG was buying me out of my contract and that in accordance with its terms and conditions I was on 'gardening leave' for the next twelve months. I would be paid in full and I couldn't work for anyone else. My non-compete clause would also stay in place for a further twelve months. It was effective immediately and there was no need to return to the office in Hong Kong. I was free.

It was to be years later before I found out what had made IMG change their strategy towards dealing with me, and I am not able to reveal what that was. At around the same time both Fern and Massimo were also to leave the business. As part of the conditions of IMG buying me out of my contract I was to have no involvement in the day-to-day management of the business for the next twelve months, even though I was officially still considered an employee. I was allowed to attend the 15th Anniversary of RAFW but as I indicated I was not allowed to speak to the media. An official announcement was made that I would be departing IMG but would still attend RAFW Spring/Summer in the May. That's when I was told that at RAFW I would only be allowed to attend six shows.

Everybody knows I attend every show on the official schedule. I have done so since Wayne's first show in 1996, up until 2010. I went to all individual shows, group shows and off-site shows with just one exception, the Paablo Nevada show at the NSW State Library when I was called away before it started to deal with the drama that was about to unfold at Wharf 3. In total, over those fourteen years I attended close to six hundred shows. Attending all of them was very important to me because I had made a commitment to the Australian designers that if they showed at RAFW I would be in the audience to support them as their number one fan. Anyone who knows what a fashion week schedule is like knows what a Herculean effort it was to attend every show, every season. No one to my knowledge in the global fashion industry had ever made a commitment like this. I wore this achievement as a badge of honour. The powers-that-be at IMG knew this and I think it might have given them great pleasure to rip it from me.

In my last year, still technically the head of RAFW, I was permitted to select the six shows I would attend. At all other times I was told not to be on-site. If I broke this condition I would be in breach of my employment contract and would potentially not receive salary payments that were due to me and also face the possibility of being sued. From IMG's perspective they saw an opportunity in 2010 to phase out my involvement in a way they thought would be the least harmful to the event. Letting me attend a few shows to show the industry that IMG had some sort of respect for me but gagging me to prevent me from telling the media and the industry what was going on gave the impression that I didn't care in my last year. Many designers that showed that year were very upset and thought

I had turned my back on the industry. My phone was running hot with media enquiries. I just had to sit through the few shows I was allowed to attend and slip out quietly without speaking to anyone. It was a soul-destroying week. But there was more.

Graeme Lewsey and I had planned a retrospective exhibition, called Frock Stars, in the lead-up to our 15th Anniversary. We thought of no better place to stage this than the venue where we held our first Opening Ceremony, and where I would subsequently donate the AFI archive of Fashion Week, the Powerhouse Museum. At first I thought the official opening would be a good opportunity for me to thank all those in the industry who had supported me and helped RAFW get off the ground, and then drove it through fifteen years of development. This seemed a very fitting and digni-fied exit. But I was told that while I could attend the event I was not allowed to have anything official to do with it and in no way would I be permitted to speak. Attending that event was again extraordi-narily difficult, with many people commenting about my lack of involvement in the official proceedings. Even though the smallest acknowledgement possible was made in the official speech, given my omnipresence throughout every single aspect of RAFW for the past fifteen years the industry was at a loss to explain why it seemed I had turned my back on them. It was my version of a dead man walking. It was hell.

To maintain some semblance of self-esteem and to try to gain control of the situation, especially as it related to my key staff, I held a private cocktail party following the official opening. With close family and friends gathered around I told them how sad the situa-tion was and in a gesture of thanks I presented Jodi Pritchard, Jarrad Clark, Graeme Lewsey, Lucia Labbate and Lorraine Lock each with a beautiful Tiffany & Co. silver key. I presented it to them individu-ally, telling them they now held the keys to their future without me.

Over the following days I continued my 'dead man walking' impersonation until my last appointed fashion show at RAFW, fittingly the New Generation Collections. This is the show I had conceived and it was the launching pad for so many great designers. In my usual way, I couldn't resist going to one more show than I was allowed during the week and this was duly noted. I was told that if I now attended the New Gen show the terms of my employment contract would be breached. I went anyway. New Gen was my final one. Staff had been told not to acknowledge this in any way. I had also been banned from speaking to the media. Moments before the show was due to start I was asked by Dan Hill to move from my usual spot at the end of the runway because I was blocking the media's view of someone more important. I adamantly refused. I watched the show with my heart beating so hard I thought it would explode. It was a combination of anguish, frustration, sadness and anger. I rose at the end of the show as proudly and as composedly as I could. I turned to face the media pit where Graeme and Jarrad had been watching the show and caught their eyes for a moment. Jodi was not there. I turned, walked through the side entrance of the Overseas Passenger Terminal and unceremoniously got on my Lambretta and drove away. I was heartbroken. All my staff was told to basically stay away from me during the week and there were to be no events or send-offs behind the scenes. My key people, as I discovered later, were hurting as much as I was but out of fear of upsetting their employer they could do nothing.

At this point in time I was feeling real animosity towards IMG. I still don't understand why people behave the way they do when they are within a corporation. The hierarchical structure seems to make them act often against their better judgement or what is fair and responsible. Executives seem to copy the behaviour of others so they can justify their actions, and the people within seem to be forever looking up to see who they can jump over on the next rung rather than trying to reach down and help others pull themselves up. The holy grail is profits at all cost and the corporate hole they all disappear into, with absolute disregard or recognition of loyalty. I just can't understand it. I certainly do recognise the achievements of IMG. However, I don't think Maureen Reidy is a particularly cruel person; she was just acting on instructions from above and was trying to impress. I don't think Peter Levy took any great joy in being the hatchet man. I don't think Dan Hill enjoyed being the watchdog over me at RAFW. I don't think Jodi, Graeme or Jarrad took any pleasure in having to stand by and watch the hand I was dealt. I don't believe Chuck Bennett or Martin Jolly wanted to personally hurt me. I'm sure it was all just business and for the best of the corporation, and in the end perhaps it was.

As for me, how did I want to be treated? I wanted to continue my record-breaking commitment to the industry I love and sit in the front row of all the designers that showed that year. At the launch of the 15th Anniversary Frock Stars Exhibition I wanted to personally recognise those who helped over the last decade and a half to put Australia on the global fashion map. I wanted to publicly acknowledge the contribution to the industry made by Jodi, Graeme, Jarrad and Lucia. I wanted to recognise the role IMG Fashion had played and was expected to play in the development of RAFW, and tell the industry to support them. I never got the opportunity to do that and I'm happy to be able to do it now. I really don't think IMG or the event would have suffered by allowing me the time and the dignity to do this.

I'm happy being an entrepreneur and I am now back in control of every part of my destiny. I care for people more than profits when I need to. It means I can invest my own money in my vision and play Don Quixote when I feel like it. It means I'm free to stand on my soapbox and tell the world exactly how I think, being fully aware of the ramifications. I like being me and I don't think I was ever going to be comfortable being anyone's senior vice president.

Selecting the shows I would attend at RAFW Spring/Summer 2010 was a really difficult decision. In the end I gravitated towards where I thought my support would be best placed: in the emerging talent of our industry. The shows I attended were by Christopher Esber, Dion Lee, Ellery, Ksubi, Romance Was Born, the TAFE show and New Gen—yes, all seven of them. For the rest of the schedule I had to be content with watching online, like everyone else did. It was interesting to see the increasing impact that online video was having on our industry by 2010, and the immediacy of often being able to access collection shows from the convenience of a laptop. Other highlights that season, those I wasn't able to personally experience, were the debuts of two designers who were to go on and establish great businesses: bassike, who introduced a new take on easy dressing to critical acclaim, and the delightful Bianca Spender. Bianca is Carla Zampatti's daughter and she stepped out of her mother's design studio to take on the catwalk herself. It was a beautiful collection but I was really embarrassed when I bumped into her after her show and she asked me why I wasn't there. I wasn't able to tell her the truth and just made up some feeble excuse. Fleur Wood also made her solo debut that season to great reviews and Aurelio Costarella's star continued to shine with Jennifer Hawkins, Myer ambassador and fan, in the front row. On the model front Bambi Northwood-Blyth really made her presence felt on the catwalk as well as with Dan Single from Ksubi—years later they were to marry.

The day after the New Gen show at RAFW Spring/Summer 2010 I jumped on a plane to Hong Kong to contemplate my future. I still couldn't work for anyone else or undertake any activity that could be conceived as competition to IMG. The past twelve months had been very difficult. The harassment I received left me full of self-doubt and had shaken my business confidence. The RAFW experience had also left me shattered and emotionally exhausted. So I did what I always do at difficult times in my life: I went to the mountains and skied.

Following the infamous call from Peter Levy I spent as much time as I could that winter in Japan skiing with my kids. I returned there for the next season in late 2012, moving in with a great friend of mine. I joined the NISS Ski School and gave private powder lessons. I immersed myself in the local community and culture and Hannah, Jules and David came to stay with me, spending as much time as their school and university timetables would allow. For many years I'd had a vision about building the ultimate six-star ski lodge and then I discovered a wilderness area near Hanazono, one of the resorts that make up the Niseko region, that I thought would be perfect for this. Perhaps my future was building that dream lodge after all, and being the entertaining host and lead ski guide. With that in mind, The Lodge @ Hanazono was born and I threw myself into securing this amazing parcel of land and designing The Lodge from the ground floor up. I found a great architect based in Los Angeles who had a lot of really cool alpine experience. I flew him to Japan to start working with me on the design and I also started to work with one of the huge Hokkaido developers. The Lodge @ Hanazono was on its way to becoming a reality.

Over the years in Hong Kong I had also become very close to my good friend Morgan Parker. I originally met Morgan when the company he was then working for, Taubmans, sponsored MasterCard Luxury Week. We hit it off on a number of levels and became close confidants. Morgan, given his property development background, also provided some advice on The Lodge. Coincidentally, around the time I left IMG he was made an offer he couldn't refuse to leave Taubmans, where he was Asia Pacific CEO. Morgan had ambitions to undertake some major charity work and had dreamt up a concept called Wheel 2 Wheel, similar to Ewan McGregor's Long Way Down initiative. The idea was to ride a motorbike from Hong Kong to Australia through ten countries en route, raising money for a designated charity in each country. He wanted to also create a television series of the journey to promote the charity and raise awareness. Morgan asked me to join him on the ride and I thought it was just the perfect opportunity. I could continue to develop The Lodge and do this charity work as well.

Having the opportunity to pay it forward given the fortunate life I have always had seemed appropriate during my gardening leave. We immediately embarked on a rigorous training regime and brought together a team to help organise this complicated undertaking.

I bought a huge BMW GS 800 and learnt how to ride it—a far cry
from my Lambretta. Morgan and I hit the gym thanks to sponsor
Pure Fitness and started to identify and confirm all the charities as
well as the route and the logistics involved. Through my television
connections I was also able to help secure National Geographic as a
broadcast partner and was in the process of confirming a number of
sponsors. I really dedicated myself to this cause, the bike, the training, underwriting various costs, etc. I was finding the whole thing
worthwhile and therapeutic. Then the bombshell dropped.

To my complete dismay and astonishment I received an email
from Morgan saying that he had made a decision that he was
undertaking Wheel 2 Wheel by himself and that I was no longer his
partner on the ride or in the company we had formed together. I was
gobsmacked. I literally couldn't believe it. I had considered him an
incredibly close friend and this just seemed to come out of the blue.
I was initially devastated. For me it was like I had been punched
three times that year: by IMG, at RAFW 2010, and now by Morgan.
In the end National Geographic pulled out of being a partner on the
television series but as I understand it Morgan funded a number
of episodes himself, which I believe are on YouTube. I returned to
Japan, to The Lodge development and teaching skiing.

*

Life really does have a way of happening while you're making
other plans. Never truer words have been sung by the one and only
John Winston Lennon. There I was, happy making plans to build my
dream ski lodge and convincing my children to come and work for
me and live happily ever after in the powder paradise of Hokkaido,
but life's journey had other plans for me. An ex-IMG colleague
who had moved to Dubai called and asked me if I was interested
in becoming the creative director of Dubai Fashion Week. No way,
just not going to happen—I'm as happy as a powder pig here in
Hokkaido. He was persistent and as a throwaway line I told him I

had been invited by a friend to come to London and that if they flew me first class to London via Dubai I'd drop in and meet with them. A few days later an email turned up with a confirmed ticket.

On a lark I headed off to London via Dubai, where I got the royal treatment. The owners of Dubai Fashion Week were going all out to impress me and get me to take on their event to try to garner some international credibility for it. An interesting conversation ensued that revolved around the fact that if I was to return to the fashion industry I would be more interested in pursuing a new business model concept I had devised rather than working on a traditional fashion week again. To cut a long story short, they basically made me an offer I couldn't refuse, offering to pay me a small fortune to run their fashion week as well as agreeing to secure funding for my new fashion business model, allowing me time to pursue my dream lodge. The moral of this story is, however, 'Beware of strangers in Dubai bearing gifts'. It was going to take me forever to get paid and the funding never came through for the new venture.

I had agreed to produce Dubai Fashion Week in October of 2011 but first I was to return to Sydney for RAFW in May and then the Australian ski season, where I had made a commitment to run a private Masters Ski Program. Returning to RAFW as the founder, not the CEO, was always going to be difficult. It was now about the love affair I have always had with Australian designers and not so much about the business. IMG seemed very nervous about my return. There had been lots of comments in the industry throughout the year along the lines of 'It's just not the same without Simon.' Certainly there had been some media commentary about the rise of the corporate influence and the loss of personal passion, which was to be expected. From my perspective it was important to support IMG, regardless of how I had been treated the previous year. I was the one who had made the decision to sell the event to ensure it had a permanent home within the IMG Fashion network and I wanted to support that proposition. As I wasn't allowed to speak to the media or the industry the previous season this message was never communicated. Regardless, I wanted to be able to support IMG and the ex-AFI staff who were still working on the event.

There was sort of an uneasy truce in 2011. By this time Jodi had decided that she had had enough of everything fashion and after initially leaving Hong Kong to go back to Sydney eventually settled in Melbourne where her family is from. Graeme, Jarrad and Lucia were still with IMG and working on RAFW. IMG hadn't really pushed a spokesperson forward to take over my soapbox role so interestingly a lot of media interviews and requests for comments were coming directly to me. Everybody wanted to know what I thought of the event now. As I had always done I continued as its champion, as I will until the day I die. I applauded the changes that had been made and behind the scenes offered Graeme, Jarrad and Lucia my advice, this being that it was time to move the event again. RAFW needed to be reinvented for lots of reasons, among them that IMG needed a new venue so that the event couldn't be compared to the one they had inherited.

This year was a milestone for me career-wise. It was the first year I became eligible to be nominated for the Australian Fashion Laureate. Previously as an employee for IMG, who still produced the event, I couldn't be put forward. Graeme called me to say that I was going to be the first-ever non-designer recipient of the award and that it would be presented at RAFW 2011. To be recognised by my peers in this way, especially in the first year I could be, was both humbling and gratifying. It was a public thank you from the industry for all I had done over fifteen years to establish Fashion Week and help the industry become part of the global fashion industry. It was a magic moment made even more special by the fact that it was presented to me by Carla Zampatti. The only regrettable thing was that I was in a hiding-behind-my-hipster-beard phase and every photo of me in the media holding the beautiful Jan Logan-designed statue shows me with this hideous long beard! The Australian Fashion Laureate has been awarded on seven occasions now, and I'm in fine company with the other recipients: Akira Isogawa, Carla

Zampatti, Easton Pearson, Collette Dinnigan, Jenny Kee and Simone and Nicky Zimmermann.

I decided not to attend all the shows on the schedule in 2011, even though I now could. I just thought it would send the wrong message. I'm sure it would have upset some at IMG and the industry needed to see they had new partners now and they needed to embrace them. I directly contacted the designers and the PRs I especially wanted to see and support. As usual there were many highlights. Yasmin Le Bon, a good friend of supermodel-turned-designer Gail Elliott, walked in Gail's Little Joe Woman show. Maurice's Iceberg restaurant staged the Kirrily Johnston show. Dion Lee again knocked it out of the ballpark with his show at the Opera House. Toni Maticevski returned from showing in New York and presented another beautiful collection. Yeojin Bae made her debut and Lover celebrated ten years in the business. On the special guest front bloggers Susie Bubble and Tommy Ton made their global influence count and Graeme really pushed hard on increasing RAFW's social media impact.

The number of designers showing was down again in 2011. I think this was a combination of the follow-on impact of the GFC and the fact that many designers were just over the OPT venue. The most concerning factor, however, was the lack of international buyers. This was a trend that had really started to worry the industry. Certainly IMG cutting the event's international marketing budget was an element in the drastic drop-off but it also reflected broader global trends.

*

Not long after RAFW 2011, I was in Dubai producing Dubai Fashion Week along with our international team. I had put together a great crew, including many who had been with me at AFI and IMG, such as Troy Daniel, Jack Bedwani and Selina Robson as well as my son David. I also did a deal with Chic Models and brought a group of great girls over from Australia to work at the event. In the lead-up, though, something very unexpected happened. At the media launch, for which I had been reluctantly dragged back to promote the event, Troy introduced to me one of his friends from Australia, who was now working as a fashion editor in Dubai. Enter Miss Kirsten Doak. I literally fell off my soapbox. That chance introduction changed the course of my life in the most wonderful and unexpected way. Thanks, Troy.

Kirsten and I fell in love almost immediately. We became inseparable. Dubai Fashion Week was only a few weeks away and Kirsten very much hosted the event with me, sitting in the front row alongside me and helping me to entertain the government officials and VIPs. It was a match made in fashion heaven: the fashion entre-preneur and the fashion director. As the story of our lives unfolded in front of each other we had the amazing realisation that Kirsten had been with Mrs Fish all those years ago and we had never met. I still don't think Victoria can get over the fact that we are together.

Following Dubai Fashion Week in the lead-up to the 2011–12 ski season I spent most of my time in Dubai and it wasn't long before Kirsten and I moved in together. We had become regulars on the fashion scene there and had also started to travel a lot together. Kirsten came with me to India when I was asked to speak at an international conference and to Edinburgh, where I judged the Scottish Fashion Awards. I travelled with her to London for a beauty conference, to Abu Dhabi to meet Gwyneth Paltrow at an event, to Cairo to do a review for the Four Seasons Hotel and to Oman to review the Chedi Muscat resort. Kirsten also came with me to Niseko to understand firsthand why I loved this place so much. She fell in love with it as well. This latter trip was the catalyst for a pretty important discussion that was ultimately going to set our priorities for the next few years.

Kirsten couldn't really see herself at this stage in her life retiring to help run a ski lodge in the wilds of Japan, and sourcing develop-ment funding for it had proved to be really difficult following the terrible Japanese tsunami in 2011. While I had been continuing to pursue the building of The Lodge @ Hanazono, the new fashion business model I'd had in mind had been slowly taking shape. Together we decided to put The Lodge on the backburner and continue to work in the fashion industry by developing the new venture.

There had also been another tsunami-like factor that had a major effect on The Lock Group. During my IMG phase the partners in The Lock Group, including me, decided to divest our three existing operating divisions, being Spin, Propeller Productions and Tropfest. The Tropfest decision was really made for us when founder John Polson decided not to renew our licence agreement with him, which was very disappointing after the success we had had over the previous eight years. We rolled Propeller, our film and television production company, into a company called Stella and for a while it continued to be the direction vehicle for Simon Bookallil. Then we made our big move: floating Spin on the stock exchange.

I was the largest shareholder in Spin and this was basically going to be my retirement fund; well, The Lodge fund at least. As part of a group of marketing communications agencies called Blue Freeway we launched the stock at a dollar and it quickly rose to $3. I had a note on my fridge saying, 'Don't be greedy—sell at $5.' Always the risk-taker I hadn't taken any money out at the initial public offering and so all my equity had been transferred to Blue Freeway shares. After seventeen years of operating Spin I now put all my chips in it on the table. Then the perfect storm hit. The aggressive acquisition program Blue Freeway had embarked on didn't generate the revenue projected, and the GFC really hit home. Institutional investors pulled out one by one. The shares plummeted. There was absolutely nothing I could do as all my shares were in escrow and couldn't be sold before twenty-four months from the launch. Two months before the escrow was up a takeover bid was made to privatise the company at four cents a share. Seventeen years of gut-wrenching hard work just evaporated along with my retirement and lodge funds.

Following this, and as a result of the residency I now had in Hong Kong, I moved The Lock Group's global headquarters there and, along with Kirsten, embarked on career number four—the first being Pro Ski, the second as a health administrator, then The Lock Group Mark 1, and now The Lock Group Mark 2. I established a consulting division, TLG Consulting, as a way of funding the new fashion business model we had decided to develop and away we went, again!

Our first big job since Dubai Fashion Week was going to be a big test for Kirsten and our newfound love. This came in the unlikely form of Heidi Klum! Earlier in the year I had been asked to be a judge of *Austria's Next Top Model*. Go figure! Apparently they had seen my roles in the Australian version of *Project Runway* and *Australia's Next Top Model* and wanted to shoot some episodes at Dubai Fashion Week, thus the connection. I did one episode in Vienna and another in Dubai. Heidi Klum was the executive producer of both the Austrian and German versions of the program and she and the team liked what I did. They asked me if I wanted to help produce three further episodes, working with Heidi directly on *Germany's Next Top Model*, with the episodes based around challenges in Dubai. It was like the time when I was asked to be Gisele's date: 'Yep, I can do that!'

My brief was to organise and style three huge photo shoot challenges, a fashion show, manage certain elements of local sponsors and appear in episodes alongside Heidi and the other judges. The first shoot was to be an incredible stunt where we strung the twelve contestants from a wire suspended from the roof of Meydan Racecourse ten storeys up with the skyline of Dubai in the background. Internationally renowned photographer Rankin was flying in for the shoot. The next was an Arabian-inspired setting in the searing heat of the desert, and then we did an underwater shoot among the sharks in the world's biggest aquarium at Atlantis Resort. We also produced a fashion show with Dubai's leading designer Amato Haute Couture at Nasimi Beach Club.

I had put together our international team to help me as executive producer and Kirsten came on board as fashion director to work with Heidi and Rankin and across all the other elements. It was to be our first time working together and as great fortune and fate would have it we turned out to be a natural team. Our experience and expertise were a perfect complement. It was an amazing few weeks with the highlight for me being MC for the fashion show alongside Heidi. The funniest thing happened when months later the episodes went to air in Germany, where it is one of their highest rating programs. I got a message from one of my ski instructor buddies surprised to see me in his lounge on the television screen in a fashion show! But this really cool job did certainly cement in both Kirsten's mind and mine that we could work together and that we wanted to.

Following this it was time to head back to Sydney for RAFW 2012. It was a season I was very much looking forward to as I was now starting to distance myself from the painful year of 2010, especially with a new love in my life. To my absolute delight IMG had been able to extend their global partnership with Mercedes-Benz and they returned as the naming-rights sponsors. This time around, however, the powers-that-be in Stuttgart weren't going to allow the event to be referred as Mercedes Australian Fashion Week, without the Benz. It was now going to be part of the global portfolio of fashion weeks they sponsored and the new name was to be Mercedes-Benz Fashion Week Australia, MBFWA. I took great personal pride in this because these worldwide partnerships had all started in Australia. We took the idea to Stuttgart, it spread around the world and it had now come back home.

IMG also pulled out all stops and brought Jessica Stam to Sydney. At the time she was the face of the Mercedes-Benz fashion campaign globally. The Harbour Pavilion had returned to the Overseas Passenger Terminal site and there was a bit of a rise in designer numbers participating, up from the all-time lows of 2010 and 2011. The season once again featured the second wave of Australian designers who were now setting the pace, including Alice McCall, Bec & Bridge, Camilla, Christopher Esber, Ellery, Gail Sorronda, Ginger & Smart, Manning Cartell and Michael Lo Sordo. There were also some really important debuts, including By Johnny, Khalo, Song for the Mute and We Are Handsome. There were, though, two very obvious issues that couldn't be ignored. Clearly the industry was over OPT and the venues it had used every which way over the past nine seasons! The other was the fact that yet again international buyer and media numbers were down. There was no bounce back after the GFC and there had been no increase in international marketing by IMG. Certainly the rise of the blogger and social media was a great distraction but it couldn't disguise the fact that export orders just weren't being generated as they once were.

Once 2012 was over we travelled straight back to Dubai to build TLG Consulting so we could generate the seed funding for our new fashion business model, which became known as Project Aeon, Aeon meaning for the next 'era'. One of the first clients to jump on board was Australian Wool Innovation, the Woolmark company. We helped to establish the strategy for the International Woolmark Prize and I became a judge for three of the five global regions, including India and the Middle East, Australia and Asia. Over the next few years I had the great honour to work alongside a number of international colleagues on the IWP, including Angelica Cheung (*Vogue*, China), designers Richard Nicoll and Kevin Carrigan (Calvin Klein), Bartley Ingram (Joyce), Imran Amed (the editor of *Business of Fashion*) and good friends Tim Blanks and David Bush. It is a brilliant initiative, not the least of the reasons being that it continues to put one of Australia's greatest fashion assets in the global spotlight, fine Merino wool. I have always been of the belief that if our founding fathers in Australia had the foresight to add value to our wool through the establishment of spinning mills and fabric manufacturers that we could have been an important fashion destination much earlier. Our wool for many years made the Italian industry famous for its fine fabrics. As a judge I was pleased to be on the panel that sent Dion Lee to the global final and as disappointed as he was that he didn't win, maybe more so. I was, however, on the panel that sent Rahul Mishra to the global final and he won.

While Kirsten and I were still based in Dubai, TLG Consulting was approached by the Qatar Government to develop a strategy to set up a regional fashion incubator. I'm very proud to say we beat some pretty big international competition, including the London College of Fashion, to win the tender. The project was to create the strategy to found a world's best-practice fashion incubator to assist local and regional talent to establish sustainable businesses. The strategy we created was broad ranging and incorporated an amazing studio to be situated overlooking the Arabian Gulf in the Pearl Development, as well as full-time support staff, production sup-port, internationally experienced mentors and export sales structure, including showrooms in Paris and New York. This could happen only in Qatar, given the gas-rich nation's ability to do anything it wants, including hosting the World Cup.

We were then approached to work for the Venetian Casino in Macau, alongside Troy Daniel's new events company Bespoke, to create a strategy for a new consumer fashion event for VIPs, similar to what I had done previously in Hong Kong. It was to be called Macau International Fashion Week. This, along with the fact that more and more leads to generate additional funding for Project Aeon were coming from Hong Kong, confirmed the rightness of the decision Kirsten and I had made to have Hong Kong as our new base. For Kirsten, however, it couldn't have come at a worse time as she had just been appointed to her dream job as style and beauty director for *Harper's Bazaar Middle East*. But by then we had clearly decided our future was Project Aeon and the best place for us to be was Hong Kong.

There was one more thing to do before we left Dubai. As is often the case in that city a car was sent to pick Kirsten and me up from our apartment in Dubai Marina to whisk us off to a private party at the impeccable Armani Hotel at the Burj Khalifa, the world's tallest building. On arrival we were met by the concierge and escorted straightaway to level 39, the home of the world-renowned Armani Suite, designed by Mr Armani himself and favoured by Tom Cruise during his filming of *Mission Impossible*. We were led into this incredible apartment with stunning views and to Kirsten's surprise we were the only ones there. She turned around to find me alone—the concierge had mysteriously disappeared—and I was down on my knee: 'Darling, will you marry me?'

Without hesitation she said yes. For my marriage proposal I presented her with a book I had written about the ring that was now on her finger. Its single central ruby had a long history in our family and had been left to me by my beloved grandmother, the one who all those years ago had instilled the intrigue for the fashion industry in me that had eventually led me to Kirsten. Unbeknown to me my grandmother had left it for safe keeping with my mother with instructions that she would know the right time to give it to me. To my great delight that was the moment when I told my mother I was going to ask Kirsten to marry me.

*

Following our engagement we embarked on another partnership. Given our increasing focus on Project Aeon and the inevitable need to use social media to promote it, Kirsten and I decided to jump in head first to this brave new world and learn from the inside. After much consideration we launched KirstenmeetSimon.com. It was a blog as well as a Facebook, Instagram and Pinterest platform. It basically chronicled our life, loves and travels together through our fortunate fashion journey. It was an instant success and after a series of launch initiatives we built our global followers pretty quickly to around three hundred thousand. We ended up with a publisher arranging commercial deals and the feedback from our KMS followers was really positive. We ran it for about eighteen months and together learnt a lot about the interaction between various social media platforms. Many of the KMS subscribers still follow us primarily through Kirsten's Instagram account, Kirsten Lock.

When MBFWA 2013 came around, Kirsten came with me to support the event, and to report for KMS from the front row. To my complete surprise and great honour I had been approached by *The Australian* newspaper to write The Verdict, the column Marion Hume had made famous. Marion first came to MBFWA as an international delegate for *The Financial Times*, fell in love with the country and, when the editorship of *Vogue Australia* became available, was recommended by Anna Wintour to take up the post. She did, but it was short-lived. Her journalistic approach, particularly her coverage of MBFWA, had the industry up in arms and advertisers heading south. *Vogue* is a magazine where the best commentary is made by who is not included within its pages and its readers were not used to the press-coverage style of a journalist who actually knows how to call it. Soon after leaving *Vogue* Marion found her rightful place as the writer of The Verdict. In 2013 she moved on and it was a great honour for me to fill her shoes. I took great pleasure in writing it, taking the *Vogue* approach!

KMS hired Julie Healy as our official photographer and set about letting all our followers around the world know about the event I had founded. It was amazing to be working with Julie again in a totally different capacity. She has now traded her career on the catwalk as a model for being one of Australia's new breed of emerging fashion photographers. Given her insider's edge the shots she took for us were beautiful, really adding a new dimension to our blog. Kirsten had been away from the Australian fashion industry for five years and it was very exciting for me to not only show her around the event but for her to touch base with a lot of old friends. The media also loved having her in the front row, sitting next to me with her great sense of style.

IMG had been listening closely to the industry and had finally decided to move venue. As Jarrad and I originally proposed as early as 2011, the Carriageworks in Eveleigh was the perfect choice. It has lots of venue options and endless configuration possibilities for collection shows—it is going to take a while for the industry to get bored in their new playbox. Aside from the new venue, there was much else to celebrate in 2013 and it was all reported on a daily basis by KMS. Both Jayson Brunsdon and Camilla and Marc celebrated their ten-year anniversaries at the event with brilliant shows. Aurelio Costarella celebrated thirty years in the industry and Lisa Ho her eighteenth. There were also some killer solo debut shows from Vanishing Elephant, Khalo, Emma Mulholland, From Britten and Phoenix Keating. With this talent the future was looking really bright. This year was also the first time that *all* the shows were streamed live, with Nicole Warne from Gary Pepper Girl, a newly signed IMG blogger, hosting the links. There was also a live pop-up screen in Martin Place, spreading the word on Australian designers, and a small online retail trial allowing certain items to be purchased direct from the catwalk. The highlight of the season, though, was the ingenious show produced by kaftan queen Camilla in Centennial Park.

In a giant Indian-inspired tepee Camilla brought the theatre of presentations back to MBFWA, which hadn't been seen for a number of seasons. The setting was a perfect backdrop to the never-ending cavalcade of colours and the catwalk playfulness of Georgia May Jagger. The other big superstar model to grace MBFWA this season was Joan Smalls, who had followed Jessica Stam as the face of Mercedes-Benz.

Kirsten and my days at MBFWA 2013 were a whirlwind of attending shows, media functions and designer parties and then writing until the small hours of each morning to keep the KMS family up to speed. It really added a new excitement and perspective for me. After spending a few years in the wilderness, so to speak, it gave me back a meaningful role at the event and I felt I was once again making a contribution to the industry through both KMS and The Verdict. Little did everyone know then that this was just the tip of the iceberg for what was about to come.

Back at our base in Hong Kong we continued our focus on Project Aeon, which was now really starting to gather momentum. AEON International Holdings Ltd was now registered in Hong Kong and we were developing two new business models for the fashion industry globally: the business-to-business model that would eventually become ORDRE.com and a new consumer model that is an internet fashion channel incorporating 'Shop the Runway' interactive video technology, a project named FWTV. ORDRE's inspiration really comes from the current limitations of fashion weeks and showrooms around the world to connect designers directly with fashion retailers and provides an additional online platform. Much of the development in its early days was as a direct reaction to the drop in buyer attendance at MBFWA. This is a trend that we are seeing around the world as buyers are travelling less and less to key markets and have precious little time and budget to explore secondary fashion weeks and new markets.

As has always been the case with The Lock Group, its companies are often established because of an opportunity that arises that is just too good to resist. Such was the case with the birth of our BRAND X. Now that I was based in Hong Kong a number of old and new clients approached me to handle their marketing communications. One in particular was Oroton, who were looking to expand their impact around the region. Kirsten had also been approached to style for *Tatler* magazine in Hong Kong and we decided to launch BRAND X together to manage all these projects. The Lock Group now consisted of three companies again, TLG Consulting, BRAND X and AEON. AEON continued to grow and take up more and more of our time, as we moved from concept to start-up mode, and so I invited my eldest son David to come to Hong Kong to take over BRAND X. David already had a number of years as a venue manager at MBFWA, had studied event production at Swinburne in Melbourne and worked with me on Dubai Fashion Week and was working in communications in Melbourne when the offer was made. In the tradition of the Lock family entrepreneurial spirit, David jumped at the opportunity and moved immediately to Hong Kong with his fiancée Kes. We lucked out again when Kes, who was an admin guru with a law firm in Melbourne, agreed to come on board with ORDRE. David and Kes are now married.

The balance of the year up until MBFWA 2014 was spent juggling the development and funding requirements of ORDRE. Even given the growth of The Lock Group over the past few years with the success of TLG Consulting and BRAND X, there was no way we were going to be able to cash flow the development of AEON ourselves. Much of the year was spent learning how to raise money in the world of venture capital, an area as foreign as Mars to me. I had always grown our businesses out of our own cash flow without any debt—well, except to those long-suffering MAFW creditors back in the early days. AEON was a completely different beast and we were now making a global play. By May 2014 we had made some great inroads and had travelled the world to pitch to investors in London and New York as well as Hong Kong.

Kirsten and I were also constantly back and forth to Sydney working on AEON but one trip stood out from all the rest: our wedding on 2 December 2013. Originally planned to be in an ice chapel built in the snow in Niseko it moved to Sydney given my father's ailing health and the fact that in the end it was going to be easier for other family and friends. Having said that, an international contingent flew in from all around the world for our special day. The ceremony was held in Marks Park, Bondi, on the headland overlooking the azure Pacific Ocean, thanks to the wedding planner of the century—well, really, events guru—and close friend Nikki Andrews. My son David was my best man supported by his younger brother, Jules. Kirsten's bridesmaids were her sister Mia and my daughter, Hannah Emily Rose. A real new-age family affair! My mother and father, Joy and David, joined Kirsten's parents, Mark and Lynn, in the most important front row of our lives. The wedding party then strolled along the ocean pathway to where else? Icebergs.

This restaurant has been the home of many special celebrations over the years for me. Maurice and his team once again presented a sublime feast and my brother, Rich, had us all in tears of laughter as our MC. Kirsten's cousin Phoebe Bacon—listen out for that name— presented us with a very special singing tribute and old friend Alex Dimitriades had us all on the dance floor with his fine grooves. The pictures from the day are so special, made all the more beautiful by amazing flowers thanks to another friend who has worked on many Fashion Week shows, ably assisted on occasion by Hannah, the talented Saskia Havekes. We were also really pleased to be able to share the pictures of the day with *Harper's Bazaar Bride*, thanks to Kellie Hush and her talented team.

It wasn't long before I was back again at MBFWA in April 2014, where I would be solo as Kirsten was engaged on a major fashion shoot. I was there with a very different agenda from previous years. We were now in the lead-up to the global launch of ORDRE and it was time to select which Australian designers we would invite to be part of our Designer Portfolio. ORDRE allows a global retail network of invitation-only buyers from prestigious department stores, multi-label boutiques and leading online retailers to access a curated portfolio of designers from the world's best fashion weeks and industries. It is an online channel that will sit alongside the traditional channels of fashion weeks and showrooms. I originally developed the concept as a result of the difficulty designers partici- pating in MBFWA and other fashion weeks around the world were experiencing because buyers weren't travelling as much. Creating an online wholesale channel just seemed obvious to me.

The development of ORDRE was now well underway and what better place to start inviting designers to be part of the portfolio than in Australia, I thought. MBFWA was the perfect vehicle to select those designers who had the ambition to export, were capable and also had the digital assets required for the platform, including fashion show videos and catwalk images. So that year at MBFWA it was back to what I do best: attending every show on the schedule.

It was a great way to really critique all the best Australian designers and identify those to invite to be part of ORDRE.

In only the second year at the Carriageworks the industry already felt really at home with the venue and the spaces. Unfortunately two very familiar faces were missing from the team. Graeme Lewsey had left IMG the previous season to take up a position in the Australian fashion industry that was always his destiny: CEO of the Virgin Australia Melbourne Fashion Festival. Lucia Labbate, who had risen through the ranks from receptionist at The Lock Group through to event director at IMG, had also departed and was now a senior account director working for Jack Bedwani at the projects. We were all really pleased when long-time Spinner Elle Persson was appointed by IMG to take over the reins in Sydney. Elle had started way back when, cutting her teeth on the MBFWA group shows. She was somewhat of a mentor to my daughter, Hannah, who did work experience with her at MBFWA, lining up models and working backstage for a number of seasons. Elle also worked with us freelance in Hong Kong and had done some work for Jarrad on IMG Fashion events in Istanbul, so it was great to have an old-school team member at the helm of our event.

I guess that is also how a lot of us in the Australian fashion industry feel about MBFWA, seeing it as 'our event'. It is. It might have been built by me with the support of thousands, but a lot of people, from designers, models, production specialists, hair and make-up experts, marketing and PR to buyers and media, now feel they own a piece of it given their direct involvement in this very special event. It is something we can all feel proud of as we reach our milestone 20th Anniversary celebrations in April 2015.

The 2014 season delivered a number of standouts for me. The best was the debut of the talented boys from Strateas Carlucci. I had been a champion of theirs from my involvement in the International Woolmark Prize, when they broke international precedent by winning both the men's and women's regional finals in Australia in 2014. Alex Perry secured the incredible model Alessandra Ambrosio to walk in a slick show. Alice McCall celebrated her tenth anniversary and We Are Handsome presented an inspiring show, complete with live snakes—a popular theme over the years—at Reservoir Gardens in Paddington. Other rising stars to watch included Haryono Setiadi and Phoenix Keating. The event also broke new ground in the consumer arena by presenting Mercedes-Benz Fashion Weekend Edition at the Carriageworks immediately following the industry event. It was a real sign of the times. IMG has also done a clever partnership deal with a huge social media platform in China to distribute the videos from MBFWA in the hope of growing the profile of Australian designers in the world's fastest-growing consumer market. For me the season crystallised the choices we made in which Australian designers to invite to be part of ORDRE. They included bassike, Camilla and Marc, Christopher Esber, Dion Lee, Ellery, Ginger & Smart, Josh Goot, Khalo, Lover, Toni Maticevski, Strateas Carlucci and Zimmermann.

Since the end of MBFWA in April, Kirsten and I have been on the road. Following presentations to the Australian designers on ORDRE we embarked on a series of market visits to secure designers for the platform and brief key retailers in preparation for our launch in November 2014. ORDRE initially will curate from eight markets around the world, including Australia, Shanghai, Seoul, Tokyo, New York, London, Paris and Milan. Designers include well-established houses looking to develop new markets and emerging designers looking to break into key markets. As creative director, Kirsten works with a number of really clever people around the world, including Julie Gilhart in New York and Yasmin Sewell in London, to identify and create the right balance in the portfolio. Both Julie and Yasmin are MBFWA alumni. Julie, when she was at Barneys New York, was one of the first US buyers I convinced to come to the event and her support went on to break a number of Australian designers into the NY market. Yasmin was originally also a buyer and then went on to a stellar career based in London, including stints at both Browns working for Mrs B and at Liberty.

It is now late in 2014, Kirsten and I have done three complete circumnavigations of the globe, spending a week at a time in each of the key markets as well as in Hong Kong where our global head-quarters are. While on the road I have been writing this book, on speeding trains, early in the mornings, in Parisian cafés, in lofts in New York, sitting on pebble beaches on the French Riviera—our honeymoon, which was cut short from two weeks to three days!—overlooking The Bund in Shanghai, from a bookshop in Tokyo and at the foot of my father's bed in Avalon, Australia. This has made the book less a retrospective about MBFWA and more about how the Australian fashion industry used the event to grow up. I wanted to capture what is happening now in the industry globally and my thoughts on where the Australian fashion industry goes from here.

It can sound a very glamorous life being on the road, travelling between the great fashion capitals of the world. While it is incredibly exciting the logistics of working constantly out of a suitcase and crossing multiple time zones are not without their challenges and frustrations, but we do love it. On 12 November 2014 WWD.com headlines announced that ORDRE was live and is now slowly and carefully building what I believe is going to be the defining global platform for the industry to do business. The trials and tribulations of building a business in the digital age are not dissimilar to those I experienced over twenty years ago when I founded MBFWA, and the analogies I noticed along the way are intriguing. For me it is all about helping the industry I love and am inspired by, surrounded as I am by innovation and creativity, building a team culture where everyone loves coming to work and going the extra yard and, hopefully this time, building that ski lodge in Japan.

*

As for the 20th Anniversary Year MBFWA in April 2015, while I am finishing these last chapters of my book Emily Weight at IMG will be pulling her hair out putting the schedule together. Thank heavens she is another Spinner who joined IMG a few years ago. At this time of year the team will be pitching the schedule and juggling the days and dates as much as I did for fifteen years. Designers will be demanding this and that, all insisting they have the right to a particular time slot and on-site or off-site location. Sadly, for only the second year out of the past nineteen, Jarrad Clark won't be there as he resigned from IMG in 2014 to take up a role as senior vice president of KCD Worldwide.

In the lead-up to the 2015 event new supporting sponsors will be announced. I imagine the continuing enthusiasm for the role of Mercedes-Benz Fashion Weekend Edition will be at play, potentially a new online distribution deal will be announced and the year's Australian Fashion Laureate will be presented. As it is our 20th Anniversary, I'm sure this will encourage more designers to participate than last season, but you can be reassured at some point that the media coverage somewhere will feature a 'who is not showing' story, as well as a skinny-model story on about day three. There will be lots of amazing shows from Australia's leading designers, who still see the event as relevant to their business, and fresh recruits who will make their debuts, hopefully to one or two rapturous applauses from the industry. Media coverage will be significant and will continue to build awareness and consumer demand for Australian designers, and orders will be written. As they should.

13

A Future for
Fashion Week

THIS SECTION HAS been hard to write, in more ways than you can imagine. Firstly, my amazing father, David Price Lock, passed away while I was working on it. You would understand from the early chapters what an inspiration he has always been and will continue to be for me. He had a glorious life and is one of the few who left this world with few regrets. This book is dedicated to him.

Secondly, I have struggled with how honest I can be with expressing my thoughts about what I see as the future for the Australian fashion industry—I don't want to upset anyone or burn any bridges in the Australian industry I love so dearly. Thirdly, I'm concerned the reader might perceive a self-interest in regard to my new business ORDRE. However, through everything I have written here it is evident that the business of fashion globally will turn more and more to selling wholesale collections online and that is why I have established ORDRE. To not talk about it in the context of where the industry goes from here would be wrong. Online ventures will solve the current dilemma faced by both designers and retailer buyers alike: that of connecting conveniently to each other. This doesn't mean the complete demise of fashion weeks or showroom networks. It can be an additional channel that sits alongside and complements the complete madness and logistical nightmare of the international fashion week circuits and designer showrooms and the many benefits the industry derives from these initiatives. For Australian designers it will put them on an equal platform with the best designers around the world and that is what I have been trying to do for the past twenty-five years!

*

In 1996, when I was producing the artwork for the very first delegate brochure for MAFW, the copy had to be painstakingly set through the use of bromides, and photographic negatives were used to produce chromaline proofs of the final artwork before it was sent to the offset printers. Once produced, the options were to post it to media and buyers, fax it and lose the coloured artwork and definition in the process, or hand deliver it to the right people. It was an expensive process and we could only afford to use about a dozen coloured photographic examples of the best Australian designers to encourage attendance at the event.

In 1996 Hotmail was launched. In 1998 we went live with afw.com.au. By 2001 half of the western world was using email and we could send low-res pictures as attachments. In 2000 Net-a-Porter was born. In 2004 Facebook was launched. In 2006 YouTube posted their first video. In 2010 Instagram was up and running. In 2014 ORDRE was launched globally. In the early 1990s, a computer with the processing capabilities of the iPhone today would have cost $3.87 million. In just twenty short years the world of fashion has been completely changed by the internet and the digital revolution that surrounds it. The $64 million-dollar question is, will MBFWA survive? I for one hope so but I believe it will be in a very different form.

MBFWA and its former incarnations as MAFW and RAFW has had a huge impact on the Australian fashion industry. The event has been a catalyst for so many things: growing the profile of Australian designers, generating national consumer demand, creating hundreds of millions of dollars of publicity for the designers and their stars, helping to start the Store Wars, and growing and developing aligned industries in modelling, hair and make-up, as well as production and marketing. It has provided work experience and industry exposure for countless thousands of fashion students and has introduced Australian fashion to many key industry influencers throughout the world. It has helped Australian designers expand internationally and has carried with them a very important message: that as a country we are creative, innovative and sophisticated, and can make a mark in one of the most competitive global industries, ready-to-wear fashion. The event and its designers have shown the world another aspect of our lucky country, one I believe relates to most Australians and many other people around the globe.

From my perspective my journey through the past twenty years of Fashion Week has been a joyous one. It has given me the foundation of all my business endeavours, allowed me to work with a team of people, many of whom I now count as great friends, provided me with an opportunity to meet supermodels and prime ministers, seen me travel the world countless times, share hilarious moments with my family and see my children grow up backstage and in the front row. I've met Anna Wintour and Suzy Menkes. I've partied with some of the best designers in the world … and Wayne Cooper! I helped put Australia on the fashion map globally, which I take great pride in. My journey through Fashion Week also led me to Kirsten, of all places in the middle of the desert, and it wasn't even an Australian one!

I have always loved being involved in the industry and its creative and innovative take on so many things. I do currently, though, find this attitude at odds when it comes to the business of fashion. I feel the industry needs to dismantle some of its edifices and embrace the digital age in a meaningful way to prosper. The current business-to-business models that exist and that are at the core of any fashion week strategy are an ongoing frustration to designers and fashion buyers around the world. I live and breathe them every day of my life as we build the ORDRE business. Let me share with you two real-life examples from both a designer's and a buyer's perspective.

A classic designer example is that of a highly credentialed Korean designer we work with. We recently arrived in his atelier in Seoul to find him and his staff frantically packing his new season collections into suitcases to accompany him and his team to Paris for showings. Each garment had to be documented for customs and then packed tight into a suitcase to fly more than halfway around the world. On arrival the designer and his head of sales and an assistant will check into a fashionable hotel they really can't afford after suffering the jet lag that only economy-class travel can provide. They will spend the next day unpacking the crumpled collection and steaming each piece to within an inch of its life to make it look picture perfect, like the photographs taken of the collection back at the Korean studio over two twelve-hour days for both the look books and individual product line sheets.

The collection will be shown in a leading Parisian showroom, sitting alongside another eight designers, a number of whom will have a significantly higher profile. The hope is that these designers will attract buyers to the showroom and they will be introduced to these lesser-known brands. It has taken a number of seasons of lobbying the queen bee who runs the showroom in Paris just to be accepted onto the roster. This is fashion week in Paris at the end of the international fashion circuit.

Along with my friend from Korea another ninety designers will present their collections on the runway as part of the official schedule. Approximately another two hundred designers will also be represented in competing showrooms just like he is. This includes the London Showrooms, which are almost completely sponsored by the UK Government and the British Fashion Council, where over thirty British designers are showcased in a very well-marketed and aggressive approach, following on from London Fashion Week two weeks before. A number of the major designers from New York Fashion Week and Milan Fashion Week are also re-showing their collections in Paris to try to get buyers who didn't attend the other fashion weeks to take a look now.

My Korean friend can only afford to stay in Paris for the five days of showings. The head of the showroom has assured him there is interest but everyone is so busy while they are in Paris. She hasn't been able to secure him any appointments but has reassured my friend that the buyers will be flooding through over the five days. Each day from 10 a.m. my Korean friend and his team sit patiently in the showroom waiting for the buyers to arrive. More often than not they are sent off to the corner café pending the arrival of a big buyer coming to see one of the more established designers. They are told that rather than waiting eagerly in their corner to pounce after the main designer has presented, the showroom sales assistant will quickly direct the buyer's attention to his new collection. Unfortunately time and time again the big buyers just don't have the time to stop and talk to him. In fact, after having really only a passing glance at the main designers they request the look book and other information documents be emailed through so they can consider sending an order by return email when they get back to the office.

The five days continue on as such and eventually six buyers have seen our Korean designer, who arrived in Paris with so much great expectation. Each of these buyers spent about seven to ten minutes quickly reviewing the collection before they departed for the Chanel show or some such designer, or for another fleeting showroom appointment. By the end of the five days no confirmed orders have been made. All the clothes are then packed back into the suitcases, ensuring the customs forms are correct. They head back to the airport for a connecting flight through Heathrow to Seoul.

Two weeks later, after the final seasonal orders have been sent out to the makers, a US$12,500 order comes from a multi-label boutique in Russia who saw the collection in Paris. The showroom takes 15 per cent commission on top of the fee for service over the showing days and fortunately the order makes it to the Korean studio in time for the makers to include it.

Our Korean friend also shows his full collection at Seoul Fashion Week but apart from a few regional buyers from China no other international buyers attend, which is the reason for the showings in Paris. Not deterred by the results in Paris, the Korean designer is now considering securing a showroom in New York as well to target the US buyers. He is also considering moving from Paris to show in Milan. The future could potentially involve showing seasonally in Seoul on the catwalk to support the important home market and then shipping the collection around the world to various locations to try to get in front of those elusive buyers, just like the other top five thousand ready-to-wear designers around the world who rightfully claim their collections are suitable for luxury department stores, speciality multi-label boutiques and prestigious online retailers. The competition is off the scale!

From the buyer's perspective, ever since the myth about consumers never buying online without trying things on first was completely obliterated by the success of Net-a-Porter and the likes, the retail industry globally hasn't been the same. Basically the amount of available outlets for clothes doubled overnight. Now there are offline bricks-and-mortar stores as well as online outlets, both competing for the same market. At the same time there is the worldwide phenomenon of the fast-fashion chains, which have positioned themselves around ready-to-wear trends at a fraction of the cost of the original and promote the idea that it is all right to mix luxury with fast fashion. Added to this scenario is the fact that leading designers are using their fashion week shows to grow their consumer profiles and are then capitalising on this by doing less expensive diffusion ranges with any number of fast-fashion chains. Then there is the ongoing fallout of the GFC.

With so many more doors open, more obstacles and the same market size the result has been a predictable one. Retailers have had to become more competitive to survive and one way they can do this is to reduce procurement costs. The end result is fewer buyers, reduced orders and cuts to travel budgets. It is interesting to look at the current buying process through the activities of an actual buyer to try to put the role of all fashion weeks into perspective. The issues and frustrations buyers from around the world feel are universal and perhaps best summed up by a good friend of ours who buys for a leading department store in New York.

She has been with the same organisation for the past ten years and has weathered the changing environment. Ten years ago she had a substantial travel-buying budget that allowed her to travel to London Fashion Week, Milan Fashion Week and Paris Fashion Week, usually extending her stay in Paris for follow-up meetings, twice a year. She would start buying the season in New York when market week opened about ten days before New York Fashion Week. In all, the buying process went on for about six weeks, often extended by perhaps another ten days when she got back to her office to finalise all the orders from the European designers. Ten years ago she was also allowed to accept invitations from second-tier fashion weeks, where she could discover new designers to secure exclusively for the New York market. She actually attended MBFWA twice about eight or nine years ago. She also accepted invitations from São Paolo Fashion Week and had visited Tokyo Fashion Week once in 2007.

In 2008, continuous bad economic news was topped off in September when Lehman Brothers went bankrupt. As we now know, it sparked the global recession, which would last until 2012. This financial situation, and the continuous media reports that went along with it, had a profound impact on consumer spending and confidence. The ready-to-wear fashion industry around the world in some areas was in free fall. In the United States in particular, multi-label boutiques literally shut overnight as big-spending customers tightened their belts. Those that soldiered on pulled back to the basics and the most established designers, no longer wanting to experiment with emerging designers. For many Australian designers and other designers from non-core ready-to-wear markets the effect was devastating. As an example, Collette Dinnigan's stockists in the United States dropped from a high of about thirty stores to only five. Department stores played it safe and the big designers were extremely cautious, not only about keeping collections sellable and commercial but also in slowing down or completely stopping franchised-owned stores. Many of the big international houses turned their attention to China over this period, where the GFC was having limited effect on the enormous domestic growth.

From a retailer's perspective, when Net-a-Porter broke new ground in online shopping in 2000 and had grown both its reach and impact globally by 2008, it legitimised the purchasing online of ready-to-wear designers. Consumers began turning to the internet in the hope of finding better value than at bricks-and-mortar retailers. The online shopping world was exploding and in response department stores started to stock very conservatively because you could now find every designer you had ever heard of online. Designers were also opening more and more online stores so they could earn double the margins and even at discounts could still achieve decent profits. Given the reduced overheads of establishing an online shop designer sales and close-outs were more competitive than traditional department stores and multi-label boutiques. With the sheer number of online retailers their combined effect had an enormous impact on the logistics of the business worldwide. DHL, UPS, FedEx and many other delivery services began to offer three-day turnarounds to anywhere in the world, and today same-day delivery is available in more and more markets. Simple return policies meant the focus on having to try something on first slowly but surely disappeared and traditional retailers started to become showrooms by de facto. Customers would try on expensive ready-to-wear pieces then turn around and purchase the item at the best online price in the world, which was then delivered to their front door almost immediately.

Fast-fashion retailers or high-street retailers that copy runway designs and reproduce them in cheaper fabric and at a certain price point always existed before but the GFC gave them a new reason for being. Not only in the past decade has the quality of mass production increased tenfold but also the speed in which a garment can now be brought to market is astounding. From the moment of ripping off a top designer on Instagram or Style.com to its arrival in a flagship fast-fashion store on Fifth Avenue in New York can be just four to six weeks. The original piece from the designer won't arrive in their Fifth Avenue boutique until eighteen weeks later and it could be ten times the price. Our fast-fashion friends, however, understand what consumers want and they don't want to wait another six months for the new season's merchandise to arrive. They want the look they saw on Instagram from the runway at Paris Fashion Week now, and they also want something new again next week when they walk back into the same store.

Trends and new designers are being shown somewhere in the world every day and the design teams of the fast-fashion retailers are experts at scouring the world for inspiration and producing a never-ending series of new collections to arrive quickly in-store. Our department store friend who had relied on two major seasonal drops a year is now faced with a customer who expects new merchandise and collections every time they walk into the store. Fast-fashion chains have perfected their business model through globalisation, which has allowed production levels and turnaround times to be established to sustain this new consumer-purchasing pattern. To add insult to injury my now long-suffering department store buyer has had to deal with an ongoing series of collaborations by her most loyal top designers as they produce brilliant diffusion collections in collaboration with any one of half a dozen fast-fashion chains to present consumers with the designer's look at a fraction of the price.

The GFC helped put a focus on the relevance and role of online sales because of more competitive pricing. Consumer confidence and spending capacity helped to support the double-digit growth of the fast-fashion industry and at the same time a little thing called social media exploded around the world. Thanks originally to the likes of Style.com the industry pretty much knew what was happening on the runways as soon as a new collection was released. I'm pretty sure the fast-fashion chains thought Style.com was really cool but then Facebook and Instagram took the runway looks to the consumers of the world. When Instagram was launched, every want-to-be fashionista following their favourite fashion celebrity or designer could sit front row with them as the world's best designers presented their new season's collections. I actually know within seconds sometimes what the latest collection looks are thanks to friends and people I follow who post video on Instagram from the front row. For millions and millions and millions of fashion-forward consumers around the world this generates one simple response: 'I want to buy that NOW.'

The season before last Karl Lagerfeld presented his Chanel supermarket-inspired show. Apparently it generated two billion social media impressions around the world. The calls of 'Where can I buy those amazing trainers from the show?' was deafening. So what happens to this pent-up consumer demand? The fashion-savvy crew head straight to Moda Operandi, where with a 50 per cent deposit they can pre-order the original for delivery in six months' time, being one of the first in the world to buy the original. For many others they will keep an eye on their local brand of the global fast-fashion chain to see if an 'inspired' version of the same thing shows up at a fraction of the cost. For the balance it will be about unrequited love and the hope that maybe in six months' time they will be reminded about their fashion crush when they shop online or walk into their favourite department store.

So what of my friend the buyer? What does this mean for their business and the designers they deal with, who pretty much still present collections at a traditional fashion week somewhere in the world? Firstly, they have had to respond to the competition of online sales by trying to play to potentially their biggest asset: the physical theatre of fashion that can't be replicated online. This has seen many department stores and multi-label boutiques upgrade their merchandising design and layout to generate more appeal to customers, as well as a number of inspiring new interior design layouts and the inclusion of lifestyle aspects into traditional retail spaces, including cafés and restaurants. Some of my favourite modifications are Selfridges in London, Le Bon Marché in Paris, and Opening Ceremony, Jeffrey and Barneys in New York. It has also put new emphasis on the importance of customer service, both on the floor and after sales. However, one of the biggest changes to the industry has been the pressure department stores and multi-label boutiques have put on designers to increase the number of drops or deliveries each year, a direct result of the strategy implemented by the fast-fashion retailers who constantly have new season collections arriving in-store. This is now the norm in regards to customer expectation and the days of having two seasonal drops a year are long gone.

Originally the seasonal drops were spring/summer and then autumn/winter, although on occasion deliveries were split. Pressure was then put on designers to present cruise or resort collections to be delivered prior to Christmas, before mainline spring/summer arrived in February. Then the push came for pre-fall to be dropped in June/July before mainline autumn/winter is delivered in August/September. This now means that most buyers' expectations are that an established designer is producing four collections a year. There is even pressure on some designers to present six collections a year if you include pre-pre-fall and pre-cruise. These timings are focused on the northern hemisphere buying cycle and account for the majority of ready-to-wear designer orders placed around the would, perhaps as much as 75 per cent of all orders.

It is only the mainline collections of spring/summer and autumn/winter that are traditionally shown on the catwalk at a fashion week. However, in recent years some designers have been also showing cruise/resort on the catwalk around May/June. This trend has been led again by Karl Lagerfeld at Chanel, where he selects a different exotic location each season to present Chanel's cruise collection. Many others, including Dior, have now followed. So our poor buyer is now given instructions to ensure designers who are selected by the store are able to have multiple stock deliveries throughout the year. This strategy comes with the requirement to review and purchase a number of collections from the same designer, the majority now not shown on a catwalk but purely in a showroom. That showroom is more often than not located away from New York where she is based. As previously explained, from the designer's perspective they are eager to have showroom representation in multiple cities to address this issue.

Ah, but at least the buyer has some respite when it comes to the tradition of buying at fashion week, especially New York Fashion Week. She can rely on an efficient schedule of centralised shows and the ability to review collections on models. She can then directly select from the catwalk the best outfits for the seasonal buy after seeing how fabrics and silhouettes fit and drape on real people—well, models at least—and not just hanging on a rack in the showroom. It is a nice thought that has driven the international fashion week circuit for a number of decades. The reality, however, is now very different.

The largest catalyst for change at all international fashion weeks has been social media, with perhaps Instagram being the biggest culprit. For many designers it has changed the focus of these once industry-only wholesale events into content generators for social media to directly engage consumers. Once a designer would put a few mad outfits at the end of a catwalk show to try to get page three in the newspaper but now it seems the production of entire collections is focused towards generating the greatest social media coverage possible. This has become a game where designers are trying to outdo each other with unique venues, over-the-top production techniques and often collections that only vaguely resemble what is back at the showroom and will ultimately go into production. The social media coverage is phenomenal. All the fashion bloggers have been moved into the front row so they can take better pictures and video. This also moves them closer to the A-list celebrities who have now been crammed in to provide even more content for social media. Venues have been selected to provide incredible visual backdrops to the collections and the themes in the collections have been pushed beyond their commercial applications to emphasise the designer's new direction. The pared-down and saleable version is left back in the showroom. Our friend the buyer has now been pushed to the second row to make way for the likes of Anna Dello Russo and her 680,000 Instagram followers.

It doesn't stop there. Many designers have become disillusioned with the central venues that have been used in New York at the Lincoln Center and have decided to show off-site, selecting one-off venues that provide better creative imagery for social media. A number have decamped to Made Fashion Week downtown, which actually underwrites production costs for emerging designers through their very successful corporate sponsorship program. Remember Westfield Wharf 3? Mercedes-Benz has now pulled out of New York Fashion Week because of lack of investment returns as a result of designers moving away and the impact of Made Fashion Week. At the same time the new owners of IMG, William Morris Endeavour, who own New York Fashion Week, have announced that they will be buying Made Fashion Week. February 2015 was New York Fashion Week's last outing at the Lincoln Center. The Council of Fashion Designers of America have bought the New York Fashion Calendar that for years has been the arbitrator of the schedule of shows. What the future now holds for one of the powerhouse fashion weeks in the world is unclear.

Meanwhile, last season my buyer friend had to endure the completely unrealistic challenge of having to buy as best she could with reduced numbers in her buying team and travel budget. This only allowed her to attend New York Fashion Week, where she is based, and Paris Fashion Week for ten days. Her season went something like this. All the New York designers opened their showrooms a week before New York Fashion Week, and every designer and their dog was in her face to make an appointment. In addition, a number of showrooms promoting designers from Milan, London and Sydney were presenting collections before fashion week. The week was beyond hectic, running uptown and downtown and on average spending twenty minutes with each designer, with no time to actually write orders in the showroom. New York Fashion Week then started and it was back-to-back fashion shows all over town, as few wanted to use the Lincoln Center. In between shows salespeople were trying to drag her into showrooms for appointments. Late nights started to kick in as this was the only time she had left to try to draft orders from the many inadequate line sheets that had been handed out or emailed through from showrooms.

My friend was really looking forward to seeing the Alexander Wang show. The invitation arrived for a venue in Brooklyn, another first on the schedule. As the show was outside Manhattan buses had been laid on but it was a nightmare and many guests had to miss both the show before and the show after on the schedule. My friend arrived at the warehouse venue that could have really been anywhere and its production set-up was in the round, a buyer's nightmare. The set was full of metal shapes to add to the industrial feel of the sports luxe vibe of the collection. The girls charged out, walking in all sorts of configurations through the maze of shapes, one through the middle, one across the back, and another around the outside. My buyer friend didn't know where to look as clothes flashed by her. Marco would not have been happy! She couldn't even get a clear shot of the clothes on her iPhone. It was difficult anyway from the second row because there was no tiered seating and the fashion bloggers had clearly taken up permanent residency in the front row.

The Instagram videos, however, were amazing, given you didn't even need to edit them as girl after girl flashed by. About fifty people posted videos directly from the front row, with the total combined number of followers being approximately ten million viewers. This didn't even count the Facebook impressions, that of Style.com or hundreds of other online sites. Consumers around the world were clambering for a collection they couldn't buy for six months. However, have no fear, as Alexander Wang for H&M, inspired by this collection, was to drop before Christmas. But the originals would not arrive in-store until the following February.

Meanwhile, my buyer friend headed back to the Alexander Wang Manhattan showroom to draft an order, as it was not possible to do so at the show as it only provided a fleeting overall impression of the collection and not all the pieces were on the runway. When the shows in New York eventually came to an end the fashion pack moved off to London and Milan, where my buying friend had also gone in years past but budget cuts meant that Paris was her only option. She now had a ten-day break before she was to arrive in Paris. The New York–based showrooms were on her case to complete her appointments and place orders, and the London designers and those in Milan, who were also showing in Paris, were also on to her to lock down appointments while she was in Paris. Her email inbox was getting clogged with line sheets, look books and images from shows already held. Paris was going to be a nightmare.

Her bosses at the department store had also engaged the services of Lambert And Associates, one of the world's leading sourcing agents, to help set up appointments with potential key designers and suppliers in Paris. The itinerary was looking hellish, with fashion shows and showroom appointments from dawn until dusk, while fighting the Parisian traffic every inch along the way. Outside of the existing designers she already stocks and has to visit, the new appointments and shows she wanted to see and the must-attend appointments that Lambert And Associates were organising, there were perhaps another three hundred or so aspiring designers showing in Paris who just weren't going to be able to break into her itinerary. Many, in fact, are the future of her business. One was our designer from Korea.

*

Do you sort of get the feeling the system is broken? Try to put this into perspective and realise that the above scenario is just for mainline shows. This process has to be repeated for at least four collections a year, if not more. People try to tell me that the life of an international fashion buyer is a glamorous one. The reality is stale baguettes at midnight alone in a hotel room looking at line sheets.

Where does MBFWA fit into this chaotic world and what of its future? There are a number of facts that need to be addressed. The reality is that given the situation of the present industry environment very few international buyers will attend MBFWA. There are no travel budgets and even less executive time to be dedicated to a fashion week away from the main game. Our designers who have international ambitions realised this long ago. While they might have grown up through MBFWA, launching themselves in Australia, their international wholesale aspirations mean that many either show in New York, London, Paris or Milan or have an agent in one of these cities. This includes a range of designers like Zimmermann, Ellery, Dion Lee, Josh Goot, Toni Maticevski, Akira Isogawa, Camilla and Marc, Christopher Esber, bassike, Ginger & Smart, Romance Was Born, Song for the Mute, sass & bide, Alice McCall, Strateas Carlucci and Haryono Setiadi, among others. They don't use MBFWA to drive international sales at all. If they participate in the event it is to support their Australian business and consumer fan base.

The other reality is that if designers are using the event legitimately to generate wholesale orders from Australian-based retailers then the timing of the event is too late. Originally I established the timing as a compromise between being late in the Australian spring/summer buying season and early in the international cruise/resort season in May. While the event has been brought back to mid April it is now still too late for the Australian department stores and multi-label boutiques to use to buy spring/summer. Most of the orders have been placed during February and March because of their insistence that designers deliver spring/summer in-store in August—too early in my opinion. Any orders generated from

MBFWA are usually just topping up what has already been ordered from the showroom previously. The event obviously still provides a very effective platform to launch new designers, where buyers often watch a designer develop over a number of seasons before they place a first order. The event is still invaluable for shining a media spotlight on our industry and for producing incredible content for social media and online distribution.

On top of all that, I am very concerned about the impact of Mercedes-Benz pulling out of New York Fashion Week. They have sent a message around the world that each fashion week they sponsor will be judged on its own merits and against certain investment-return parameters. Hopefully if IMG can both bring together the schedules of Mercedes-Benz Fashion Week New York and Made Fashion Week and find a new central venue, such as the proposed new Cultural Shed by the Hudson River, then they might be able to pull Mercedes-Benz back in. In Australia IMG's influence and global partnership with Mercedes-Benz was instrumental in getting them to return to the event for what I believe to be a contract that expires after 2015, but what then? If Mercedes-Benz doesn't see the content that generates the media coverage of the event in Australia being worthwhile will they also leave our fashion week? If that happens could a replacement be found? Without a replacement could the event commercially stand on its own two feet? I know from experience it can't. Is the writing on the wall for MBFWA? After twenty years and all it has done to promote and launch the careers of countless Australian designers and grow the industry, is it all over? Could MBFWA continue to exist as a trade event based on wholesale collections and still have an effective role on the international fashion week circuit in light of the incredible changes that have happened over the past twenty years? I think it can and this is exactly what would need to be done:

Step One: (SPL to fill in blank)
Step Two: (SPL to fill in blank)

Step Three: (SPL to fill in blank)
Step Four: (SPL to fill in blank)

If IMG would like to contact me and pay me a small fortune as a consultant I would be happy to fill in the blanks. Ha!

I would, however, like to propose a different future for Australian Fashion Week and I'm happy to tell anyone who will listen. We were the mouse that roared twenty years ago when we launched the first fashion week in the southern hemisphere on the international fashion week circuit. It is time to again be global leaders. My opinion is that in the future all fashion weeks will be of more value to the industry if they focus on consumers rather than, as they do currently, the industry. A radical shift of perspective and timing is required and the collections shown need to change from wholesale collections to those that are available retail and in-store. In Australia this means that MBFWA should continue to be held in Sydney but move to a time in August or September when the majority of the new season's spring/summer collections have arrived in-store.

I truly believe that over the next decade all fashion weeks around the world will start to focus more and more on consumers and show collections that are immediately available for sale. We are already starting to see this. Burberry has been leading the charge and recently Moschino presented a collection that was already in-store and available online to take advantage of the social media coverage of their fashion show. The billions and billions of social media engagements currently made from fashion week shows are basically going to waste as consumers can't buy these clothes for six months. Can you imagine if Karl Lagerfeld delivers his show from Paris Fashion Week, it is instantly beamed around the world and then those clothes are already available to buy? There will be a stampede and queues around the block at Chanel stores and a realisation of the direct-investment return from what has been spent on the show. King Karl has already intimated to the press that this is what might happen. I wouldn't be surprised if his parting legacy when he leaves

Chanel is that he moves his spring/summer show from October to the following March, when that collection has arrived in-store, and does a similar shift with his autumn/winter and cruise collections.

When MAFW burst onto the scene every city around Australia was basically jealous. They all had fashion industries to varying degrees and they wondered why they couldn't have an international fashion week too. The answer is obvious, but it created a new movement spearheaded by Melbourne with the development of a number of consumer-focused fashion festivals. Australia as a result is the only country in the world where almost every major city has an established fashion festival supporting the local industry. These mainly consumer-focused events picked up on the opportunity that Fashion Week in Sydney created and the consumer eagerness to attend shows as the industry did in Sydney.

The March autumn/winter-based Melbourne Fashion Festival and its sponsors—originally L'Oréal and subsequently Virgin Australia—embraced this philosophy and led the charge. I absolutely applaud what the Melbourne Fashion Festival has achieved. It is, at the moment, without peer the best fashion festival in the world and made all the better by having my friend and boy genius Graeme Lewsey running it. Perth, Adelaide and Brisbane should also be acknowledged for the valuable fashion festivals they have created to drive fashion retail in their respective cities. It is now Australian Fashion Week's role to become the spring/summer bookend in Sydney.

While MAFW/RAFW may have been the catalyst, its legacy in the response from other capital cities in creating fashion festivals is in my opinion one of the most valuable things the event has done for our industry. It is time that Australian Fashion Week became Australia's best fashion festival and gave Melbourne a run for its money—sorry, Graeme. This should be based around the rightful promotion of autumn/winter collections in Melbourne in March and the spring/summer collections in Sydney in August/September and this will be of huge value to the Australian fashion industry, much more so than the contribution MBFWA is currently making. IMG have made attempts to develop the Sydney Fashion Festival, an event I created and which is based at the Sydney Town Hall, but it will always be seen as an after-thought as long as MBFWA exists in April. It will never develop the momentum it needs from the industry to be in every way the equivalent of the Virgin Australia Melbourne Fashion Festival.

Australian Fashion Week could be reinvented around a central schedule of individual designer shows and retail shows. As has happened in Melbourne it could embrace every aspect of the fashion industry and fashion retail. It could create a point of difference and positioning to Melbourne to be the ultimate complement to it. It could be used in exactly the same way as the current industry event is used, to showcase new talent, to provide work experience for various aspects of the industry and to invite international guests to be exposed to the Australian industry. Let's also finally bring back the nationally televised Australian Fashion Awards and make it an anchor event in the week of the show. The list of ideas and components that might be added could go on forever—give me a call.

Then we need to get Team Australia back together. Let's not just build the event as a national fashion retail event but as a global one. Let's use the event as Melbourne does to be a catalyst for international shopping tourism and add even greater value for the industry. Let's get the backing of government departments and anyone else who can help build Australian Fashion Week into the biggest powerhouse fashion retail event in the Asia Pacific.

While I'm back on my soapbox, I'd like to make a shout-out to the newly formed Australian Fashion Chamber. Not much has happened since its launch, apart from a few well-meaning mentoring lectures and another round of awards for the chosen few. The Australian Fashion Chamber should on behalf of the industry be creating strategies for growth and development and leading from the front. It should be helping IMG sort out the future of MBFWA or Australian Fashion Week, and figuring out, given the changing global marketplace, how it can help grow business for Australian designers. Do we need a showroom strategy like the British Fashion Council? Do we need an incubator program like I developed in the Middle East or like the one run by the Council of Fashion Designers of America in the United States? Do we need to produce international showcases for Australian designers at international fashion weeks as we have done in the past? What digital and social media platforms can benefit the industry? The government and industry will only support clear, well-articulated strategies that have broad industry support and the Australian Fashion Chamber has the capacity to do this, as I suggested it could when I first approached the current chairman to jointly establish the initiative. As is on the record, my support was rejected at the time but I'm always happy to help. Again, give me a call.

While I think about it, my old rival Mrs Fish had it right, back in the day with Wharf 3. Well, partly. Westfield does have a very important role to play in the development of the Australian fashion industry and the establishment of Australian Fashion Week as the country's and the region's potentially most important fashion retail event. They failed all those years ago at sponsoring an industry event but their rightful role is as the principal or naming-rights sponsor of a consumer-focused Australian Fashion Week held annually in August or September. To me they are the perfect partners as they are the equivalent of the United Nations of fashion. They love everyone from Zimmermann and Dion Lee to Myer and David Jones. They umbrella every Australian designer brand in their centres throughout Australia and would significantly benefit from driving a consumer frenzy nationally around the arrival in-store of the new season collections of Australian designers. Just imagine what they could also do as the digital and broadcast partner of the Australian Fashion Awards and the role they could play in international showcases for Australian designers along with Team Australia. I think their new outlets in New York and London could be a real help there.

Fashion weeks should now belong to consumers and this will best benefit the industry in the long run to sell more clothes. Fashion weeks are not needed purely as a way to sell wholesale collections. There is a new thing called the internet for that! My hope is that in the very near future Westfield Australian Fashion Week will herald the start of the new spring/summer season of Australian designers across the country. The excitement of thousands upon thousands of consumers attending the event and millions engaged through social media will have a direct result at the cash registers. The event will be made even more special by all the celebrities sitting front row, the fashion bloggers going berserk outside taking shots of street style and the media having a feeding frenzy when Lara Bingle turns up with her new baby! It will help Australian designers compete against imports and the fast-fashion chains. It will herald new stars and promote them through the nationally broadcast Australian Fashion Awards. It will attract leading global influences in the world of fashion to help open doors for our designers overseas. This is where the value of the event lies now, not in selling collections six months prior to a handful of buyers. That can already be done online. My hope is that consumer demand created from Westfield Australian Fashion Week will grow wholesale orders anyway.

At the same time the Australian Fashion Chamber needs to become more strategically and business focused. It needs to expand its current directors to include individuals who are currently at the cutting edge of business designer development nationally and internationally, who have specific experience relevant to the job that needs to be done. It needs to establish a showroom, incubator, international showcase and digital platform programs as a starting point. It needs to become the ringmaster and the catalyst for Team Australia. It needs to quickly establish a funding model and immediately appoint a full-time CEO and executive team. As per my original plan!

So there you have it, that is what I think and as everyone knows I'm always around to help. In reflecting on this last chapter I can't help but recall the words of my father, David P. Lock, to provide the inspiration for the future of the Australian fashion industry: 'Don't be afraid to change and don't be afraid to fail.' This philosophy has been my touchstone for the past twenty-five years.

As for me I'll always be in the front row, still the biggest fan our industry has ever had.

MAFW Participants (1996–2014)

9, 96, 2 for the Show, Aanchal Chanda, Adagio, Adam Wore Short Pants, Adele Weiss, Ae'lkemi, AG by Arthur Galan, Ageman, AJE, Akira, Alannah Hill, Alexandra Barter, Alexandra Nea, Alex Perry, Alice McCall, Alistair Trung, Alpha60, Am Eyewear, Amanda Cummings, Amanda Garrett, Amadio for FOX14, Amar, Amber & Thomas, Ammo, Anaessia, Ananya, An Ode To No One (Haryono Setiadi), Andre Laurent, Andrea Cainero, Andrea Moore, Andrea Rembeck, Andysoma, Ania Fabjanczyk, Anna & Boy, Anna Quan, Anna Thomas, Anna Westcott, Annah Stretton, Annie Who, Annoyingly Enormous, Anthea Crawford, Anthony Leigh Dower, Ant!podium, Anupama Dayal, April Marie Swimwear, Aquintic, Arabella Ramsay, Archit Agarawal, Arlene Clement, Arnsdorf, Artsu, Arx, Asanovski, Ashe, Ash to Gold, Aurelia Santoso, Aurelio Costarella, Autonomy, Avatar, Ayaka Ichikawa, Ayako Goto, Azzolini, Baboon, Bambam Clothing, Bang, Bare, Bare by Rebecca, Barney Cheng, Base, Bassike, Baylene, Beat Poet, Bec & Bridge, Bei Na Wei, Bela Voce, Belinda Fairbanks, Bella Mia Design, Ben Smith, Benjamin Mach for Robyn Caughlan, Benjamin Lau, Bernard Chandran, Bettina Liano, Betty Tran, Bhalo, Bianca Spender, Billion Dollar Babes, Bikinii Five Oh, Blanc + Delta, Blanchet, Bless'ed Are The Meek, Blue Australia, Body, Bondi Bather, Bonita Cheung, Bowie, Bowie Genus, Breathless/Self, Brent Wilson, Brian Rochford, Brigid McLaughlin, Bracewell, Bronx & Banco, Brooke Benson, By Johnny, Byron McGilvray, By Weave, Cable Melbourne, C-design, C People, Cameo, Cameron Dunlop, Camilla, Camilla and Marc, Caravana, Carena West, Carl Kapp, Carla Zampatti, Carli Turland, Carlie Waterman, Carlson, Caroline Fuss, Caslazur, Catherine Maple-Brown, Celia Loe, Ch3mical Three, Charlie Brown, Charlotte O'Carrigan, Charmagne Mewing, Chitra's Closet, Chloe Fitzjames, Choul Kim, Christina Exie, Christopher Baldwin, Christopher

Dobosz, Christopher Esber, Cibella, Ciara Nolan, Circus Girl, Claire Tout, Claude Maus, Clean Cut (sustainability group show), Cleonie, Cohen et Sabine, Collecting Pretty Boys, Collette Dinnigan, Constance & Violet, Country Road, Covers, Curtis, Crystal Tsoi, Cybele, Cynthia Thai, D'oreen, Daniel Avakian, Daniel Cho, Daniel K, Daniel Yam, Daryl, Davis Eyes, DearDenim, Deborah Pak, Defy Fashion, Desert Designs, Dev r Nil (India), Devious, Dhini, Diane Freis, Diet Coca-Cola Little Black Dress Show, Dion Lee, Diyana Kosso, Dizingof, DNA, Donna Sgro, Dorian Ho, Doris Lee, Dot & Herbey, Doublen Nekola, Doris Q, Duvenage, Dylan Cooper, Dyspnea, Eastern Block, Easton Pearson, Ed And Bek, Eduardo Calucag, Eileen Kirby, Elena Verdiants, Elissa McGowan, Ellery, Elliatt, Ellin Ambe, Elliot Ward-Fear, Emily Cheong, Emma Malady, Emma Milikins, Emma Mulholland, ericaamerica, Erin Loh, Ess.Laboratory, Estate, estate red label, ezzavezza, Faddoul, fait a main, Fani Lei Ka Yu, fashion assassin, Fernando Frisoni, Fischer Von Meszlenyi, Flair, Flamingo Sands, Flannel, Fleur Wood, Flora Cheong-Leen, Flowers For A Vagabond, Fonda Johenson, Fox 14, Franciz, Friedrich Gray, Friend of Mine, Frisoni Finetti, From Britten, Fru Fru, Funkulo By Sam Elsom, Funky Threads, Fuschia, Gabriel Lee, Gabriel Scarvelli, Gail Sorronda, Galanni, Garment, Gary Bigeni, Genevieve R, Geoffrey Parker, George Chen, George Gross, George Wu, Gina Kim, Ginger & Smart, Glamour Pussy, Glen Rollason, Gorman, Goodone, Guy Hastie, Gwendolynne, Gypsea, Hallican Boodie, Hannah McNicol, Han, Hana-Lia Borovik, hansel, Happy Beads, Hardwick, Harry Who, Hayley Dawson, Hayley Elsaesser, Helen Cherry, Helen Talevski, High Tea with Mrs Woo, Holic, Honey Hartley, Hotel Bondi Swim, Howard Showers, Huong, Hussy, Illionaire, Inder Dhillon, Injury, Inksoffjohn, Indjapink, Ingrid Verner, Isaiah, It Girl, Ixiah, Jac Allen Couture, Jaclin Chouchana, Jacqui Alexander, Jae Lingerie, Jain, James Cameron, Jamie Ashkar, Jane & Eleni, Jane Lamerton, Jayson Brunsdon, Jeenenun, Jenny Bannister, Jenny Kee, Jessica Holmes, Jessie Hill, Jets Australia, Jill Fitzsimon, Jimmy D, Joanna Chu Liao, Jodie Boffa, Joe The Taxi Driver, Johanna Johnson, John Cheung, Jonathan Ward Couture, Jon Hewitt, Joseph Li, Josh Goot, Joshua Granath, Jovani Couture, Joveeba, Jozette, Jtah, Julianne, Juli Grbac, Julia Chao, Justine.Taylor.Made, Kalb & ETIW, Karen Walker, Karla Spetic, Kate Hurst, Kate Reynolds, Kate Sylvester, Kathryn Beker, Katie Graham, Katya Grokhovsky, Kaylene Milner, Kelly Love, Kerry Grima, Khalo, Khoon Hooi, Kiaya Daniels, Kim Deters, Kirby Purrs, Kirrily Johnston, Kini Bikini, 'Kitten', KLUK, Konstantina Mittas, Kooey, Kornerd, Kowtow, Kristi Rose,

Ksubi, LAB Gallerie Local Art Base, lalesso, Lan Yu, Laurence Pasquier, Leah Hibbert, Lee Mathews, Leigh Schubert, Leona Edmiston, Leonie Levy, Leonardo Salinas, Leonard St, Leopold, Leroy Nguyen, LF Markey, Liam Revell, Liam Wellstead, LIFEwithBIRD, Lili, Limedrop, Lisa Blue, Lisa Ho, Lisa Maree, Little Gracie, Little Joe Woman, Little Ramonas, Liu Designer, Logvin Code, Longevity, Lorena laing, Lorinda Grant, Lorna Jane, Louise Dale, Louis Philippe, Lover, Lucy Hinckfuss, Luci Torres, Lucette, Luela, Lui Hon, Lu Lu Cheung, M J M Lifestyle, M-ONE-11, Macgraw, Mad Cortes, Madame Marie, Magdalena Velevska, Maidenlove, Maiike, Mandarin Chilli, Manifesto, Manning Cartell, Marajoara, MARCS, Marcus/ Baby Doll, Marnie Skillings, Marsha Vetolskiy, Material Boy, Maticevski, Matthew Eager, Maurie & Eve, Maus, Mayson, Megan Salmon, Melanie Cutfield, Melinda Looi, Melissa Polynkova, Mellissa Simone, Melly, Michael, Michael Lo Sordo, Michelle Jank, Midesko, Milich & Morton, Milk, Milk & Honey, MILS, Mimco, Mime, Miok Kang, Mischa, Miss Gladys Sym Choon, Miss Unkon, Mjölk, Moiselle, Moocha Bella, Moontide, Morrison, Morrison Hotel, Morrissey, Mouth, Ms.Couture, N/A by Nicole and Aaron, Nana Judy, Naomi Raggatt, Nara, Narendra, Natalie & Sarah, Natalija Kucija, Nathan Paul Swimwear, Natasha Gan, Nelson Leong, Nevada Duffy, Nevenka, NF, Ngami, Nicola, Nicolangëla, Nicholas Blanchet, Nicholas Christensen, Nicole Collins, Nicola Finetti, Nina Field, NLP, Nobody, Nookie, Nylon Flocks by Nicola Finetti, Nyou, Obus, Olive, One Fell Swoop, One Teaspoon, Ophelie, Oroton, Oscar & Elvis, Ovna Ovich, Ozone Aware Beachwear by Wendy Heather, Paablo Nevada, Pacino Lee, Pacino Wan, Pani, Patrick Li, Paul Nathaphol, Paul Scott, Peggy Hartanto, Pervert, Peter Dwyer, Pfeiffer, Phillips, Phoenix Keating, Phos Phoro, Pia Interlandi, Pieter Kapp, Pigsinspace, Piper Lane, Piras Soetedja, Pizzuto, Platform, Pleasure State, Posse, Prateep Laoteppitak, Preacher, Preston Zly, Princess Highway, Prudence Todd, Purr, Rachelalex, Rachael Cassar, Rachel Gilbert, Rahul & Firdous (India), Ranee_K, Rebecca Dawson, Rebecca Thompson, Red Smith, Renee August, Renee Warner, RICH, Robin Alexander, Roger Grinstead, Romance Was Born, Robert Burton, Roopa Pemmaraju, Rosie Ryder, Roy, Ruby Li, Ruby, Ruby Smallbone, Rufus Green, Rukshani, Ruth Tarvydas, SABA, Sabatini, Sable & Minx, Saint Teresa, Saffron Craig, Sally Smith, Sally Watts, Sam Fisher, Sample Only, Sandra Thom, Sara Algars, Sara Aljaism, Sara Phillips, Sarina Suriano, sass & bide, Sauce, Scanlan Theodore, Seafolly Australia, Seduce, Serjiant, Serpent & The Swan, Seventh Wonderland, Sewn, Shakuhachi, Shaun Collins, Shem, Show off!, Silence is Golden, Silk Road,

Silvia Car, SKYE & Staghorn, Sonam, Song & Kelly, Song For The Mute, Sonya Zutic, Sophie Penberthy, Spencer Webber, Spook, SpppsssP, Spy, Spy Henry Lau, Sretsis, St Augustine Academy, Staple the Label, State of Georgia, State of Grace, Stephanie by Conley + Cranford, Stephanie Conley, Stephanie Cranford, Stephanie Goerlach, Stevie, Stitch Ministry, Stolen Girlfriends Club, Story by Tang, Strateas Carlucci, Subfusco, Suboo, Su Design, Sunjoo Moon, Surface too deep, Susan Rep, Susan Scarf, Susie Mooratoff, Steven Khalil, Stand, Sven, Swarovski, S!X, Tallow Gallery, Talulah, Tea Rose, Terri Dean, Terry Biviano, Thang Dang, The Browns, The Cassette Society, The Letter Q, The N, The Social Studio, Therese Rawsthorne, Third Millennium, Thousand Reasons, Thurley, Thys Collective, Tiffany Treloar, Tigerlily, Tight Knickers, Tim O'Connor, Timovsthang, Tina Borg, Tina Kalivas, TL Wood, Todd Robinson, Toi Et Moi Sydney, Tom Abang Saufi, Tom, Dick and Harry, Tour, Tovah, Trelise Cooper, Trevor Chard, Trimapee, Tristan Melle, Tsubi, Tu, TV, Ty + Melita, Uberchic by Kirrily Johnston, Ugur ile Alijan, UNIF.M, United Constructions, (Un)NakeD, Urban Originals, Uscari, Valerie Tolosa, Valerija, Vanguard, Vanishing Elephant, Vasiliki, Verduci-Smith, Vicious Threads, Vicki Fung, Victoria Loftes, Victoria & Timothy, Villiam Ooi, Vinh Nguyen, Virginia Killory Liu, Virginia Lau, Vixen, Wallace Rose, Watersun, Watson x Watson, Wayne, Wayne Cooper, We Are Handsome, White Kitten, White Sands, White Suede, Whitney Eve & WE By Whitney Eve, Who Am Eye, Will & Roth, Will Be., Willian Chan, Willow, Winnie Ha, Winson Tan, Woods & Woods, Wool Protégé, World, Workshop, Xenheist, Xu's, Yan Pothin, Yekaterina Peker, Yeojin Bae, Ying Yuan, Yousef Akbar, YPV, Yu, Yuliy Gershinsky, Zaicek, Zambesi, Zanerobe, Zanthus, Zhigang 'Del' Chen, Zhivago, Zimmerman, Zocky, Zoe Mahony, Zsadar.

Acknowledgements

EVERYTHING I HAVE done over the past twenty-five years was only made possible by the help of a cast of thousands. I would truly like to personally thank all the wonderful staff of The Lock Group since 1989 and those in the fashion industry who have contributed to making particularly Mercedes Australian Fashion Week and its incarnations as Rosemount Australian Fashion Week and Mercedes-Benz Fashion Week Australia such a success. Obviously this is just not possible, although a number of individuals have been recognised in the telling of key stories in this book. Many others have had a positive impact on my life in a very tangible way and I thank them for the dedication, enthusiasm and passion they have contributed to my vision. It would, however, be remiss of me not to publicly thank a few special groups of people.

First, the partners and shareholders of The Lock Group over the period of 1989–2010, when the company still had a direct involvement in Fashion Week, including Marguerite Julian, Simon Bookallil, Greg Gleeson, Martyn Pointer, Lorraine Lock, Karson Stimson, Jodi Pritchard, Graeme Lewsey and Annalise Brown. Their support, particularly in the early years, gave flight to a huge idea. Special thanks must also go to all the staff of Spin who were dragged in to help on the event.

Then, all the key staff and contractors of Australian Fashion Innovators responsible for producing Fashion Week from the company's inception in 1991 through to when it was sold to IMG in 2005. They included Jodi Pritchard, Graeme Lewsey, Jarrad Clark, Lucia Labbate, Vanessa Van Zyl, Sophie Miller, Fiona Chaloner, Mariela Castillo Demetriou, Kate Lovery, Tess Glasson, Cat Rodwell, Richard Jones, Karyn Westren, Louise De Francesco, Annie Kelly, Nat Ratard, Kannon Rajah, Orlando Reindorf, John Flower, Phillipa Scott, Christine Bookallil, Iain Reed, Troy Daniel,

Jack Bedwani, Elle Turner, Marco Maccapani, Jennifer Sourness, Selina Robson, Lara Karamian, Craig Claridge, Robert Fischer, Nikki Hodgeman, Zanthia Harvison, Miro Kubicek, Barry Wafer, Nell Schofield, Simon Haywood, Andy Glitre, Skye Campbell, Mic and Tim Gruchy, Antonia Leigh, Graz Mulcahy and Ali Newling.

Also, the global group of people from IMG Fashion and other divisions who are the current owners and caretakers of the event, and particular those I worked with during 2005–10 including Chuck Bennett, Martin Jolly, Fern Mallis, Massimo Raedelli, Ivan Bart, David Cunningham, Jenny Rose, Francesco Suarez, Dan Hill, Chris Gilbert, Phil Stoneman, Max Davis and more recently Elle Turner, Emily Leiding Weight and Louise Iselin.

I would also like to thank the very special people who at various times had the role of being my executive assistant—probably the hardest job in the fashion industry. Thanks to Alana Burmeister, Sara Langham, Lucia Labbate, Bec Calder, Vanessa Van Zly and Tania Arpadi. An extra thanks to Vanessa, who helped me directly on *In The Front Row*.

Without the support of my immediate family I would not have had the energy and momentum to carry on when the mountains seemed impossible to climb. My three amazing and talented children David Lock Jnr, Hannah Lock and Jules Lock, my ex-wife Lorraine, my incredible brother Richard, his wife Kate and their children Jackson and Tallulah. A very special thanks to my mother, Joy—who in many ways has been my biggest supporter through her continuous and unwavering belief in me—for her creativity and wisdom, which continue to amaze me. Thanks also to the Doaks—Mark, Lynn, Caleb and Mia—for their recent encouragement.

Thanks to all the team at Melbourne University Publishing for their guidance, advice, patience and expertise, especially Colette Vella, who initially helped set me on the right path, along with Sally Heath, Cathy Smith and Monica Svarc.

This book is dedicated to my father David Price Lock, who passed away on 1 January 2015. Without the lessons I learnt from him while I was growing up, through his words and actions, I would never have had the drive, determination and skills to do half the things I have done so far. He will always be an inspiration as my journey in life continues.

To my darling wife Kirsten. Thank you for allowing me to share this story and for your encouragement, careful judgement and guidance. I am so grateful that we are now in the front row together continuing this amazing fashion journey. I can't wait to see where we end up. Love you.